History of the Book

by

SVEND DAHL

First English Edition

THE SCARECROW PRESS, INC.

NEW YORK   1958

Preface

This book comprises a series of lectures held at the beginning of the 1920's and considerably expanded for publication here.

Most of the existing works on the history of the book present its various phases: manuscripts, printing, binding, illustration, the book-trade and libraries separately. In this work I have attempted to present them all in a unified account so that their interrelationship will become apparent and the history of the book will appear in perspective as an essential factor in the history of culture.

The earlier editions of this work have been out-of-print for many years. This new edition incorporates the results of recent research, and brings the account down to the present day.

I wish to thank those specialists who have so kindly examined various parts of the book: Dr. J. Christian Bay, former Librarian of the John Crerar Library in Chicago, Palle Birkelund, State Librarian of Denmark, Ejnar Philip, printer, and H. P. Rohde, librarian at the Danish Royal Library.

I also thank Otto Andersen, book-dealer, for various helpful suggestions and for the warm interest that he has shown in this new edition.

1957   Svend Dahl

iii

Table of Contents

ANTIQUITY

The history of the book extends over more than five thousand years. There are, however, few and scattered facts from the first two-thirds of this period to guide us in forming a picture of books and their place in the ancient world. Archeological investigations of the last generation have, it is true, made many new discoveries in this as well as in other fields, but there is still much that is unknown or uncertain, and the classical Greek and Roman writers, who are usually our best source for the history of culture, give very little information about books.

Hence it must be with a great deal of caution that we venture on this uncertain ground; it is all too tempting to draw general conclusions from isolated finds, conclusions that may be completely refuted by later discoveries.

Egyptian Papyrus Rolls

When seeking the earliest available evidence in any phase of cultural history one will seldom seek in vain in ancient Egypt. Productive literary activity, to judge from archeological finds, developed to a high degree in the kingdom of the Pharaohs; not only were religious texts produced, but scientific and literary works as well.

In the still, swampy, waters of the ancient delta of the Nile there grew large quantities of a plant which the Greeks called papyros, a word of uncertain derivation. The papyrus plant belongs to the family of the sedges, and at the present time the extent of its growth is very limited. The Egyptians used it for many purposes, but we are concerned here only with the use they made of the stalk of the plant. This stalk is triangular in shape and may reach a height of 10-15 feet; the pith of the stalk was cut into thin strips, which were dried and laid out in a row alongside one another with the edges overlapping slightly. Over these strips another row was laid cross-wise and the two layers then moistened with water and pounded together into an integral unit (see Fig. 4). This gluing process was extremely stable and in most of the papyrus sheets that have been preserved we

7

find that the two layers still are firmly bonded together.

After the strips had thus been combined into a sheet,
the sheet was presumably sized so that the ink would not run,
and it was then dried in the sun and glazed to produce a
glossy surface. The finished sheet, when it was of good
quality, was very supple and flexible, and in general this
flexibility has been retained amazingly well through the centuries. The sheets were glued together side by side to form
long sections. The production of papyrus seems to have become a regular industry at an early period, and the product
was sold in large quantities, like paper from our modern factories, in the form of bales or rolls from which sheets could
be cut off as needed. Ordinarily the sheets used were 6 to
7 inches high, but later we find sheets up to three times this
size. The better grades of papyrus were light in color, being yellowish or almost completely white, while the poorer
grades were more or less brownish.

The manufacture of papyrus was well developed as
early as the third millenium B.C., and it soon reached a
stage of technological perfection that was not to be surpassed
later. It is possible that there were some differences of detail in the methods used in different periods, but nothing definite is known about these. There are a number of uncertain-
ties about the manufacture of papyrus; the description that is
usually given is not based on Egyptian writings but is derived
from painted reliefs found at Thebes and especially from the
account by the Latin author, Pliny the Elder, supplemented
by the investigations of modern Egyptologists.

One characteristic of all papyrus, whether it is of the
fine hieratic quality or one of the poorer types, is that there
is a difference between the two sides of the sheet because the
two layers of strips lie at right angles to each other. The
side on which the strips run horizontally is called the recto
side, and this was the side usually preferred for writing,
while the other side with the strips running vertically was
called the verso side and was less frequently used. A material as pliable as papyrus was eminently suited to being
rolled, and when this was done the recto became the inner
side and the verso, with no writing on it, the outer side.

The Egyptian book was in the form of a roll. In reading it was gradually unrolled so that the writing appeared little
by little. As a rule, the writing was divided into columns,
thus making the lines quite short and dividing the book, in a
sense, into "pages," which came successively into view as
the roll was unwound. One famous papyrus roll now in the

University Library at Leipzig is about 65 feet long and is divided into 110 "pages." The text begins at the extreme right and the pages then follow one another from right to left.

The system of writing that was used was not, except in certain religious books, the original hieroglyphic as we know it from inscriptions, but a more rapid and easier form of writing that had been developed as early as the middle of the third millenium B.C. for use on papyrus and was, like the fine grade of papyrus, called hieratic ("priestly"). In a later period we find papyrus sheets with another type of writing, the so-called demotic ("popular") which is further simplified. The oldest papyrus known dates from about 2400 B.C., but there is evidence that papyrus was used for writing when hieroglyphic was in use because there is a hieroglyphic symbol for the papyrus roll.

1. Papyrus roll with Greek text in columns.

The writing tool used by the Egyptians was a reed
stalk cut at an angle, with the one end frayed by chewing so
that it acted as a soft brush. By turning it thick or thin
lines could be produced. In the third century B.C., however,
a stiff pointed reed, the calamus, came into use making it
possible to write a finer line. This became the common writing tool, and like the ruler for making straight lines it was
part of the equipment of every scribe. The ink he used was
made from lampblack or charcoal by adding water and an ad-
hesive. It was superior to our present-day ink -- the writing
has often preserved its deep black sheen through the ages.
Red ink was also used, especially for titles and chapter headings. The scribe kept his pens and his ink on a sort of pal-
ette, a thin oblong piece of wood with a slot to hold the pens
and two or three depressions for ink. The papyrus rolls
were kept in clay jars or wooden boxes. Since the outer part
of the roll would necessarily be subject to wear it was often
made of better material or was protected by a covering, and
the edges of the roll might be reinforced by gluing on strips.

The fact that papyrus has been preserved down to the
present day, and in considerable quantities, is not due to in-
herent characteristic of the material. From statements made
by ancient writers we know that when a roll lasted a couple
of hundred years it was considered to have reached an honorable old age. We often find complaints about the fragility of
the material and its poor keeping qualities. Destruction by
insects was quite common, and attempts were made to coun-
teract this by dipping the papyrus sheet in cedar oil. The
worst enemy was moisture. It is, of course, impossible for
us to estimate how many papyrus rolls have been destroyed;
all we can say is that what is now preserved represents only
a small fraction of what originally existed. An indirect proof
that moisture must bear the major part of the blame for this
destruction is seen in the fact that by far the greater part of
the papyri that have been found come from excavations in
Egypt; although, as we shall see later, the Graeco-Roman
world used papyrus to a greater extent than did the Egyptians,
for almost a thousand years, yet only a very few papyrus
finds have been made in these countries. The reason lies
primarily in the destructive effect of their climate. For this
same reason, even in Egypt, only a few finds have been made
in the humid Nile delta; the major finds are from the dry
sand of middle and upper Egypt. Egyptian graves have been
excellent repositories for this fragile material. In the last
centuries B.C. it became the custom to make mummy coffins
of discarded papyrus sheets glued together and covered with a
layer of plaster; several papyrus texts have come to us in this
manner. A far greater number, however, have been preserved

through the general religious custom of placing various sacred texts, prayers, etc., in the grave as protection during its journey into the realm of the dead; among these the "Book of the Dead" was especially common.   This book is known from about 1800 B.C.; it gradually acquired a conventional content, and copies were apparently made by priests on a production basis with spaces left for the name of the deceased -- an industry of the same type as that which later developed for the letters of indulgence issued by the Catholic Church.

The trade in Books of the Dead was probably the only book trade that existed in ancient Egypt.   Some of these books were extensively illustrated, and the illustrations were presumably drawn by an artist before the scribe wrote the text. In most instances the pictures form a border that runs the entire length of the roll above the text.   Their artistic value varies greatly, but all exhibit the stylistic features so well known in Egyptian relief carvings.   A few Books of the Dead have colored illustrations or have been given special treatment in some other way.   These were presumably intended for persons who had been very prominent or very wealthy, while the ordinary man had to be content with much smaller and more modest productions.   From all indications papyrus was expensive, even more so after it had become a large-scale export product, and consequently it was not the only writing material used in Egypt.   Among the others were leather and for shorter notations wooden tablets, pieces of limestone and potsherds.

We have almost no information about libraries in classical Egypt.   At that time there was no separation between book collections and archives; books and documents had the same outward appearance and required similar methods of storage.   In Egypt as well as in other countries of the ancient world libraries were attached to religious centers, or temples. The temple of the sun god Horus, which is still preserved at Edfu in southern Egypt, has a room where the walls are decorated with the titles of 37 books that the library had received as a gift.   In the vicinity of Thebes two graves have been found with inscriptions in which the word librarian appears as a title; a father and his son are buried here, who presumably belonged to the priesthood and had accordingly been teachers of learning and writing.

Early Chinese Books

While the papyrus sheet became the prevailing writing material in the Nile valley and thus determined the outer form

2.   Fragment of an Egyptian Book of the Dead, intended
for a person of rank.   Above the text there is a colored pic-
torial frieze with artistically drawn figures. (British Museum).
Most Books of the Dead, however, were less elaborate, many
having no illustrations, and since the text was not intended to
be read it was often full of errors.

of the book in Egypt, an equally high culture had simultane-
ously developed in far-away China.   China possessed the art
of writing and produced literary works as early as the third
millenium B.C.   During the next thousand years or more we
know that the country had imperial historians; the great philosopher Lao-tze, who lived about 500 B.C., was said to have
been archivist at the imperial archives.

The materials used for writing at that time were bone,
tortoise shell, split bamboo stalks and later wooden tablets
on which lines were drawn with a stylus; the writing began in
the upper right-hand corner and ran vertically downward, the
lines following one another from right to left, just as in Chinese books of the present day.

Almost no wooden manuscripts are still in existence.
One major reason for this was the edict to destroy all books
issued by the Emperor Tain Shihuangti in the year 213 B.C.
This was done to punish authors who had dared to criticize
his political actions.   Only a few books escaped destruction
by fire, and most of the wooden books that were produced
thereafter were probably destroyed by rot.

This book-burning incident, however, served to introduce a new period of great literary activity; efforts were
made to replenish the supply of books by seeking out and re-
issuing those works of classical literature from the time of
Confucius that had escaped destruction.   Writing was no longer
restricted to wooden tablets but was also done on silk cloth,
either with a bamboo pen or a camel's hair brush.   The ink
used was a black substance obtained from the varnish tree
and later india ink made from lampblack mixed with glue.
Silk possessed several of the properties of Egyptian papyrus
-- it was pliable and had a smooth surface, but it was more
expensive.

Cuneiform Tablets of the Near East

Besides Egypt and China there was a third region that
had a highly developed culture in ancient times.   This region
was the Near East, and in particular Mesopotamia.   In the
fourth millenium B.C. at the latest, a people called the Sumerians migrated from the east into the southern part of the
country between the Tigris and the Euphrates and then gradually spread northward.   The culture they developed is known
to us through the excavations at Ur, Lagash, and especially
at Nippur, which had obviously been a great religious center.
There is no doubt that the Sumerians had a system of writing

and an increasingly significant literature, and they are generally considered to be the originators of cuneiform writing,
an original pictographic form that early changed to a phonetic
system.

The true cuneiform characters, however, were first
introduced by the Semitic Akkadians, who toward the close of
the third millenium B.C. put an end to Sumerian rule as they
gradually adopted the Sumerian culture. To these peoples belong the Babylonians, and together with the Assyrians, a Semitic people of northern Mesopotamia, they attained a dominant position in all of the Near East. In the 15th century
B.C. their language became the diplomatic language of the
time; even in the royal archives of the Egyptian city El-
Amarnas many cuneiform tablets in the Assyrian-Babylonian
language have been found.

At Nippur, mentioned above, parts of a large temple
library and archives containing clay tablets have been discovered; these date partly from the Sumerian period and partly from the Babylonian and Assyrian period. The temple of
Nippur has several rooms, of which some were undoubtedly
used for the library and others for the archives. When the
clay tablets were found they were in unorganized piles and
many were broken; but originally they must certainly have
been contained in clay or wooden boxes or in woven baskets
set on clay bases or on wooden shelves along the walls. To
protect them against moisture these boxes were coated with
asphalt and the same was probably also done with the baskets.
In other instances, however, the tablets had merely been tied
together and placed directly on the shelves or in niches in the
walls; these as well as the boxes and baskets were undoubtedly marked with small clay labels.

In writing on the tablets the characters were impressed
in soft clay by means of a blunt triangular instrument of metal, ivory or wood, thus giving the characters their wedge-
shaped form. After the writing was completed the tablet was
dried in the sun or baked in an oven and became as hard as
brick. Some of the larger tablets have small holes in their
surface through which steam could escape during the baking
process. Some of the tablets that have been found, however,
were not adequately baked and have consequently been difficult
or impossible to separate and decipher.

A total of nearly half a million tablets, including fragments, has been excavated to date from the ruins of the Near
East and Mesopotamia, and many of them are now in European and American museums. The tablets are rectangular in

3.   Cuneiform tablet containing a hymn to the Babylonian
king Dungi (University Museum, Philadelphia).

shape and vary greatly in size; some are 12 inches wide by
16 inches long, but the majority are only half that size. The
tablets were written on both sides; the back was slightly con-
cave while the face was flat or convex. The back of the tablet that lay on the top of each stack was turned up, and on it
was written the title of the work and often also the names of
the owner and the scribe, with an admonition to treat the tablets with care. The latter might well be necessary, for if a
tablet fell to the floor it was easily broken. It was customary when the contents of tablets were no longer of interest to
use the tablets themselves as material for roads and floors,
or to stack them together in solid piles.

Literary activity flourished among the Babylonians and
the Assyrians and there was plenty of clay in the country between the two great rivers. There were undoubtedly writing
rooms in conjunction with every temple. The period of Assyrian greatness, which follows that of the Babylonians, falls
in the 8th or 7th century B.C., and the archives and library
of King Ashur-bani-pal (Sardanapalus?) in the Assyrian capital city of Nineveh are famous. This site was excavated a
hundred years ago by British archeologists and more than
20,000 complete tablets and fragments are now preserved in
the British Museum. The clay of the tablets found here is
finer and more carefully baked than that found elsewhere, and
the writing is generally clearer and more elegant, for which
the credit must go to the large staff of calligraphers at Ashur-
bani-pal's court. This king was evidently a great collector
and gathered texts from all places, both inside and outside
his kingdom; these were then reworked and copied, just as
was later done at the library of Alexandria. Babylonian-As-
syrian literature is extensively represented in the library of
Ashur-bani-pal, but there are also Sumerian texts. A large
part of the library was destroyed when the Medes, allied with
the Persians, conquered Nineveh in 612 B.C. Two or three
private Assyrian libraries have also been found.

We also have collections of clay tablets with cuneiform
writing from two other Near East civilizations. The Hittites,
who flourished between 1900 and 1200 B.C. have left us a-
bout 15,000 unusually large clay tablets in their capital, Bog-
hazköl, which lies east of Ankara. Catalogs that have been
found give the titles and the number of tablets in each work.
In Ras-Shamra, an important trade center of northern Syria
in the time of the Hittites, clay tablets have been found with
texts in the Ugaritic language, which is closely related to
Phoenician. They are written in a kind of cuneiform with
only 29 signs, representing an alphabet somewhat similar to
the Phoenician alphabet, the progenitor of the Greek and all

later alphabets. This Ras-Shamra alphabet, as well as the
Phoenician, must be considered to have been inspired by
Egyptian writing.

Other Early Writing Materials

We have mentioned several kinds of material that were
in use at various time and various places during the first two
or three thousand years of historical time, but we have still
not mentioned the one that was perhaps in use earliest of all,
namely bast fiber. We know that both the Greek and the Latin words for book, byblos and liber, originally denoted bast.
It is also true that palm leaves, dried and rubbed with oil,
have been used for writing in India for many centuries and
are still used there to some extent. Hence there is nothing
remarkable in the fact that a related material such as bast
was used in the same manner; the characters could be
scratched in with a pointed instrument just as is done on palm
leaves. Linen was probably also used for books. Livy, for
instance, mentions linen book rolls. Leather was used to an
even greater extent; some of the recently discovered Dead Sea
scrolls are of leather. Even in Mesopotamia, where clay
tablets were so dominant, other writing materials were also
used; in the ruins of a city near Nineveh cuneiform writing
has recently been found on tablets of wood and of ivory coated
with a layer of wax.

Greek Papyrus Rolls. The Alexandrian Library

The papyrus roll apparently made its entry among the
Greeks in the 7th century B.C. Export of this material from
Egypt to Greece then began to increase steadily, and by the
5th century the use of papyrus appears to have been general.
The fact that Herodotus does not mention papyrus rolls at all
in his description of Egypt may be an indication that they were
in common use in his own country. The Greeks called the
blank papyrus sheet chartres, which became the Latin charta
and produced our words chart and card. The written sheet
was called byblion, or biblion, in Greek They called the
papyrus roll kylindros while the Romans called it volumen, a
word that is still used in many languages to denote one book
of a set. Another word with the same meaning, Latin tomus,
Greek tomos, was originally used for a roll consisting of a
series of separate sheets pasted together.

The oldest known Greek papyri date from the 4th century B.C. The letters still have the primitive and severe

form found in inscriptions, but there are too few rolls preserved from this period to justify any general conclusions.
Not until we come to the 3rd century does our knowledge become somewhat complete and certain, supported by the numerous finds of Greek papyri that were made in the course
of the 19th century, particularly in Egypt and Asia Minor,
and largely from the Alexandrian period.

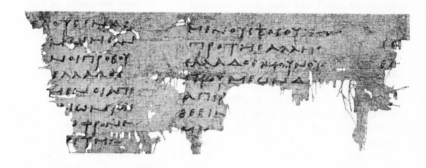

4.   Papyrus fragment from the first half of the 3rd century B.C. containing a text of Herodotus.

The fact that the finds become more extensive in this
period has its reason, of course, in the flowering of Greek
culture and religion that took place on Egyptian soil after
Alexander the Great had incorporated Egypt into his far-flung
empire.   From then on the papyrus book became a part of the
Greek world as never before.   The connection between Egyptian and Greek culture was strengthened still further when
Ptolemy I, after the fall of Alexander's empire, established
his powerful kingdom in the Nile valley and devoted himself
to giving his new capital, Alexandria, a position of leadership in the world of culture as well as of politics and commerce.   He, and especially his son Ptolemy II, invited Greek
scholars and offered them a carefree life as members of a
sort of religious brotherhood or academy with its quarters in
the new temple of the muses, the Museion, patterned after
Aristotle's famous peripatetic school in Athens.

In the Museion there was both study and teaching; the
large library that was assembled there in the course of the
third century B.C. was quite comprehensive, even containing
translations of Egyptian, Babylonian and other early literature.
This library was the larger of the two collections that made

up the Alexandrian library, the greatest and most famous library of the ancient world; the other collection was located
in the temple of the national deity Serapis, and was called
the Serapeion.

The object of the Alexandrian library was first of all
to collect the whole of Greek literature in the best possible
editions, arrange them and provide them with commentaries
-- a task to which a phenomenal amount of labor was devoted. The poet Callimachus was one of the many outstanding scholars who worked in the library. On the basis of its
subject catalogs (pinakes was the word for catalog) he compiled a sort of author catalog of the entire Greek literature
of that time, and even though we now have only fragments of
his work, these are sufficient to indicate his excellent qualifications as a cataloger.

We know practically nothing about the library quarters
at the Museion, but those at the Serapeion have been excavated along with the temple. The size of the Alexandrian library is not definitely known, but it is estimated at about
700,000 rolls in the larger division and about 43,000 in the
smaller. If these figures are correct there must in many
instances have been several copies of the same work. Large
sums of money must have been available for purchases, and
a great deal of work was certainly expended on copying poor-
ly preserved manuscripts and preparing new critical editions
to supersede more or less doubtful texts. Long works were
divided up into several rolls of approximately the same length
in accordance with the sections of the text, and on the other
hand several short texts were combined into a single roll --
all presumably done with a librarian's view to having the rolls
of a certain standard practical length.

No single complete roll has been preserved. The usual length was probably about 20-23 feet; when rolled together
this would make a cylinder 2-2.5 inches thick, which was
thus easy to hold in the hand. Rolls over 30 feet long were
certainly exceptional. The height of the rolls also varied, although here again we note a tendency toward standard measure-
ments. Only a few of the rolls that have been preserved are
over 12 inches high, the majority being between 8 and 12
inches or between 5 and 6 inches. The portion of the papyrus sheet used for writing also varied considerably; the more
elaborate manuscripts have wider margins than the plainer
ones. The length of the columns could be from 2/3 to 5/6
of the height of the roll, and the space between columns and
the distance between lines varied in a similar manner. Even
in the same manuscript the distance between lines might vary

to the extent that some columns would have more lines than others; the width of a column was in general somewhat less than its length (see Figs. 1 and 4).

The instrument used for writing literary works was a thick hollow reed stalk, cut to form a pointed pen. Only capital letters were used (the small Greek letters did not evolve until the Middle Ages) and no space was left between words, which naturally makes the texts difficult to read. On the other hand, it was customary to mark the end of a unit in the text by placing a line, the so-called paragraphos, under the beginning of the last line of the unit, and this word has continued in use to denote divisions of the text. The script was a formal type of calligraphy which the scribes were taught, but each scribe unavoidably developed individual characteristics in his writing. Every letter was made distinct, though for ordinary daily use there was a more rapid cursive script with less definite lines and with combined letters. About four-fifths of the papyri that we have are in cursive script; these represent mainly public and private documents and letters.

The scribes who wrote the literary manuscripts constituted a sizable professional class with considerable education; they were paid partly by number of lines, presumably referred to a line of standard length, and partly according to the nature of the text. When the scribe had finished his work the manuscript was proof-read either by himself or by a special "corrector," who corrected the errors and might also make various critical notations in the margin to clarify the text (the so-called "scholia") or insert signs (asterisks, etc.) to call attention to linguistic peculiarities.

The title of the book roll, when there was one, was usually placed at the end of the text, probably because it was best protected there, being innermost as the book lay rolled up. The use of specific titles was undoubtedly a relatively late practice; Greek papyri of the earlier period probably had no titles, but were identified, as Callimachus did in his work, by the name of the author and the initial word or words of the text. To tell the rolls apart as they lay or stood in their containers a sort of label did gradually come into use. It was attached to the upper edge of the roll. The word title itself comes from this label, which the Romans called "titulus" or "index," and the Greeks "sillybos." The wooden or stone jar in which the rolls were kept was called "bibliotheke" by the Greeks, but the meaning of this word was extended quite early to include a collection of books in general; in Latin the jar was called capsa or "scrinium."

Illustrations were probably not unusual in papyrus rolls, even though a few, mainly of a mathematical or similar nature, have been found. In a number of instances a portrait of the author was reproduced, and the suggestion has been made that the columns of Trajan and Marcus Aurelius in Rome are to be interpreted as large-scale reproductions of picture-rolls.

The amount of papyrus used by the Greeks and later by the Romans, who took over from Greece the papyrus roll as their book form along with the other aspects of Greek culture, must have been considerable. A number of varieties, or brands, came on the market, some named for Roman emperors (charta Augusta, Claudia, etc.). In the later Roman Empire factories were established in Rome, importing raw papyrus material from Egypt and making papyrus sheets from it.

It appears likely that the Ptolemys imposed a tax on the exportation of papyrus, and later the papyrus trade became a government monopoly; the top sheet in a bale was called "protocol" and received a sort of official stamp. This monopoly continued to exist even after the Arabs conquered Egypt.

Among the oldest papyrus finds is the one that occurred during the excavation of Herculaneum in 1752. About 1800 carbonized rolls were found in this town which had been destroyed by the eruption of Vesuvius in 79 A.D.; these are now preserved in the National Library at Naples. There are also famous papyrus collections in the National Library at Vienna (Archduke Rainer's collection of about 80,000 pieces), the British Museum in London, The Bodleian Library at Oxford, Staatliche Museum in Berlin and the Egyptian Museum in Cairo. The University of Copenhagen has a small collection of Greek papyri, still only partly processed.

But to return to the library at Alexandria, it is obvious that such a great literary center would also be important in the development of the book trade. There is indirect reference to the existence of publishers in Athens as early as the 5th century B.C., and from Xenophon's Anabasis we know that there was trade in books with the Greek colonies. With the rise of the Alexandrian library the opportunities of the book trade were expanded, partly because the library itself became a large-scale customer and partly because the library made available an outstanding collection of manuscripts from which copies could be made for sale.

Among the books acquired by the library at Alexandria
were said to be some from the collection left by Aristotle.
He had willed his library to one of his pupils, but it was
later broken up and partly destroyed; a few of the books were
said to have been brought to Rome by Sulla after passing
through various hands. Beyond this we know very little about
Greek private libraries, but that of Aristotle must certainly
have been outstanding.

When Caesar conquered Alexandria in 47 B.C. part of
the larger division of the library was burned. The final destruction of the Alexandrian library presumably came in 391
A.D. when the Christians, under the direction of Archbishop
Theophilus of Antioch, destroyed the temple of Serapis.

The Library at Pergamum

The library at Pergamum in northwestern Asia Minor
was founded by Attalus I and was expanded by Eumenes II.
It may be only legend that the latter tried to kidnap Ptolemy's
competent librarian and put him to work in the Pergamum library and that Ptolemy put his unfortunate librarian in prison
to prevent this, but the story does show that this new and
growing library must have been considered an unwelcome competitor of the older library at Alexandria.   On the other hand,
there is probably no basis for the statement by a Roman writer
that the Egyptian king at the beginning of the second century
prohibited the export of papyrus in order to prevent the library
at Pergamum from expanding and overshadowing the one at
Alexandria.

The Pergamum library very likely used the Alexandrian
library as a model in matters of organization and cataloging.
We have some idea of the library's quarters through the excavations of German archeologists in 1878-86. When they excavated the temple of Athena in Pergamum they found four
rooms, the innermost of which contained a colossal statue of
Athena and was presumably a sort of meeting or reception
room, while the three adjoining smaller rooms may have been
used for books; all four rooms opened into a collonaded arch-
way -- an arrangement that we find in many other library in-
stallations of ancient times.

Pergamum and its library probably never attained so
illustrious a position in the scholarly world of the time as that
held by Alexandria and the library there, and it is possible,
as mentioned above, that the former was actually incorporated
into the latter by Anthony's gift to Cleopatra. Pergamum has,

however, left significant traces in the history of the book,
assuming that we are correct in giving it the credit, as is
usually done, for the promotion of parchment, or vellum, as
a writing material.

Leather had undoubtedly been used for writing at various places in the ancient world even in very early times. A-
mong the Egyptians and the Jews, as well as the Assyrians
and Persians, and to some extent the Greeks, animal skins
were so used. The Greeks called them "diphthera," a name
that they later applied to other writing materials as well. It
was not until the third century B.C., however, that leather
was subjected to a special treatment to make it better suited
for writing, and it is the development of this process that we
associate with Pergamum. In any event the processing of
leather for writing purposes was done on a large scale there,
and the word parchment, "charta pergamena" is presumably
derived from the name of the city.

As a rule, sheep, calf or goat skins were used; the
hair was removed, the skin scraped thin, soaked in lime
water to remove fatty substances, dried, and then without any
other tanning it was rubbed with finely ground chalk and polished smooth with pumice stone or similar material. The
final product produced by this method was excellent for writing;
it presented a smooth and firm surface and was usable on both
sides. Its durability exceeded that of papyrus, though it was
by no means resistant to all types of destructive action. One
factor that contributed greatly to its extended use was that, in
contrast to papyrus, it permitted erasures to be made easily.
This is the reason that among vellum manuscripts -- especially from the Middle Ages and in periods when the material was
expensive -- we find palimpsests, that is, sheets on which the
original writing had been rubbed out and new text written over
it (Fig. 8; palimpsest means "re-smoothed"). The manufacture of parchment was not, like that of papyrus, restricted
to a single country, and for this reason it was presumably,
at least in the early period, not so expensive as papyrus
came to be. Nevertheless, at the beginning it was mainly
used for letters, documents, and other small items; it was
only gradually that parchment, which the Romans called "mem-
brana" was raised to the status of a book material, and it had
to compete with papyrus in this field for three centuries before it finally attained complete supremacy. From the fourth
century A.D. papyrus gradually went out of use. It is true
that in the papal chancellery there are rolls or sheets of papyrus from as late as the 11th century, but these must be
considered rare exceptions, and owe their existence to a respect for this traditional and scarce material.

Vellum can be bent like papyrus but it is less pliable,
and there is no doubt that vellum books were first in the form
of rolls the same as papyrus books. It was to be expected,
of course, that the tradition would be followed, and although
we do not possess a single Greek or Roman vellum roll there
is sufficient evidence that they did exist. The Jews also
used parchment rolls and use them even today for their sacred book, the Torah. The length of a roll was generally
limited by the length of the animal's hide, though it was possible when necessary to sew several pieces together and thus
make longer rolls. Parchment was also used as a covering
for papyrus rolls -- representing the very first stage of book-
binding.

The Roll Superseded by the Codex

However accustomed the people of antiquity may have
been to the roll they must have felt that it had disadvantages
for ordinary daily usage. One important disadvantage was
that when the roll had been read it had to be rewound before
it could be read again; in the case of a long roll this might
involve some difficulty. Even though a stick (called "umbili-
cus") was customarily used; some wear was caused by this
operation when the rolls were used frequently. As long as
papyrus was the standard material the roll was the most natural form; with vellum, however, the situation was different.

From very early times the Greeks had used small
writing tablets of wood, sometimes with a coating of wax, on
which brief notations could be scratched with a metal stylus.
School children use them for writing their exercises. Two
or more tablets of this kind were often bound together to
form small booklets (those made of two tablets were called
"diptycha") and such note-books were used extensively by
trades people or by scribes for temporary notations. When
vellum came into regular use for writing it was very easy to
adopt the form of these tablet books for vellum books, and
this step was taken in the first period of the Roman Empire.
This form was called a "codex," and it has remained essen-
tially unchanged since its adoption. A few codex sheets have
been preserved from about the end of the first or the beginning of the second century A.D. Vellum codices were certainly in use at that time, although they were probably considered less respectable than papyrus rolls. They were
used for small and less expensive editions because vellum
could be used on both sides and a text that would require a
large roll or several rolls could be contained in a relatively
small codex. In recent years a number of codices from the

second, third and fourth centuries have been found in Egypt
-- proof of the rapidity with which the codex form had pene-
trated into the very homeland of the papyrus roll. Attempts
were also made to apply the codex form to papyrus, perhaps
as early as the first century A.D., and a number of papyrus
codices have been found from the 3rd-5th centuries A.D. The
older material did not lend itself to the new form, and the
papyrus roll continued to exist alongside the codex until both
the papyrus material and the roll form were finally abandoned.

Archeological finds show that parchment codices were
in the majority by the fourth century and by the fifth century
they had taken over the field completely.

It is quite interesting to note that the oldest writings
of the Christian Church were nearly all in codex form with
only a few in rolls. One reason given for this is that the
early Christians were not wealthy enough to afford the more
expensive papyrus, but had to content themselves with the
less expensive vellum.

A certain special respect has been attached to the roll
as the most ancient book form even in our own day, as we
see, for instance, in the custom of giving documents a distinctive and formal appearance by making them in rolls --
festival speeches, honorary diplomas, etc. In expressions
like "honor roll," etc., we have a reminder of the time when
such documents were still in roll form, and the word "control" really is "contra-roll," i.e. a roll that the tax office
kept as a safeguard along with the regular tax roll.

There are several old codices in which all the sheets
have been laid inside one another in a single fold; such a
procedure naturally made the book awkward, and also made
the inner pages narrower than the outer ones. The idea of
dividing a book into several folds, with a few sheets in each
and tying these folds together with string, much as is done
with the signatures in books today, developed quite early.

The formats of books in the first four centuries of our
era were rather small; the ratio of width to height was usually about 2:3. Just as today, there were undoubtedly certain standard sizes of sheet, and the various formats were
obtained by folding the sheet once or twice. From the fifth
century on larger formats became more common. As in papyrus rolls and modern books, the finer codex manuscripts
show a tendency to wider margins, while the inferior ones
have their pages filled with writing almost out to the edge;
nearly always, however, more space was left at the outer

edge of the sheet than at the top and bottom, probably as protection against wear.   In its general features the codex book
is basically similar to the roll book.   Even the practice of
placing the title at the end of the text was, at first, transferred from the roll to the codex, even though it was of no
practical significance in the latter.   It was not until the fifth
century that it became the regular practice to place the title
at the beginning of the work as well.   One new feature, however, that was introduced along with the codex was pagination.   This device was unnecessary in the roll, where the
columns were necessarily maintained in their proper order,
but in the codex it became of practical importance.   In the
beginning, however, it was often used only on certain pages
or on the front side of each sheet; hence it cannot actually be
called pagination, but rather foliation ("pagina" = page; "foli-
um" = sheet).

As mentioned earlier, only a few rolls with illustrations are known, but we have a considerable number of codices from the first centuries A.D. with some sort of pic-
torial embellishment, including illustrations that actually represent the contents of the text (Fig. 7) as well as purely decorative designs.   The pictures are colored but have practically no shading, and the figures and faces are reminiscent of
those on monuments, coins or wall paintings.   As early as
the 4th century there were Greek and Coptic manuscripts in
which the first letter of each section was enlarged and decorated with various flourishes in color, usually red, thus intro-
ducing the initial ("initium" = beginning).   The script used in
the earliest codices was a special form of calligraphy, just
as in the rolls, and it gradually became more and more fixed
in its form.   There is a series of Greek and Coptic manuscripts from the 4th and 5th centuries, of quite different content but all written in an almost identical, beautiful, hand with
broad rounded lines, indicating a growing tendency toward uniformity in style of writing.

The implement used for writing on vellum was the hollow part of the shaft of a feather, preferably from a large
bird such as the eagle, raven or goose.   From these ancient
pens developed the later goose quill and our metal pens.   The
ink was of the same composition as that used on papyrus; it
was not until the 12th century A.D. that the ink that we know
today, made of copperas and tannic acid, came into use.   How
the early codices were bound is not known with certainty.   In
most instances a simple parchment cover was probably all that
was used, but there is a codex from the 3rd century in which
six blank sheets at the front and back were pasted together
and covered with leather.   There are examples of leather

5. Coptic binding in red and yellow leather with tooled geometric designs. (Egyptian Museum, Berlin).

bindings of the 6th-8th centuries, from Egypt, that show traces of handsome intaglio work on the covers (Fig. 5). These bindings were made by the Christian Egyptians, the Copts, and they must have been preceded by a long period of development, because of their professional quality.

Book Trade and Book Collecting among the Romans

When the Romans conquered the world and appropriated the fruits of Greek culture, the Greek tradition in the realm of books was continued on Roman soil. Roman military leaders brought Greek book collections back to Rome as spoils of war -- direct evidence of the high value placed on books.

Gradually a book trade developed in Rome, presumably conducted in large part by immigrant Greeks. The book dealer, called "bibliopola," used specially trained slaves ("servi literati" or "librarii") for copying texts; they were paid by number of lines, the standard line consisting of 34-38 letters.

In the time of the Republic the book trade still was apparently very limited and the same was even more true of publishing. An exception was the large publishing business conducted by Cicero's friend Pomponius Atticus; his text editions of Cicero's works and the works of older authors were famed for their accuracy.

With the coming of the Empire the book trade began to flourish in Rome as well as in other cities; book stores were located on the busiest streets and were often meeting places for writers and scholars. Lists of new books were posted on the walls or door columns. Booksellers were, as a rule, also publishers; the book-buying community had grown so large and wide-spread that there was need for an intermediary between the author and his readers. Not without reason did Horace boast that his verses would be read on the shores of the Black Sea and on the banks of the Rhone and the Ebro. The Roman publishing industry, however, differed from that of our day in important respects. The author received no payment; on the other hand the publisher did not have a monopoly on the publishing of a book but merely undertook the production of a certain number of copies. The author was free to arrange with other publishers to issue the same work, and anyone who wished could buy a book and have it copied; there were no legal regulations protecting the literary property of the author, and he did not count on any financial return from his writing. Only by dedicating a work to some wealthy patron could he expect pecuniary recognition.

It was the general custom for the author to gather a group of his friends to read aloud to them from his latest work; thus arousing interest in it. The great historical work of Herodotus was first made known through his own reading aloud from it in the towns that he visited on his travels. In time, however, this custom developed into something of a nuisance, especially since the less talented authors were often the most eager to recite their own product on any occasion. In the last centuries B.C. it was the publishers who began to invite the literary public together to hear new works read.

We know the names of several prominent publishers from the period of the Empire. There were the Sosii brothers, who were publishers for Horace among others, and Tryphon, who issued the writings of Quintilian and Martial. These publishers had philological scholars on their staff as

proof-readers who went through every single copy and corrected any errors.   Nothing definite is known about the size
of the editions, but works in demand could attain wide distribution within a short time.   Neither do we know a great deal
about the prices of books beyond the obvious fact that the
price depended on the size of the book and the style in which
it was published.

Wealthy Romans with literary interests had their own
slaves to copy the books that they wished to possess, though
it is doubtful that they did this because it was cheaper than
buying the books from a dealer.   There is no doubt, however,
that important books or beautifully executed copies brought
high prices; this applies especially to the original manuscripts of those authors who were most in demand among Roman collectors.

The number of private Roman collectors continued to
increase throughout the later years of the Republic and during
the Empire, and gradually the bibliophile came into fashion;
a sizable book collection was an essential part of a prominent Roman's house, preferably arranged in an elaborate setting that would add to the owner's prestige.   We have accounts
of such collections comprising several thousand rolls; they
were usually divided into a Greek and a Latin section. Wealthy
persons also had libraries at their country villas; and the
charred remains of one of these were found in the excavation
of Herculaneum.   This particular collection was in the villa
of the Pisos and contained mainly Epicurean writings, probably indicating the owner's predilection for this philosophical
doctrine.   But by no means did the owner always care about
the contents of his books; there must have been some basis
for Seneca's complaint about the many collectors who did not
even know as much as their slaves.   The Roman luxury libraries can be visualized as follows: In a room of green
marble tiles the book rolls were arranged on shelves, in
niches or in open cabinets along the walls; the rolls either
lay on the shelves enclosed in purple leather cases or they
stood upright in elaborately decorated containers.   Round a-
bout in the room stood busts or relief portraits of famous authors, a custom that Pliny the Elder say was introduced by
Asinius Pollio when he founded the first public library in
Rome.

Public libraries were also found in the Roman Empire.
With Alexandria as a model, Caesar planned to set up a similar library in the capital of his empire, but he did not live to
see the idea realized.   After his death, Asinius Pollio established the first public library in Rome, in the Libertas temple,

6.   Ruins of a Roman provincial library (the Celsus Library at Ephesus) founded 110 A.D.   At the back of the large
hall is seen an apse for a statue; along the walls there were
two rows of niches for book cases.   The outer walls are
double as protection against moisture.

in the year 39 B.C.   Under the Emperor Augustus two other
large libraries were added, the Palatine library in the temple
of Apollo on the Palatine Hill, established 28 B.C. in com-
memoration of the battle of Actium, and the Octavian library
in the hall of Octavian in the temple of Jupiter on the field of
Mars.   At each of these libraries there was a librarian with
several assistants; the library workers were called "librarii"
and belonged to the slave class.   The person in charge, however ("procurator bibliothecae") usually belonged to the eques-
trian class or was one of the Emperor's freedmen.   The salary of such a public servant in the first century A.D. was
the equivalent of about $2500 per year today.   Both of the li-
braries founded by Augustus were largely destroyed by fire
as were so many others of that time, the Palatine library in
191 A.D. and the Octavian library presumably in 80 A.D.
Shortly before this the library that the emperor Tiberius had

established in the temple he built on the Palatine Hill in
honor of Augustus also burned down, but it was rebuilt by the
emperor Domitian.   There were also public libraries on the
Capitoline Hill and at the magnificent baths built by the emperor Caracalla about 215 A.D.

All of these collections were overshadowed by the library that the emperor Trajan founded about 100 A.D., the
Bibliotheca Ulpia, which also served as the archives of the
empire.   In 370 A.D. there were said to have been no less
than 28 public libraries in Rome, and similar institutions had
gradually grown up in the provinces as well (Fig. 6).   Literary and archeological sources record a large library founded
by Hadrian in Athens.   The public libraries were, like most
of the private libraries, divided into a Greek and a Latin section.   The rolls lay in wooden cabinets set in niches in the
walls.   The long colonnades that were apparently found in
most libraries were coveted places of retreat for students who
could sit here and read or carry on their learned discussions.
There is also evidence that home loan of books was permitted
in special cases.   In the course of the 4th century A.D.,
however, the interest in libraries declined sharply and many
of them deteriorated from lack of use.

Latin literature began in earnest in the second century
B.C., and it was not long before there developed a style of
handwriting for use in literary works that differed from the
ordinary cursive writing.   The earliest Latin book script was
stiff and formal like the Greek, and like the Greek it consisted very largely of capital letters.   The oldest known example of this capital-letter form appears in a papyrus from
Herculaneum; the letters are jagged and have many corners.
In the so-called "capitalis quadrata" style the letters are almost square, while in "capitalis rustica" (Fig. 7) they are
slimmer and more elegant.   Alongside these styles of writing
there was another with broader and more rounded shapes, the
so-called uncial script.   By the 4th century uncial was fully
developed and it was the standard book script until the end of
the 8th century (Fig. 8).   Both styles, as well as the Greek,
used some abbreviations.

Invention of Paper in China

While the papyrus roll and the parchment codex were
thriving side by side in the libraries of the Roman Empire,
a discovery was being made in China, which was later to become of the greatest significance for book production.

ACUILVIILINTICYCLODESJULMINAMASSIS
CUMEAOCERANTALIITITAVRINISIOLLIBUSAURAS
ACCIDIUNTREDDUNTQUEALIISTRIDENTIATINGUNT
ALAALACUGEMIIINEOSLTISINCUDIBUSANTRUM
ILLISINTERSESLMAGNAUIBRACCHIATOLLUNT

7. An uncial (capitalis rustica) Virgil manuscript of the
4th century. (Papal Library in the Vatican). The illustration shows the smithy of the Cyclops and is typical of Roman
painting of the classical period.

8. Uncial manuscript that once belonged to the monastery
of Bobbio. The large writing is from the 4th century and is
a text of Cicero. Later this text has been erased and the
parchment used a palimpsest for a text by Augustine, written
in the 7th or 8th century in a small uncial hand. (After
Franz Steffens).

After the great book burning of 213 B.C. the Chinese began using silk cloth for writing, but silk was expensive and they therefore began making an entirely new material of silk rags that had been cut up in pieces and soaked to form a pasty mass that was then dried and became a sort of thin paper. This material was still too expensive to be widely used, so attempts were made to find something less expensive. According to tradition this search came to an end in the year 105 A.D. when Ts'ai Lun invented paper. Instead of silk cloth he used much cheaper substances as raw material: plant bark, especially bast fiber from the paper mulberry tree, discarded cotton cloth, old fish nets, etc. His invention soon met with general acceptance and in the next two or three centuries many manuscripts must certainly have been written on paper, though practically none are preserved from this early period. In a small oasis town at Lop-nor in the desert of Tibet Sven Hedin dug up several pieces of paper that may be the oldest in existence -- they are assumed to be from the second or third century A.D. -- and a number of paper manuscripts have been found in the walls of a temple at Tun Huang in Turkestan; some of these are now preserved in the British Museum, some in the Bibliothèque Nationale, and a few in the Royal Library in Copenhagen (one of the latter is dated 1016). Like the papyrus books these manuscripts were in the form of rolls.

For almost 700 years the Chinese were able to keep their method for producing paper a secret, but when Chinese paper-makers were captured by the Arabs in the middle of the 8th century the secret was discovered. From then on paper started its journey through the Arab empire and reached Europe about 1100. Before this took place, however, great changes of another nature had taken place and had set their mark on the history of the book in Europe.

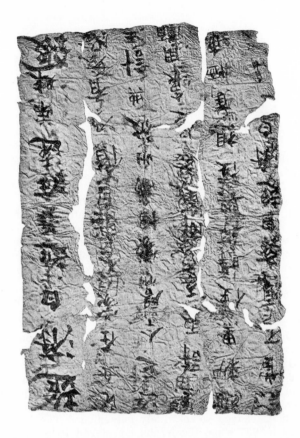

9. One of the fragments of paper documents excavated by Sven Hedin in a monastery ruin in the desert of Tibet. The paper is from the 2nd or 3rd century and is perhaps the oldest paper known. The characters were probably made with a hair brush.

THE MIDDLE AGES

Early Monastery and Church Libraries

When the Roman Empire gave way and Italy was laid waste by plundering expeditions of the barbarians, Roman book collections fared ill. A great many of them were certainly destroyed during the fifth and the beginning of the sixth century A.D. when the death struggle of the Roman Empire took place. Christianity had already begun to make its influence felt before this time; Christian literature was taking its place along with Greek and Latin literature. The churches had collections called "bibliothecae sacrae" or "bibliothecae christianae" containing the books of the Bible, the writings of the church fathers and the liturgical books that were used in the church services. Many of these libraries were destroyed during the persecution of the Christians that began under Diocletian in the year 303.

Outstanding among these libraries was the one at Caesarea in Palestine. It had been founded by the church father Origen, later reorganized by his pupil Pamphilos (who died 309 A.D.) and its importance for the Christian world was similar to that of the Alexandrian library in the world of Hellenic culture. The Bibles produced at the writing schools in Caesarea were widely esteemed. The library was destroyed in 637 when the Arabs conquered Palestine.

Information is available about book collections of other church fathers. Books were collected in the monasteries of Christian or, as it is called, Coptic, Egypt where the first communities of monks were formed as early as the second century. Knowledge of hieroglyphic writing was dying out at this period, and Greek script was used by the Christians. The Coptic language, which constituted the last phase of the ancient Egyptian language, was written in Greek letters and continued to be used by the church even after Egypt was conquered by the Arabs in the seventh century. There was considerable literary activity in these Coptic monasteries. From a number of them, especially those in the Nitrian desert, the British in the 19th century brought home many Coptic manuscripts and a number of Syrian manuscripts. The manuscripts

lay quite unnoticed by the monks at the time they were discovered, but on examination they were found to contain Christian and other texts going back to the fifth century.

Following the stormy period of the barbarian invasions
the importance of the Christian Church, and especially of the
Church of Rome, in the world of books continued to increase.
Throughout the Medieval period the church was the dominant
factor in this field and performed a work of decisive significance in preserving that part of the classical literature of the
ancient world that had escaped destruction in the great political upheavals.

Byzantine Libraries

Ancient Greek culture found a special place of refuge
in the Byzantine Empire. Just as the Ptolemys had done in
their time with Alexandria, so the emperor Constantine the
Great in the fourth century sought to make the capital of the
eastern Roman Empire, Byzantium (Constantinople,) a cultural center. Some two generations before the Alexandrian library was burned by the Christians, Constantine, with the
aid of Greek scholars, founded a library in which Christian
as well as secular literature was represented. Under Julian
the Apostate another library for non-Christian literature was
formed. Constantine's library burned in 475 and was reestablished, but its subsequent fate is very uncertain. At the
time of the capture of Constantinople in 1204 it was damaged
considerably, but there was still an imperial library in existence when the Turks captured the city in 1453; many of
the books were burned at that time or carried away and sold.

At the academy founded by Constantine in Byzantium
the study, and hence also the copying, of the Greek classics
was eagerly pursued; the same was true of the Byzantine
monasteries, which continued to be strongholds of Greek learning throughout the Middle Ages. The most famous of all these
was the Studium monastery in Byzantium, where the abbot
Theodore in the 9th century compiled rules for the conduct of
copying rooms and libraries; but there were also some 20
famous monasteries located in the mountains of the small pen-
insula Athos by the Aegean Sea, which had their flourishing
period in the 10-15th centuries. Even today these contain a-
bout 11,000 manuscripts, the older ones mainly of theological
and liturgical content, along with some musical texts. The
monastery of St. Catherine on Mt. Sinai and several others also possessed very valuable collections of manuscripts; in the
Sinai monastery was found the famous Biblical manuscript,

Codex Sinaiticus, which later came to Russia and is now in
the British Museum.

The Byzantine monastery libraries, as well as those
in Byzantium itself, became veritable mines for the book collectors of the Renaissance. In spite of this and the vandal-
ism they have suffered throughout the ages, so that almost
none of their most ancient stock is preserved, these libraries
still today contain great treasures from the early centuries
of the Middle Ages. They preserved the Byzantine cultural
tradition, which was later continued by the Greek Catholic
Church in the monasteries at Kiev and Novgorod and in the
Balkans; this applies particularly to the monasteries of Athos,
where the libraries became prototypes for those in Russian
monasteries.

Among the Byzantine scholars whose names are still
known was Photius, who lived in the 9th century. He gave
us valuable insight into the literature of classical antiquity
through his bibliography, Myriobiblon, in which he describes
the contents of the approximately 280 works in his own collection.

Arabic Interest in Greek Literature

Interest in Greek literature flourished in areas entirely outside the realm of the Christian Church. When the
Arabs were forming their great empire that extended from
Central Asia through Asia Minor and North Africa to Spain,
creative contact was also established between Greek and Arabic literature and science. In this great Islamic empire
there were large libraries attached to seats of learning,
mosques and especially to the courts of princes and rulers;
there were also private collections of importance. The art
of writing was highly respected and early assumed a decorative character.

In the first phase of the development the center for
the transfer of Greek literature to Arabic was the library of
the famous Caliph Harun-al-Raschid and his son Al-Mamuns
in Baghdad. Greek manuscripts were used, and later Iranian
and Syrian translations were made from the Greek.

The next phase of Islamic culture was connected with
the large collections of books in North Africa and Spain. A-
mong these the library of the Fatimite family in Cairo became
especially famous. It is said to have contained several hundred thousand volumes before it was plundered by the Turks

in 1068; its final destruction did not come until the 12th century. Some material from the Fatimite collection is preserved in Yemen. The contents were primarily manuscripts of the Koran and other religious books, but there were also works on mathematics, astronomy, medicine, philosophy, law and linguistics. Jewish scholars played a considerable role at that time in the transmission of the literature of ancient Greece.

This literature acquired a new seat at the library of the Umajjades in the Spanish town of Cordova. In particular, Al-Hakam II in the 10th century had books bought in large numbers from all parts of the Islamic empire, and in his palace he kept numerous scribes, editors and book-binders. This library suffered great damage through plundering and fire, and with the fall of the dynasty in 1031 it ceased to exist, but in the days of its glory it had seen lively activity in the translation of Greek classics into Arabic. Later these Arabic translations were again translated into Latin, and several famous classical authors, including Aristotle, Hippocrates and Galen, were, in part at least, made known to European scholars of the Middle Ages in this round-about way. After the fall of the Umajjades this translating activity found its home in Toledo.

Enormous destruction of books accompanied the storming of Samarkand and Baghdad by the Mongolians in the 13th century. After that period the various ruling dynasties of Islam paid more attention to Persian literature and history, and under the Sefavids in the 16th century Persian book production reached a high point.

The fact that the Islamic world was able to develop such a great literary activity is due in part to the circumstance that it had a writing material that was cheaper and better than papyrus or vellum. As mentioned earlier, Chinese paper makers were taken captive in the 8th century and brought by the Arabs to Samarkand in Turkestan; here they made paper of linen rags and flax, and the manufacture of paper soon spread throughout the entire caliphate. In the time of Harun-al-Raschid, at the close of the 8th century, there were factories in Baghdad and in Arabia, and in the 10th century the manufacture of paper reached Egypt.

Pieces of cordage and especially linen rags were used, and the paper produced in Islam can accordingly be called rag paper. The raw material was shredded, soaked in lime water, dried in the sun and thoroughly rinsed with clear water. It was then spread on a netting stretched over a frame and was

rubbed with fine flour and wheat starch. To make the sheets
suitable for writing they were dipped in wheat flour paste or
in a pasty residue of cooked rice, and finally smoothed with
a burnishing stone.

The art of paper making came to Europe about 1100,
when the Arabs introduced it into Spain. One of the first
places where paper was made was the current literary center, Toledo, though the earliest known place was in the vicinity of Valencia.

Libraries of the Roman Church

In general, it was the Church of Rome that through its
monastic orders and eccleciastical institutions continued the
care and use of books after the fall of the Roman Empire and
the triumph of Christianity. A peculiar figure in this period
of conflict between the old and the new was Cassiodorus, a
man of distinguished Roman ancestry who lived at the end of
the 5th and the beginning of the 6th centuries. He entered the
service of the Ostrogoth king Theodoric the Great, during
whose reign the reading of the ancient authors had its final
flourishing. In his old age Cassiodorus withdrew from the
life of the world, founded a monastery, the Vivarium, in
southern Italy and there established a sort of Christian academy. In the rules that he laid down for its conduct he ad-
monished the monks to serve God also by diligent study and
careful copying of texts, and by these he meant not only ecclesiastical texts but secular literature, both Greek and Latin
as well. Cassiodorus was the first to charge the monastic
communities specifically with the task of transmitting learning
and the scholarly tradition. After his death part of his monastery library is said to have come to the papal seat at Rome.
There, as early as the 5th century, books were being collected as part of the papal archives in the Lateran, but almost
nothing is known about this first papal library.

In this troubled period there were also instances of
concern for literature among prominent ecclesiastical and civil
officials outside of Italy. The archbishop of Clermont, Si-
donius Apollinaris, in his letters provides a glimpse of several
libraries in southern Gaul from the period following the inva-
sion of Attila; he describes in particular the beautiful collection that the prefect of Gaul, Tonantius Ferreolus, had in his
villa Prusiana near Nimes. This collection the bishop considered as good as any in ancient Rome. With the supremacy
of the Franks, however, a period of cultural decline began in
this region and was not followed by a revival until the end of

the 6th century. It was at about that time that the learned
Spanish bishop Isidore collected his extensive library in Seville and used it in writing his works, one of which, the Ety-
mologiae, was a sort of encyclopedia and was widely used as
a textbook for several centuries.

Books among the Benedictine and the Irish Monks

Among the monastic orders there was none more interested in working with books than the Benedictines. Benedict himself had in 529 founded the monastery on Monte Cassino in Italy which later became so famous, and in the regulations that he laid down for the life of the monks he placed
very great emphasis on reading. The brothers were to spend
their free time in reading, and two of the oldest among them
were to see that the others perform their duty in this respect.
Benedict himself had in mind pious rather than scholarly literature, but in the many Benedictine monasteries that sprang
up throughout Europe in the latter half of the 6th century, after his disciple Maurus had founded the monastery of St. Maur-
sur-Loire, the study and copying of classical authors was pursued along with that of religious works. It was, perhaps, not
their interest in ancient literature as such that led the monks
to work with it. Knowledge of Greek and Latin was necessary for their reading of church literature and they developed
proficiency in these languages by working with the classical
authors. These monks thus created an international literary
culture which, though primarily religious in character, still
maintained the connection with the intellectual life of classical
antiquity. The Catholic Church of the Middle Ages must be
given credit for the continuing influence of classical civilization down to our own day.

The work done by the Irish monks is particularly interesting. Although Ireland was far removed from the countries of the classical world this island, more than any other
place, became a refuge for classical culture in the early
Middle Ages. Ireland had been Christianized in the 5th century by the holy Patrick, who came from Gaul, and one century later there were said to have been about 300 monasteries
in Ireland and Scotland. In these there developed a literary
culture that far surpassed that of the monks in the monasteries on the mainland. The Irish monks, who had a knowledge
of Oriental and Byzantine culture as well as of the Greek language, were eager practicioners of the art of writing and book-
making. They evolved a special national style in script and
decoration, which will be considered later. The originals for
their manuscripts were obtained on pilgrimages to Rome and

by exchanges with French and Italian monasteries. In the 9th
and 10th centuries all the monasteries of Ireland were destroyed by the Vikings, and the old Irish manuscripts that remain are nearly all from the monasteries which the Irish had
established on the European continent.

Missionary zeal was characteristic of the Irish monks;
it brought them at an early period to both England and the
continent. Around the year 590 the famous Irish abbot Columban together with twelve other monks founded the first monastery in Gaul (France) at Luxeuil, bringing along manuscripts
to start a library. For more than a century Luxeuil continued
to be one of the chief centers of French intellectual life. St.
Columban later became the founder of a no less famous monastery in Italy, at Bobbio, and thus brought the distinctive
Irish manuscript tradition right down to the fatherland of the
Church, while some of his monks, among whom was Gallus,
founded the present monastery of St. Gallen in Switzerland,
with a library that later attained great repute.

The influence of the Irish monks was felt in England
as well; at the monastery Lindisfarne in northern England, for
instance, when envoys from the papal seat were also laboring
there as missionaries. The monastic libraries that were
founded in England, among which that at Canterbury took the
leading position, did in part escape the ravages of the Viking
period. Most famous among the English ecclesiasts of that
time was the church historian Bede, bishop Benedict, who
journeyed to Rome six times and brought back books, and
Boniface, who travelled to Germany and introduced Christianity there. One of the monasteries that Boniface founded, Fulda, later had a considerable library and a famous school of
writing and painting. A pupil of Bede, Egbert, became archbishop of York and there founded a library, where Alcuin
later became librarian, before he was called to the continent.

Luxeuil gave rise to another famous monastery, in
Corbie in Picardy, and from the latter came in turn the Saxon
monastery Korvey with its library in which Widukind in the
10th century wrote his chronicle. Many more examples could
be given of the propagation of monasteries, and geneological
tables could even be worked out for the monasteries of the
various orders; we note that the daughter institution usually
received a collection of manuscripts from the parent monastery
as the basis for a library.

Evolution of Book Script

As this great literary culture developed in the monasteries, with Latin as its linguistic form of expression and
Lating literature as its special field of study, the handwriting
itself also underwent evolution.   It began with the Latin cursive form which had taken its place in the first centuries A.
D. alongside the capital and uncial forms mentioned earlier.
This cursive style was the ordinary, everyday, script used in
ancient Rome, and it consisted almost entirely of small letters (minuscules) in contrast to the two other forms which
consisted mainly of capital letters (majuscules).   Little by
little the cursive script found its way into books, and in the
early Middle Ages it developed into individual national styles
at the various monasteries (Fig. 10a).   The West Gothic form
was common in Spain from the 8th to the 12th century.   The
French or Merovingian form was originally used by the Mer-
ovingians in their documents; it had a number of variant forms
as seen in the Luxeuil and Corbie manuscripts.   The Italian
style appears in many manuscripts from Bobbio, and the Beneventan form, developed at Monte Cassino, reached its high
point in the 10-11th century.

Both the Italian and the French forms of handwriting
were partly influenced by still another national style, already
referred to, namely the Irish-Anglo-Saxon, or the insular
form as it is also called.   The Irish form did not, like the
others, develop from Roman cursive but from another Roman
form, the half uncial (Fib. 10b), a broad rounded style which
the Irish monks gradually revised into a more angular and
compressed minuscule hand, while adopting features of the
still current runic alphabet.   This special Irish style was disseminated by the monks on their missionary journeys, and was
used in the monasteries that they founded, Bobbio, Luxeuil,
St. Gallen, etc., along with a more fluent Irish minuscule.
English monasteries likewise used both an Anglo-Saxon half
uncial and a minuscule form, and these were brought to the
continent by English monks.

A common feature of all these styles of writing is the
use of abbreviations, or abbreviatures as they were called.
Even in the manuscripts of the ancient period a few constantly
recurring words or syllables were shortened, but in Medieval
manuscripts, first in ecclesiastical and then later also in secular texts, abbreviations became more common.   They did
not become very frequent until the 12-14th, centuries when
they gradually became systematized.   Originally, quite different abbreviations were used in the different types of handwriting -- the insular manuscripts, for example, had several

West Gothic script of the 10th century.

Merovingian script of the 7th century.

Beneventan script of the 11th century.

Irish script of the 7th century.

10a.   National forms of Latin minuscule script of the 6th century.   (After Franz Steffens).

10b. Half-uncial script in a manuscript of the 6th century. (After Franz Steffens).

peculiar abbreviations of their own. Later the system became more fixed and uniform. Considerable practice was required to master this system, and regular lexicons were compiled of the abbreviatures and their meaning. At first abbreviation consisted in condensing the word, so that only a few of its letters were written; i.e. DS = deus (God), DNS = dominus (lord), EPS = episcopus (bishop), etc.; in ecclesiastical manuscripts this was done rather to emphasize the words than to save space, as was the case later. Besides these condensations, there also came into use a series of fixed symbols for frequently recurring words -- a sort of shorthand that had its origin in old Roman legal documents: 3 = eius (his), γ = et (and), $\wp$ = pro (for), ρ = per (through), etc. Still another type of abbreviation was superscription; the latter part of a word was shortened by writing a single letter above the first part of the word, as $\overset{\circ}{g}$ = ergo, $\overset{\cdot}{m}$ = mihi, etc.

When a monk was to write a manuscript he first cut the vellum to size, squaring it with the aid of a knife and a ruler; then the surface was smoothed and lines ruled on the sheets, the distance between the lines being marked by small holes punched in the margin with a divider. The lines were scratched with an awl or drawn in red ink, later often with a graphite pencil. When he was finally ready to begin writing, the scribe (calligrapher) sat down at a sloping desk in which there were two inkwells, one for red and one for black ink, and equipped with his quill pen and his erasing knife he started to work. The red ink was used to draw a red vertical line through the initial letters of the text; this was called rubricating (Latin rubrum = red).

When the scribe had finished copying a text he added
a few lines at the end (subscription or colophon, as they were
called) in which the title of the book was included. These
lines usually began with the words "explicitus est," or simply
"explicit," a peculiar reminder of the time when manuscripts
were still in the form of rolls, since these words mean that
the manuscript has been unrolled. However, the title could
also be found at the beginning of the manuscript, starting with
the words "hic incipit" ("here begins") followed by a statement of the text involved. At the end the scribe also frequently noted when and where and for whom the work had been
done, etc., and he might add his own name to be remembered
by posterity.

A number of Medieval manuscripts are palimpsests, as
has been pointed out. From the 7-9th centuries in particular,
when there was a shortage of vellum, there are many manuscripts with theological texts, underneath which modern photographic techniques have discovered earlier texts of works from
classical antiquity that have been erased but are still legible
(Fig. 8).

Manuscript Decoration

As has been noted, illustrations occurred even in the
manuscripts of the ancient period, although mainly in works
on natural history and medicine, and in the Hellenistic period
there must certainly have been entire books of pictures with
only an explanatory text. Papyrus was not a good material
for book paintings, but vellum was much better. Ancient vellum manuscripts did in fact display the beginnings of artistic
book decoration, which continued its vigorous development in
the Medieval period.

Up until the 12th century illustration was mainly of
Gospels (evangeliaries). They were ornamented with pictures
of Christ surrounded by the four Apocalyptic beasts and by the
four evangelists, Matthew, Mark, Luke and John, each with
his own symbol. The so-called canonical tables -- tables
compiled to show the inner harmony of the Gospels -- were
arranged in columns and surrounded by a colonnade with
arches. Another major object of decoration in manuscripts
was the letters (initials) at the beginning of the various sections or chapters. Even in Roman times these letters were
made larger and were often set off in red by the use of red
lead or cinnabar. This custom developed rapidly in the Medieval monasteries; the initial letters were made larger and
larger and were adorned with scrolls and borders of greater

11.   Canon tables in a manuscript of the 12th century, made either in the Helmarshausen monastery near Diemel or at Lund for the Cathedral there. (University Library, Uppsala). (From "Golden Books").

and greater artistry. These large decorative letters were
painted in various colors, and often gold or silver was used.
In the case of letters that permitted it a further step was
taken by painting an entire scene within them.

    Besides these splendid initial designs many manuscripts
from the later Middle Ages have a number of independent illustrations called miniatures, from the Latin word "minium"
meaning red lead. If gold was used in addition to the other
colors they are called illuminations (Latin "lumen" = light),
and the manuscripts thus adorned are often designated as
"golden books." The paints were either opaque colors or
water colors; gold was used in the form of very thin polished
leaves or as a powder; in the early period it usually had a
yellow brass sheen, later a more reddish shade.

    It was seldom true that the same monk or nun who
wrote the text also made the initials and the illustrations. The
scribe simply left space for the latter and often wrote directions in the margin, in a light hand that could be erased, relative to the decorations and illustrations. The "miniator" or
the "illuminator" then took over, equipped with his supply of
colors, his brushes and his gold. The outline of the picture
was drawn in fine lines with a pen before the colors were
painted and the gold laid or sprinkled on.

    In the decoration of initials as well as in the execution
of miniatures and illuminations, as in the case of the handwriting itself, different styles, often with more or less local
variation, can be distinguished. The so-called Merovingian
ornamentation, for instance, which was general throughout
western Europe in the 8th century, was characterized by initials showing fishes and birds and by the use of red, green
and yellow colors, but this standard pattern was varied in different ways depending on whether the paintings were made in
German, French or Spanish monasteries.

    An entirely different style is found in Byzantine book
decoration, which reached its highest development in the 11-
12th century. It was characterized by extensive use of gold
and of purple and other dark colors, producing a rather som-
ber and mystical effect at times; the influence of Syrian and
other Oriental art is apparent. The Byzantine style in turn
affected some western European book painting, as seen, for
instance, in manuscripts from Ireland and northern England.
Here book artistry flourished in the 8th and 9th centuries, and
is recognizable by its Celtic braided work and ribbons, often
embellished with heads of birds, dogs and various mythical
beasts; gold and purple occur frequently among the colors. In

12. Byzantine book painting in a manuscript from the end of the 10th century, made in Constantinople. It is presumed to represent Solomon seated on the throne and behind him a woman symbolizing wisdom; at the left Jesus Syrach. (Royal Library, Copenhagen). (From "Golden Books").

13.   Miniature from the Codex aureus, the work of a
southern England miniature school, probably at Canterbury, a-
bout the year 750.   The decoration combines English-Scandi-
navian features with strong Byzantine traits.   (Royal Library,
Stockholm).   (From "Golden Books").

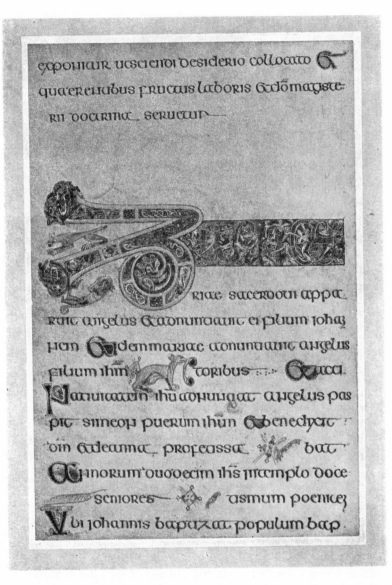

14. Page from the "Book of Kells," the book of the Gospels made at the Irish monastery of Kells about 800, in Irish script with Celtic features in the decoration.

southern England in the 10-11th century book decoration is
characterized in particular by profusely branched foliage borders and other special features.

Among the famous manuscripts executed in the styles
described above there are the Gospel produced at the Irish
monastery Kells about 800 A.D. (the Book of Kells, now in
Dublin; Fig. 14), also the Gospel from the northern England
monastery Lindisfarne (about 700 A.D., now in the British
Museum). Another is the manuscript with silver and gold letters on purple-colored vellum, called Codex Argenteus (the
silver book) which is now in the University Library at Upsala
in Sweden. It contains part of the translation of the Bible into Gothic made by Bishop Ulfilas in the 4th century; it was
written in Italy in the 6th century and later disappeared, re-
appearing in the 16th century in a German monastery, then
taken to Prague, and from there the Swedes carried it home
as booty in the Thirty Years War.

We must not forget, however, that alongside these and
other illustrious manuscripts there were many that had only
a limited amount of decoration or none at all, and that not all
the monks or nuns who executed the decorative work were e-
qually gifted. Nevertheless, it can be said, in general that
decorative art in the Middle Ages found one of its most significant expressions in book painting, supported in large measure by book-loving princes.

Charlemagne's Attempt at Centralization

An event of great significance for the entire literary
world occurred when the emperor Charlemagne, in the 8th
century, invited foreign scholars to his court in the interests
of promoting knowledge and scientific activity in his empire.
From Italy, came Paulus Diaconus, from York in Northumber-
land came Egbert's pupil Alcuin, whose work has left its mark
at the Abbey of St. Martin in Tours; the school that he established there later became the model for many other monastery and church schools. One of Alcuin's pupils, Hrabanus
Maurus, became a leader in the monastery library of Fulda.
Charlemagne maintained a staff of scribes at his court in
Aachen and collected a sizable library there; the scholars attached to the court were assigned the task of working up phil-
ologically correct editions of classical as well as theological
works, just as was done in the library of Alexandria in its
time.

In line with these efforts at cultural centralization

genera hoftium · proponamuf; Pagani dicunt; Quid eft
quodnof ex or retif adq; abicicif· tamquá multof colentef
deof· ecce uof dm qué pdicaaf colendú · filium habere di
cicif· & fine alterruf con mixtaone fexuf· patú eé confin
gunf; Iudei dicunt; Quomodo unú colicif dm · quando &
homine qué parref nri · crucifixerunt · dnm dicentef ·
hominib; excor queaf· ut camquá filium dei uenerantur·

15. Carolingian minuscule script in an Augustine manuscript of the 11th century. (After Franz Steffens).

Charlemagne and his circle also instituted reforms in the style
of writing in use. In the course of time there had necessarily
come to be felt a need for greater uniformity, in place of the
various regional styles of script, and gradually the Carolingian (or Caroline) style was established as the standard form
(Fig. 15). It was a minuscule hand that probably evolved from
the Merovingian. Gradually it superseded the various national forms, though it did, of course, take on certain special
features in the writing rooms of the individual monasteries.
In general, however, it maintained a uniform character as seen,
for instance, in its club-shaped vertical lines, which are reminiscent of the contemporary style in art and gave it the name
of Romance script. In the course of the 12th and 13th centuries it underwent a transformation; the letters became narrower
and more angular, and the contrast between thick and thin lines
became more pronounced -- the result was Gothic script (Fig.
16) corresponding to its contemporary Gothic style in art.
Writing had thus followed the evolution from the round Roman
arch to the pointed Gothic arch. The letters were written so
close together that two adjoining ones were often run into one
(e.g., the d and e). In large liturgical manuscripts the letters
were usually made quite large and heavy and given a rather
decorative appearance; this style was called missal script
(from the mass books, or missals); the name lattice script
was also given to it because the crowded letters made it re-
semble lattice work (Fig. 17). For more ordinary use there
was a Gothic cursive which was the ancestor of the script that
is still used in Germany and until a generation or two ago was
also in general use in Denmark ("old Danish" script).

16. Gothic minuscule script in a manuscript from 1339. (After Franz Steffens).

The Carolingian movement likewise had its effect in the field of illumination. An attempt was made to fuse the various regional characteristics that the manuscripts gathered from various sources. In the history of the book, as well as the history of art as a whole, this can be characterized as a Carolingian period or a "Carolingian renaissance." In books arts this movement is influenced not only by the earlier national styles, especially the Irish, but also takes many of its motifs from the plant world as well as from Roman decorative art.

Following a period of decline around the year 900, book arts blossom forth anew. In the development called the Ottonic renaissance after the emperor Otto the Great, which took place mainly at the monasteries in Fulda, at St. Emmerau in Regensburg and on the island of Reichenau in Bodensee; book ornamentation represented a mixture of Carolingian and Byzantine elements along with a tendency to exaggerate the form and movement of the figures. At this same period in England, especially at Winchester, book illustrations featured flowing drapery and ornaments in which acanthus friezes are prominent.

In the following period, particularly in the 12th and 13th centuries, the embellishment of the Psalms of David became the most important function of book painting. About 100 psalters, as they were called, have been preserved from these two centuries; many of them, especially the French and English, have both large and small initials and a charming series of scenes from the story of David or the life of Jesus. Often these psalters were made for royal personages, such as the beautiful psalter that belonged to Ingeborg, the daughter of Waldemar the Great, and is now in the Condé Museum at Chantilly. The pictures in it show Byzantine influence, but the beautifully rounded curves of the figures and their dress are typically French.

Manuscripts and Monastery
Libraries in Scandinavia

Alphabetical writing came to Scandinavia, as well as to the other countries north of the Alps, with the introduction of Christianity. Ansgar, the Apostle of the North, taught his disciples to read and probably also to write, and as the church became more and more firmly established the art of book production followed along with it. The oldest preserved books that can with certainty be said to have been written in Sandinavia do not, however, go back farther than the 11th century. The oldest Old Norse or Icelandic writing shows the influence of Carolingian as well as Irish and Anglo-Saxon styles; the latter in particular has set its mark on Norwegian manuscripts, where runic forms, as in insular manuscripts, are found while Icelandic writing has mainly been under the influence of the Carolingian style. Both Norwegian and Icelandic manuscripts show extensive use of abbreviations. Through Norway, Swedish medieval writing received a definite Anglo-Saxon influence, while Danish medieval writing was influenced by the Carolingian style and later followed the same transition to the Gothic style that took place in the course of the 13th century everywhere on the mainland. The oldest Danish manuscripts that we have were written in Gothic script: the Laws of Skania, Zealand and Jutland, Henrik Harpestreng's Book of Medicine, etc.

In the Scandinavian countries monastic culture and monastery libraries developed as in other countries, and the churches also had more or less extensive book collections.

ſtam ſua durat uutute ap
tuuam: tubue qͥs. ut bona q
pͣapib: ſuis contuht. lar
giatur et nobis ut xpiſtus

17. Missal or canon script with pointed, close-set letters
giving the page the appearance of a lattice-work. From a
French missal of the 14th century. (Royal Library, Copenhagen, Thott Collection).

        In the Scandinavian countries monastic culture and mon-
astery libraries developed as in other countries, and the
churches also had more or less extensive book collections.
In Denmark there were libraries in Øm monastery (Cara Insula) at Ry, in Sorø (there is still a Justinus manuscript in
the Royal Library that was presented to the monastery of
Sorø by Absalon), also at Herredsvad, Naestved, etc. The
cathedrals in Lund, Roskilde, Ribe, Aarhus, Slesvig and other
places also had relatively large collections. The ordinary
parish churches, of course, had much smaller collections,
perhaps only a few volumes. In Norway, where the oldest
Latin book was written about the middle of the 11th century
and the oldest books in the native language toward the end of
the same century, there were book collections at the bishop
seats of Bergen, Trondheim and Stavanger, and in Munkeliv
monastery in Bergen. In Sweden the monastery collections
were overshadowed by the library of the Birgittiner monastery
in Vadstena, which contained some 1500 volumes and was the
largest medieval library in the Scandinavian countries.

        When Scandinavian medieval manuscrips are compared
with those of other countries, such as Italy, France or England, they are clearly inferior in workmanship and appearance.
The initials and miniatures that were produced in the Scandinavian countries did not come up to the contemporary level of
book art elsewhere. In addition, especially in the case of
Icelandic manuscripts, there is the fact that they have been
transmitted to us in a rather unflattering condition; in many

of them the vellum is rough and dark, discolored by smoke
or spotted by fat and other dirt, almost completely covering
the text in some places. A glance at the two famous Edda
manuscripts and the Flatey Book, the largest medieval manuscript from Scandinavia, all three of which were written in
the 13th and 14th centuries and are now in the Royal Library
in Copenhagen, or at the manuscripts in the famous Arnamagnean collection which belongs to the University of Copenhagen,
gives the general impression that they were made and spent
a good deal of their time in a society where the esthetic sense
was not highly developed.

But even though Scandinavia was inferior in this respect, the development of medieval book arts in these countries illustrated more or less closely the pattern in other
countries. In the quiet writing room, the scriptorium, where
the noises of the world did not penetrate and where life was
controlled by the strong bonds of regulation, monks and nuns
applied themselves to their task of copying for the glory of
God. The labor of years was expended on many of the old
manuscripts (one of the most industrious Danish monks, Johannes Paschae of Roskilde, is known to have spent over a
year and a half writing a Bible in two volumes) and it would
scarcely have been possible to complete such a work except
in a monastery where life was lived "sub specie aeternitatis."
Several monks often worked together on the same codex, each
taking a separate section. Additions to the monastery libraries came primarily from the work of the brothers. They
could not own books themselves, but everything they wrote belonged to the monastery. Gifts were also made to the libraries by prominent persons or high church dignitaries, who in
this way achieved the honor of having their names inscribed
in the monastery gift book (liber daticus) and mentioned in the
brothers' prayers. At the great church meetings in Constance
and elsewhere there was the opportunity to acquire books, but
no regular trade in books, such as existed in ancient times,
is found until toward the end of Middle Ages.

Not many of the monastery libraries had more than a
few hundred volumes. The library of the Bobbio monastery,
which in the 9th century had about 700 volumes, was one of
the largest of its time. Of course, many of the volumes contained more than one text. Two of the brothers functioned as
librarian and director of the scriptorium ("armarius" or "li-
brarius" and "scriptuarius" they were called). They took care
of the cataloging and shelving. The catalogs were simply in-
ventories, intended merely for finding a particular manuscript
and contained only brief information for this purpose. The
books were placed in cabinets and only in the later part of the

18. Page of the Elder Edda (Saemundar Edda), written at the end of the 13th century; presented to King Frederik III by the Icelandic bishop Brynjólfur Sveinsson. (Royal Library, Copenhagen).

Middle Ages were these partly replaced by sloping desks (Fig. 22). In the shelving arrangement the Bible and the Church Fathers came first, then followed theology and classical literature, and finally came the other subjects such as history, law, medicine, etc. One of the librarian's duties was to supervise the use of the books. Among the Benedictines books were exchanged once a year, while the monastery regulations of Augustine and Isidore of Seville provided for daily loan of books to the brothers in the morning and return of them in the evening.

Early Medieval Book Binding

One of the monastery brothers ("ligator") took care of the binding of the books. The oldest type of binding from the Middle Ages, however, was quite different from what we now understand by book binding. It was goldsmith and jeweler's work. In the time of the Empire the wax tablets (diptycha), mentioned earlier, which the Romans used for short notations, were specially made of ivory for festive occasions, such as when a consul was to be installed, and their outer sides were artistically decorated. There are also several examples of such special diptycha from the Middle Ages, when they served as bindings for ecclesiastical manuscripts. Hence it is with good reason that these are considered the progenitors of the gem bindings of the early Middle Ages, which consisted of flat wooden boards embellished with reliefs in ivory or in hammered silver and gold and even with precious stones, pearls and enamel work. These bindings were made chiefly for the so-called altar bindings. Often the front side, which lay uppermost, was more richly decorated than the back. The motifs for the reliefs were usually taken from pictures in the manuscript itself and usually represented episodes from Bible stories, with perhaps a crucified Christ as the central figure. In the surrounding border stylized flower and leaf ornaments are often found.

These fine bindings, in common with the miniatures in the manuscripts themselves, exhibit various styles according to the time and place where they were made. Thus there are characteristic Byzantine enamel bindings, silver and bronze bindings with the easily recognizable Irish dragon patterns, ivory bindings that show the marks of Carolingian art, and others that are just as clearly in the Romance style. There are bindings in which the borders set with precious stones are the most conspicuous feature, others in which the central panel, with its high relief in hammered gold dominates. In short, a diverse multitude of artistic fantasies is represented

19.   Jeweled binding from the 10th century, containing the Echtenach Gospels (Landesbibliothek, Gotha).

in these bindings, which are still preserved in quite large numbers in libraries and museums, though often greedy hands have robbed them of their gold and their precious stones.

Leather Bindings

In contrast to the preceding, ordinary monastery manuscripts had either a plain parchment cover or a leather binding. In the course of the 14th century jeweled bindings became scarcer and in many liturgical books, less elaborate, being made of velvet or leather with metal limited to the corner pieces and the bosses that came into use in the late Gothic period so that the book could then rest on those bosses when it lay flat and the face of the binding would not be scratched.

Leather binding, as mentioned earlier, was known in ancient times but it did not come into general use in Europe until the Middle Ages. The covers of the book were usually made of beech, oak or maple wood across which leather was stretched. Dark brown calf-skin was commonly used and it could be decorated in various ways. There is evidence that deerskin and the skin of other wild animals was used.

From the older medieval period there are a number of bindings embellished with leather tooling; a pattern was drawn on the damp leather and the lines then cut into the leather with a knife and spread or punched out with a blunt tool. The technique of leather carving was used in the Coptic monasteries, but its flourishing period came in the 15th century when its home seems to have been primarily in southern Germany and Austria. The decoration usually consisted of plant designs and the grotesque late Gothic animal figures, but included representations of angels, saints, and later of knights hunting or of love scenes.

Far more common, however, are the pressed leather bindings, which did not require as fine a touch as leather carving. Hot stamps with the designs engraved on them were pressed down on the leather to make the ornamentation stand out in relief. No gilding was involved, whence the process is called blind stamping. Like leather carving it is also found in the early bindings from the Coptic monasteries. The basic pattern used in this process consisted of a series of borders within one another, composed of small square, triangular, round or heart-shaped figures. As a rule there was a difference in the design of the outer borders and of the middle section, where the stamps were either arranged in small geometric groups or in less formal patterns. In the Carolingian

20. Tooled leather binding made in Nuremberg about 1470.
The decoration consists of noble personages with flower gar-
lands; the binding has bosses and clasps. (Stadtbibliothek,
Leipzig).

period the variety of stamps was rather limited, but in the
Romance period the number increased considerably, with the
sides of the binding filled with plant and animal designs, figures of saints, knights and other human forms.   In the Gothic
period the trend was back to simpler decoration.

The corners of the binding were, as before, usually
protected by brass mountings with bosses, and the book was
kept tightly closed by metal clasps.   In addition to this, in
the later Middle Ages, iron chains were attached to the upper
or lower edge of the binding and the books thus fastened to
the desk or the shelf so that they could not fall down or be
removed from their place.   No importance was attached to
decorating the spine of the book; the books usually lay on a
desk, or if they stood on shelves it was with the spine toward
the wall; our practice of placing them with the spine forward
dates from the 17th century.   The title of the book was therefore often written in ink either on the bottom edge where it
could be seen when the book was lying down, or on the fore-
edge where it could be seen when the book was standing on
the shelf.

It should not, of course, be assumed that all the bindings made in the monasteries were as artistically executed as
those described here; many were quite plain, and not all the
monks that acted as ligators were above the level of dilettantes.
But in just as many instances the artistic sense and precise
workmanship exhibited in the use of the stamps seems mar-
velous.

Libraries of the New Monastic Orders

The Rise of Universities

As has been noted, the Benedictines placed special emphasis on literary activity, and in the 12th century the oldest
of their monastery libraries, Monte Cassino, attained high renown.   Other monastic orders also made their contribution.
Among these was the Cluniac offshoot of the Benedictine order,
among whose principle seats were Canterbury and the Abbey
of St. Albans in England.   The new monastic orders of the
later Middle Ages, the Carmelite brothers and the mendicant
friars, the Franciscans and the Dominicans, also took part in
this work.   In England, where the Mendicants came in 1224,
they built up large collections of books at London and Oxford;
likewise at Annaberg in Saxony, in Venice, Basel, and other
places.   It is interesting to note that such a modern device as
a union catalog was compiled even at that early time by the

21. Late gothic binding; blind-stamped squares and circles inside rhomboids; corner bosses and chain. (Royal Library, Copenhagen). The decoration shows that it was made by a rather unskilled monastery binder.

Franciscan monks. At the end of the 14th century requests
were sent out to no less than 186 English monasteries for information concerning their book stock, and on the basis of the
replies there was formed the Registrum librorum Angliae (catalog of books in England), which is now in the Bodleian Library at Oxford and can be considered the oldest known attempt at compiling a common catalog for a group of libraries
to show in which of them a particular book was to be found.

The Franciscans and the Dominicans also became important through the influence they exerted on the formation of
the first universities. Universities began to arise in the 13th
century in close connection with the churches. The best known
of the early universities were in Paris, Padua and Bologna.
In Paris the first collegium was founded by a churchman,
Robert de Sorbona (it is still called the Sorbonne), and Bologna became a famous center for the study of Roman law.
All these universities had their book collections or libraries,
although these differed greatly in size and content. The largest seem to have been those attached to the various collegia
in Paris; Robert de Sorbona presented his own collection to
one of them.

With the establishment of the universities it became possible for a book trade to develop. That was not possible in
the Middle Ages. Book dealers were usually called "station-
arii" (the word stationer is still used in England) and they and
their scribes were appointed or at least controlled by the university and had to agree to keep in stock correct editions of
the books that were used for instruction and rent them out for
a fixed fee to students for copying; they could only sell books
on commission. Book-selling was thus a strictly limited and
regulated business, yet it must still have paid well, to judge
from the large number of stationers that quickly gathered at
the new seats of learning, especially at the one in Paris.
Rules for stationers appeared in 1259 in Bologna, and in 1275
in Paris. Privileged book binders were similarly attached to
the universities. A stationer at a university could also sell
manuscripts to other universities and to scholars in foreign
countries; books on medicine came primarily from Salerno and
Montpelier, scholastic literature from Paris, and law books
from Bologna.

As in the monastery libraries the books of the university collections usually had to be used in the library where
they were chained to their places (Fig. 21). If a book was
loaned, another book had to be left as security. Additions to
the collections came in large part through gifts by royal persons or other prominent individuals, from high ecclesiastical

22. Late medieval library interior at Zutphen near Arn-
heim in Holland.   Books chained to desks.

officers or from professors.   The college at Paris was especially fortunate in this respect.   Gradually as more universities arose in the course of the 14th century -- at Oxford
and Cambridge, Prague, etc., libraries grew up in a similar manner along with them.

Private Book Collections of the Middle Class

In the Middle Ages books were not very common outside churches, monasteries and universities or the courts of
kings and nobles.   To an even greater degree than in ancient
Rome, literary culture belonged to the upper classes, and the
practical reason was the high cost of books.   Vellum had grad
ually become expensive -- one indication of this is the fact
that several texts were written in a single codex if necessary
to use up the sheets.   Copying was a tedious task that could
not be performed by as cheap labor as that represented by the
slaves of ancient Rome.   In the tenth century a countess of
Anjou is said to have given 200 sheep, three barrels of grain

23. German paper mill, run by water-power. The water-
wheel drives the stamping mechanism on the ground floor,
where the rags are ground to a soft pulp, which is then treated
in the vat on the upper floor.

and some marten furs for a single book of sermons, and at the
end of the 14th century a prayer book in two volumes was
bought by the Duke of Orleans for 200 gold francs, to mention
only two examples.

It was not until the 14th and 15th centuries that the middle class in the towns attained a cultural, social and economic
level that made it possible for them to own books. Nor did
these bourgeois book collections have the predominant Latin
character of those in the churches, monasteries and colleges.
Books in the national language of the country, law books, medical and herb books and the emergent poetical literature were
by no means unknown in the institutional libraries, but they became the dominant elements in the bourgeois collections. With
the flowering of the middle class, book-binding began to develop into a craft independent of the monasteries.

One contributing factor to the wider distribution of books
in middle-class circles was the introduction of the use of paper instead of vellum. As noted, the Arabs had brought paper-

making to Spain in the 12th century, and in 1276 the first paper mill was established in Italy. A mill of this type was
driven by water power; the water-wheel operated a number of
heavy beaters that tore up the raw material -- linen and cotton rags, cordage, etc. -- under water and mashed it to a
thin pulp, which was then poured into a vat. A frame was
dipped into the vat and on this frame the paper sheet was
formed; the frame was made of wood with brass wires stretch
across it. Felt pads were used to draw off the water from
each sheet; the sheets were then pressed, dried, and finally
sized to make the paper suitable for writing. The sizing
liquid was made from a boiled extract of animal hides, bones,
etc. The brass wires in the frame left lines in the paper
that were plainly visible when it was held up to the light, and
the idea soon developed of bending some of the wires to form
various designs. These so-called watermarks, could contain
the initials or the name of the paper-maker. The oldest know
water-mark dates from 1282. For the first hundred years
thereafter the marks were still rather crude but later they
were more artistic. The motifs used were flowers or animals, such as fish and birds, or often an ox head, as the
symbol of the paper maker. In Holland one of the marks
used was a beehive. In England a jester's head with cap
(foolscap) appeared. Several of these marks have continued
to the present day and they are now also used to indicate specific formats. From Europe the custom of watermarks extended itself to the Orient, whence the paper had come to
Europe.

     In the 14-15th century Italy became the principle pro-
ducer of paper. The new art was brought to France by Itali-
ans and the oldest known paper mill on French territory dates
from 1338. From France the manufacture of paper spread to
Germany toward the close of the 14th century and from there
in the course of the 15th century to England and Holland,
where it later made great progress. In 1690 it came to A-
merica. The Scandinavian countries got their first paper mills
in the 16th century, by way of Germany, with the first one in
Stockholm about 1540, followed by others in Scania and on
Zealand (at Hvidøre) and one on Tycho Brahe's island Hven.

     In the 14th century manuscripts began to appear on pa-
per and in the course of the 15th century they became more
and more common. Paper was considerably cheaper than vellum (at first about one-third the cost of the latter, later one-
sixth) and hand-made paper (or vat paper as it was called from
the method of manufacture) was of excellent quality, even thoug
it was not entirely white in appearance and had a slightly rough
surface. It is well preserved in the old books that are extant

24. Various water-marks from early hand-made papers. At left of second row from top, the ox-head, one of the oldest and most frequent marks in early paper. At lower left, the "fools-cap," which was much used in Italy and France at the beginning of the 14th century, and later came to England, where it is still in use.

except where it has been attacked by book-worms.

Royal Book Collections

The great bibliophiles of the 13-15th centuries were found especially among royalty. These included Otto III in Germany and Frederick II of Hohenstaufen; in Bohemia King Wencelaus. In France, which throughout the entire later Middle Ages was the leading country in book illumination, the outstanding collectors were Phillip the Good, and other Burgundian lords, as well as a number of the kings of France: Charle the Bald, Louis IX (Saint Louis), and Charles V (the Wise). The last of these must be considered the real founder of the French royal library, the present Bibliothèque Nationale. The catalog of his library, dated 1373, lists about 1,000 volumes which were housed in the Louvre. A bibliophile on an even grander scale was Charles' brother, John of Berry.

At this period the art of miniature painting was no longer confined to the monasteries; a class of independent illuminators had arisen. They did, it is true, sell part of thei work to churches and monasteries, but primarily they worked for royalty and other men of worldly importance. For the most part the manuscripts that they decorated were prayer books (breviaries), particularly the excerpt from the official ecclesiastical prayer book intended for the laity. This abbreviated prayer book was called "hora" in Latin, "livre d'heures" in French, "tidebog" in Danish, [and in English Book of Hours,] because the prayers in it were to be read at certain times of the day. These books were usually in small format (octavo or small quarto) and the pictures in them represented not only scenes from the life of Christ but also landscapes, hunting and battle scenes, festivals, incidents from civil and peasant life, etc., with no relation to the contents of the book.

The names of only a few of these lay illuminators are known. The greatest of them in the earlier period was Jean Pucelle, who painted flowers, animals and men in fine detail and in true naturalistic style. At the end of the 14th and the beginning of the 15th century a group of Flemish book artists moved to Paris; several of them -- Jacquemart de Hesdin, Jehannequin and Pol from Limbourg and the latter's two brothers -- worked for John of Berry, and, among other things, produced one of the most famous Books of Hours, known as "les très riches heures de Jean duc de Berry." The miniatures made by these artists give a very real lively impression of Flemish life and costumes of the time.

After this French-Flemish period the Paris artisans continued to produce Books of Hours in large numbers, but as time went on most of them simply became competent traditional products. In the second half of the 15th century the art experienced a revival with the painter Jean Foucquet of Tours. Among the many books that he worked on was a book of hours executed for Étienne Chevalier, in artistic respects the most beautiful of all known Books of Hours. Foucquet's pictures were not merely decoration, but illustrations related to the text. He was influenced by Italian art and was partial to large monumental compositions with many figures, landscapes, pictures of towns and battle scenes, all of which he executed with superior craftsmanship.

The style that prevailed in book artistry of the late Middle Ages was, as in the case of the writing itself, Gothic. This is indicated, for instance, in the frequent use of motifs from Gothic architecture, with its pointed arches. The figures are not, as in Romance book painting, joined with the background but stand bodily out from it, and in older period the human figures, as in the glass paintings in Gothic churches, are tall and slender with narrow shoulders and long hands and feet. Later the figures became more and more true to nature, as do also the flowers, leaves, insects and birds that adorn the margins against a background of pale gold. They were not tied in with the initials but form independent wide borders.

The Gothic style in its several variations characterized not only the Books of Hours but also the Bibles, in small handbook format, that were produced in large numbers at the universities and distributed far and wide. It likewise characterized the many late medieval manuscripts of chronicles, tales of knighthood, minnesongs and other secular literature in the vernacular. In addition there were the large folio choir books (antiphonaries) with notes, that were produced mainly in Italy, and finally Gothic style appeared in the realistic Dutch book paintings that were so beautifully executed in the Books of Hours and the other devotional books. Gradually this literature became a profitable trade item, produced by professional scribes and book painters who sold their illuminated prayer books at markets or from stalls at or even in the churches. In the small German town of Hagenau, for instance, a school teacher named Diebold Lauber ran a large shop where he kept numerous scribes, illuminators, rubricators and bookbinders busy. The Dutch and German "Brothers of the Common Life" became very active in the production and sale of illuminated devotional books. However, as more manuscripts were put on the market their illustrative material in many instances became more and more routine and lost a great deal of its ear-

25. First page of the Mass for the Dead in a Book of Hours that belonged to Count Philip of Bethune. The picture of the funeral procession in the initial letter was made by Jean Fouquet in Tours, or at least in his workshop. (Royal Library, Copenhagen).

lier artistic value. At the same time easel painting was coming into fashion and diverted attention from book painting.

Decline of Monastic Culture

Prayer books were often, particularly in Germany,
bound in such a manner that the leather of the binding extended
on beyond the lower edge of the book and ended in a knot by
which the book could be carried or hung from the belt. These
"bag bindings" (Fig. 26) must undoubtedly have been very common, but only a score of them have been preserved (five of
which are in Scandinavian collections).

It would be tempting to seek the origin of these bag
bindings in a desire on the part of the monks to make life as
easy possible. Like the small brackets that were attached to
the under side of church seats to provide something to lean
against when the seat was turned up, these bindings might be
considered an expression of the monks' growing love of com-
fort. It is well known, of course, that monastic life declined
at many places in the latter part of the Middle Ages and drew
far away from its original ideal. This process of degeneration also affected the literary activities of the monasteries and
the private studies of the brethren. From various sources
there is evidence of how sad the situation was in many instances with regard to book learning, how the monks neglected
their reading and how the monastery libraries stood unattended,
the books covered with dust or even piled away in some corner. The French statesman and book-collector De Thou found
such conditions as these in the Corbie monastery in the 16th
century, and several bibliophiles of the Renaissance period
described the sorrow they experienced at the sight of the brethren's indifference toward their book treasures. Boccaccio,
who was not only a writer in praise of profane love, but also
a great book-lover, writes that he had tears in his eyes at
the sight of the library at Monte Cassino when he visited that
monastery in the 14th century.

More dramatically than anyone else, however, the English bishop Richard de Bury expressed himself about the decline in book culture and in respect for books. He lived from
1287 to 1345, was a great favorite of Edward III, whose teacher
he had been, and held important civil and ecclesiastical positions, becoming both Royal Chancellor and Bishop of Durham.
An ardent desire to collect books had early taken hold of him,
and on his diplomatic missions in Europe he had ample opportunity to satisfy this desire. Paris with its many book
treasures was for him an earthly paradise. As bishop he re-

26. Left, "bag binding," half-opened. (Royal Library,
Copenhagen).   Right, the apostle Jacob holding book in bag
binding; figure from the 1435 altar-piece in the church of the
Benedictine nuns in Preetz (Holstein), now in the National
Museum (Copenhagen).

ceived many gifts of books from monasteries throughout England, and as chancellor he likewise received valuable additions to his library; he himself tells us about his mania for
books and how it was known that he would rather have a valuable old manuscript than a sum of money, and hence "de-
crepit folios and old quartos came creeping to me instead of
the usual fees and New-Year's gifts."

De Bury's name has come down to our time through the
treatise that he wrote in his later years under the title "Philo-
biblon." It was published for the first time in 1473 and since
then has appeared in various editions, including a Danish translation as late as 1949. In it the bishop gives expression to
his love of books in clever and picturesque language; "Philo-
biblon" is primarily a paean in praise of the book. But it
also tells how De Bury collected his books and thus provides
a sort of guide to the methods of the bibliophile. It is here
that he makes his pointed comments about those who mistreat
books. In one of the chapters he lets the books accuse the
"degenerate race of monks" and he attacks particularly the
students in the monastic schools who use the books with dirty
hands, let their vile nose drippings fall on the pages and use
grass straws as book marks between the pages. It may be
that bibliophilic fanaticism colored the old bishop's words, but
it is certainly true that decadence in the book culture of the
monasteries was spreading rapidly in his time. In the 15th
century, however, a reform movement did spring up among
the Benedictine orders with the aim of bringing monastic life
back to its earlier ideals and restoring book study and writing
to a place of honor. The revival of activity that this occasioned in the monastery libraries and writing rooms was not
of long duration. Only the ascetic Carthusians continued their
copying assiduously, even long after the invention and dissemination of the art of printing.

Dawn of the Renaissance

At this very time of monastic decline, interest in books
arose on an entirely new basis in Italy. This was the thresh-
old of that period in the history of culture called the Renaissance, the rebirth of the spirit of antiquity in a new form.
This movement did, as we know, affect all phases of intellectual and cultural life, art as well as literature and science.
And while the study of ancient writers in the monasteries had,
on the whole, been something of secondary importance to be
considered rather an auxiliary discipline, the Italian humanists
and their successors now cultivated the ancient writers for
their own sake, in order to learn their art, their philosophy

and their view of life.   Quite naturally there also developed
interest -- one is tempted to say a fanatic interest -- in collecting the works of these old authors, tracking down what
still remained from ancient times and striving to reach as far
back to the sources as possible.   Thus at the close of the
Middle Ages the Italian humanists and their followers played
as large a part in the preservation of Greek and Roman literature as did the men of the church at the beginning of the
period.

As indicated, it was first of all the texts themselves
that the humanists directed their attention toward, but this is
not to say that they lacked appreciation for the exterior features of a book.   Quite the contrary is true, for among the
most beautifully executed manuscripts that we have several
are, in fact, from the quattrocento, and the beautiful bindings
of the Renaissance period will be treated below.   The miniatures in Renaissance codices are known by their antique motifs: playful cupids, columns, vases and cameos, which are
used in borders and initials.   The handwriting is an imitation of the Carolingian minuscule; and it is from this humanistic book-hand, the Renaissance minuscule (litterae antiquae)
and the cursive hand evolved from it, that the "Latin script"
of later periods is descended; today this latter handwriting
style has everywhere, except in German-speaking countries,
displaced the Gothic style.

The man who has been given the name "father of humanism" or the "first modern man," the Italian poet Petrarch
has also with some reason been called the father of modern
bibliophilism.   One thing is certain, that from his earliest
youth he was a passionate lover of books and on his many
journeys bought and copied all that he could manage in the way
of manuscripts.   He was active in this pursuit in Holland and
Belgium as early as 1329, and on several occasions he was
fortunate in discovering hitherto unnoticed texts, such as Cicero's letters to Atticus and others, which he found in the
cathedral library of Verona.   Friends in France, England and
Germany sent him books.   He was particularly devoted to the
writers of the Golden Age of Latin literature and applied himself to their works, correcting the many errors that repeated
copying had introduced in the course of time.   He could not
read Greek, and Greek literature was known to him only
through Latin translations.   He had Homer translated, and in
the Bibliothèque Nationale there is still the copy of the Iliad
and Odyssey that belonged to him and contains his notes in
the margins.   We must not think, however, that Petrarch did
not also interest himself in ecclesiastical literature.   Despite
the devotion of humanism to pagan antiquity, it was not an

27.   Italian Renaissance manuscript of the Annals of Tacitus,
with antique designs in the decoration, made in 1448.   (Royal
Library, Copenhagen).   (From "Golden Books").

anti-Christian movement, and there were many church people
among its representatives.   Petrarch's favorite authors included Augustine as well as Cicero.

It was Petrarch's intention that his own library should
become the property of the city of Venice and be made accessible to the public, which would entitle him to be called
the father of the public library in modern times.   That this
idea was not realized and the books were scattered was not
his fault.

The Medici and their Circle

The centers of the Renaissance book world were the
large commercial cities of Venice and Florence.   In the latter city, in particular, the humanistic movement had one of
its mainstays in the persons of Cosimo de Medici and his
successors; they were supported by the untiring work of
Niccolo dei Niccoli, who through his enthusiasm for collecting
had gotten into debt to Cosimo and had then gone into his service.   With the aid of the great financial resources of the Medici, collection of manuscripts was undertaken on an impressive scale.   Manuscripts were brought home from countries
north of the Alps, where the monks were glad to deal with the
affluent Italian collectors.   The most eager of them all was
the papal secretary Poggio Bracciolini; during his stay at the
great church council in Constance, 1414-18, he made several
journeys to St. Galen and various German monasteries where
he uncovered hitherto unknown ancient works.   Veritable expeditions were sent to Greece, to Constantinople and Asia
Minor, where the Byzantine monasteries and libraries provided
an abundant supply of Greek manuscripts, which were thus
saved from falling into the hands of the Turks.   Byzantine and
Greek scholars fled before the Turks to Italy and became
guides and instructors in Greek literature; they also took part
in the work of collecting.   In 1490 Johannes Laskaris, for instance, came back from a trip with 200 Greek manuscripts,
many of which contained new texts.   The envoys of the Medici
often had instructions to look for books on their travels, and
back in Florence there were many copyists and illuminators
busy in the service of these lords of commerce.   Here lived
also the great dealers in manuscripts, the chief among whom
was Vespasiano da Bisticci; he knew both how to produce correct texts and how to give his codices an elegant outward appearance.   Once he delivered to Cosimo a collection of 200
volumes, produced in the course of two years by 45 scribes.
He also possessed copies of the catalogs of a number of large
libraries and could accordingly provide his customers with

valuable bibliographical information.

It was the Medici who carried out Petrarch's idea of
a public library -- an idea that was obviously in the air at
that time. Another Florentine, Palla degli Strozzi, had had
the same idea but he was banished by Cosimo. It was Cosimo who, in 1441, with the books left by Niccolo de Niccoli
as a basis, established the Biblioteca Marciana, so called
because its quarters were in the Dominican monastery of San
Marco. Another collection of the Medici, which had been developed by the famous Lorenzo il Magnifico, was called the
Biblioteca Laurenziana. In the years following 1525 Michel-
angelo erected a building for this library at the cathedral of
San Lorenzo, a building that is still famous for its elegant
reading room, one of the most beautiful rooms of the Italian
Renaissance. The two libraries, Laurenziana and Marciana,
were combined in 1808 and together they now form one of the
outstanding sights of Florence, the Biblioteca Mediceco-Lau-
renziana.

In the work with the Marciana library Cosimo had
sought the assistance of one of the most learned men of the
time, Tommaso Parentucelli, who on this occasion compiled
a sort of model catalog of what a humanistic library should
contain. It was this Parentucelli who later became Pope under the name of Nicholas V and the founder of a new papal
library in Rome after the one in Avignon had been dissolved.
He gathered a collection of over 1200 codices, a number that
may perhaps not seem so large to us but was presumably the
highest reached by any library of that time. The large sums
of money that were taken in by the papacy in the jubilee year
1450 were used for book purchases and manuscripts were
brought to Rome even from Denmark. Pope Nicholas also
paid particular attention to the acquisition of Greek manuscripts,
which he had Poggio and other famous humanists translate into Latin at princely fees. He did not, however, manage to
complete his great library plans. A later Pope, Sixtus IV,
at the end of the century, housed the collection, now number-
ing over 3,500 volumes and partly accessible to the public,
in handsomely furnished quarters in the Vatican.

Several of the papal cardinals also attained renown as
bibliophiles, though none more than cardinal Basilios Bessarion. He made a point of collecting Greek manuscripts, especially after the fall of Constantinople in 1453. These he obtained from Athens, Crete and the Orient. In all he is said
to have spent 30,000 gulden on his library, which in keeping
with humanistic ideals he then willed to the city of Venice,
where it now forms the core of the Library of St. Mark.

Bessarion was not the only Italian humanist who offered nearly all his resources on the altar of the book.   Poggio, and
Nicholas V, who before he became Pope had been heavily in
debt as a result of his large book purchases, and others had
done the same.

As indicated earlier, Renaissance bibliophiles also
spent large sums on the bindings of their books; the books in
Pope Nicholas' library in the Vatican, for instance, were
nearly all bound in crimson velvet with silver mountings. The
true Renaissance bindings will be considered later, but it shou
be noted here that in the 15th century the great majority of
bindings were still of the standard late-Gothic blind-stamped
type.   The material used was calf skin, deer skin, pig skin,
or the more elegant goat skin from the city of Cordova (cor-
dovan leather).   The stamps used for impressing the decorative work show great variation, though certain ones, such as
the Gothic rose and the lily, lions, eagles and deer are met
again and again.   A great deal of artistry was often expended
on the large engraved brass mountings on the corners and in
the center of the sides of the covers, as well as on the clasps
The engraved lines were sometimes colored yellow or green,
less often red.   Many such bindings can still be seen in libraries; their heavy mountings and thick wooden covers in
which bookworms have often left their tracks bear witness to
the competent craftmanship of the period when they were made.
In these as in medieval bindings there is in general a feeling
of strength and solidity, which corresponds well with the heavy
parchment sheets that made the book itself so massive that a
strong binding was a real necessity.   In France and England,
in the Scandinavian countries and especially in Germany bindings of this type were general through the 15th century.

The Renaissance movement was slow in spreading to
the countries of northwestern Europe.   At the time of Petrarch they were still living in the general spirit of scholasti-
cism, and their libraries exhibited this influence.   Such a
man as Richard de Bury did, it is true, have some contact
with Petrarch and other Italian humanists, but he himself cannot rightly be called a humanist.   Similarly, in French circles
we find no bibliophiles in the spirit of the Renaissance until
the reign of Louis XII, who in the year 1500 brought back
from Padua as war booty the library of the Dukes of Milan,
the Sforzas, and then still more under Francis I, who at
Fontainbleu imitated the Medici in book collecting and took into his service the Greek scholar Laskaris and the famous
philologist Guillaume Budé.

In Germany several great bibliophiles and scholars,
such as Baron Albrecht von Eyb and Bishop Nicholas of Cues,

were inspired by the interest of the Italian Renaissance in classical antiquity. Under Emperor Maximilian I, Vienna became a focal point for German humanistic studies. The Hungarian king Matthias Corvinus was in close contact with Lorenzo de Medici; he ruled 1458-90 and during this unsettled and difficult reign he assembled a library that was said to contain 50,000 volumes -- surely an exaggeration. He kept scribes not only at his court in Buda, but also in Florence; he had purchasing agents in the Levant just as did the Medici, and bought manuscripts from their supplier, Bisticci. It is strange to find in Hungary a person so closely related spiritually to the contemporary Italian book lords. Unfortunately the library of Corvinus was largely destroyed when Buda was conquered by the Turks in 1526. Only 125 of his books have come down to our time, and are preserved as great treasures in various libraries. Special interest attaches to their binding and, as shall be noted later, the "Corvinians" have a prominent place in the history of book binding.

The Medici's example naturally had the greatest influence in their own country. In the 15th century one Italian prince after another followed it on a smaller or larger scale. One of the most impressive of these bibliophiles was the Duke of Urbino, Federigo da Montefeltro, who provided elaborately equipped quarters for his collection in his castle and is said to have kept some two score scribes busy continually in Urbino and in Florence under the direction of Bisticci. The catalog of Federigo's books is still in the Vatican and shows how comprehensive this prominent Renaissance library was.

It is doubtful, of course, that these Renaissance book patrons acted entirely from idealistic motives. As in their attitude toward the fine arts so also in this instance where books were concerned, there was certainly a good deal of personal vanity and display of power involved, and in this sense their admirable devotion to literature and books can be said to have a political basis. But whatever the motives, it was this devotion that prepared the ground in Italy, more than anywhere else, to receive the book in the new form that it acquired with the introduction of printing. The actual discovery of this new art, however, and the very first steps in its development were made in Germany.

END OF THE MIDDLE AGES

The art of producing a number of copies of a book by printing was, like the manufacture of paper, first discovered in China. As early as the second century A.D. impressions are believed to have been made from pages of text cut in a flat stone, the characters being sunk into it. Later the pages were carved in wood with the writing standing out in relief. Impressions could then be taken in large or small number from this wooden slab; the raised text was coated with coloring matter, a sheet of paper laid over it and pressed down to transfer the writing to the paper. The oldest known woodblock printing from China in the form of a book dates from the year 868 A.D., but the method was in use a good deal earlier. In Japan, which learned all its book-making techniques from China, wood prints were made as early as the 8th century.

Wood and metal slabs were used for printing in exactly the same way in Europe, but there is no reason to believe that there was any connection between European and Chinese wood-block printing (or xylographic printing, as it is also called). The oldest wood prints known from Europe were made on cloth, and have nothing to do with books, but when paper came into general use, it was used for xylographic printing with ink made of linseed oil, varnish and lampblack. Pictures of saints, playing cards, calendars and other single-sheet items, often with a handwritten legend under the picture, were produced. Some 3,000 of these have been preserved. From single-sheet impressions it was not far to the book. About 1430 the first xylographic books, or block-books, were produced in Holland and Germany, the better ones being from Holland. Some of these were made by pressing the paper against the wooden slab with a hard leather pillow stuffed with horsehair, though in general a press was used.

Only a very few block-books have been preserved -- 33 different texts, and about 100 copies in all -- but they must have been widely distributed among the people at large since their contents were usually of a popular nature. It is true that most of them were in Latin, but their hand-colored illustrations were the predominant feature, especially in the many

28.   Page from a block book containing the "Bible Pauperum,"
issued in Bamberg in 1461, with hand-colored illustrations.
This Bible is known from many medieval manuscripts; it contains
scenes from the life of Christ.   Since it was used as an instruction book and was not intended for poor people, its name is mis-
leading.

small books that the lower clergy used for instruction and devotional purposes. Among these were the Biblia Pauperum (poor man's bible) containing excerpts from the Passion of Christ, the Speculum humanae salvationis (mirror of human salvation), Ars moriendi (the art of dying), etc. There were also block-books of secular content, calendars, planet books, books of prophecies, etc. The reason that so few block books have come down to us is that they were worn out by constant use, their pictures being looked at again and again -- the same reason why the elementary school books of the Middle Ages, the pieces of vellum that contained the alphabet and the most important Christian prayers, have disappeared, although they must have existed by the thousands. There is also a sort of school book found among the block-books, the so-called Donet, a Latin grammar originally compiled by the Roman grammarian Aelius Donatus.

Printing with Movable Type in China and Europe

In China printing from wooden slabs has continued in use right down to the present, even though in the 11th century they began making movable types from baked clay, and later cutting them from metal. Each single written character was cut as a separate type and the pages of the book made up by combining these types; when the printed impressions had been taken the types could be separated and then reassembled to form new pages. The fact that this method did not attain extensive use in China is due to the large number of characters used by the Chinese; an ordinary book required 4-5,000 different types. In Europe, on the other hand, where the alphabet had only a relatively small number of letters the art of printing with movable type represented a discovery of revolutionary import for book production.

It is obvious that block books could never come to play any very great role; it was only small books of 25-50 sheets at most that could conceivably be made by the xylographic process. When the impression was made by pressing a leather pad against the wooden block only one side of the paper could be used because the impression went deeply into the paper. For large books the method was much too cumbersome. But with the invention of movable type, or rather of the instrument for casting them, the way was paved for book printing on a quite different and more impressive scale. The idea of movable types did not, like the manufacture of paper, come to Europe from China, nor from Korea, where books printed from movable copper type have been found dating from early in the 15th century. The European discovery was made quite

independently of the Orient, and was made by Johann Gutenberg of Germany.

Gutenberg Invents Type Casting

Unfortunately our sources of information about the life
of this man Gutenberg are very limited. He belonged to the
distinguished Gensfleisch family of Mainz, where he was born
about the year 1400. His parents lived on one of the family
properties called zum Gutenberg, and this name he took for
himself. He was presumably trained as a metal-worker or
goldsmith, but during the troubles in the 1420's, between the
craftsmen and the old bourgeois families, to which Gutenberg
belonged, he left Mainz and in 1434 we find him living in
Strassburg. Here he went into partnership with three men who
advanced him money in return for which he was to teach them
his "arts and skills." It can be assumed with good reason
that the reference was to his printing, so Gutenberg was already working on his inventions about 1438. When one of the
partners died owing Gutenberg money, there was a lawsuit in
1439 of which the documents are still preserved. In these
we find mention of lead, a press and various "forms," and
one of the witnesses speaks about "that which belongs to printing." How far Gutenberg developed his invention during the
Strassburg period, which lasted at least to 1444, we do not
know.

The discovery that Gutenberg made can, as in so many
other instances, be said to have been in the air at the time.
Long discussions have been carried on as to whether it should
not instead be credited to a Dutch printer by the name of
Laurens Janszoon Coster in Haarlem. There can scarcely be
any doubt that Coster knew the art of printing with movable
types. A Cologne chronicle of 1499 mentions the Donatus
grammars printed in Holland as early examples of book printing, though these may have been block books; but his method
of casting types must have been very cumbersome and impractical. Hence even though Gutenberg may have seen Coster's
printing exhibited at the reliquary festival in Aachen in 1440
and thereby been stimulated to work with book printing, he
nevertheless could not have learned anything of significance
from Coster's work. It is just as plausible to assume that
he was led to the idea of movable types by the stamps or
dies used in book-binding. These were a kind of type that
could be separated and put together again in different ways
and bindings with inscriptions that are stamped on with separate metal letter-stamps date from the first decades of the
15th century. A Bohemian goldsmith in Avignon, Prokop

Valdfoghel, used metal types in 1444 for some purpose or
other that presumably involved inscriptions, but not for book
printing. Gutenberg is credited with being the father of the
art of book printing, because he is the one who discovered
a satisfactory apparatus for casting the types and thereby
made the method practically usable. It is probable that he
had collaborators, but what part they had in the discovery we
do not know and hence we must ascribe it to Gutenberg alone.

Gutenberg suffered the fate that has befallen so many
inventors. His life was beset with difficulties and others
reaped the greatest financial benefit from his invention.

In 1448 Gutenberg was again in Mainz where he took
out a loan, presumably to enable him to continue his experiments with printing. A year or so later he again borrowed
money -- 800 guldens on two occasions from a wealthy merchant, Johann Fust; this was a very large sum at that time,
and was to be used for materials and equipment presumably
needed for printing a large Latin Bible that was completed in
1456, and which we shall come back to later. At this period,
however, there arose some trouble between Gutenberg and his
financer, resulting in a legal process of which we do not know
the final outcome. However, Gutenberg had to pay back the
first loan with interest, and part of his material became the
property of Fust. The following years were an unsettled period in Mainz; a struggle took place between the former archbishop and his successor, Count Adolph of Nassau, and the
town was captured and plundered by the Count's troops.
Whether under these conditions Gutenberg had been able to replenish his equipment and resume printing is not known; on
the other hand, it is certain that in 1465 he was accepted into Adolph's court and was thus, among other things, exempt
from taxes. Gutenberg died in 1468 and was buried in the
Franciscan church of Mainz, which was later torn down.

We have no printed work that bears the name of Gutenberg, nor any of his that gives the date of printing. Only
by studying the types in relation to historical and chronologi-
cal factors is it possible to assign a number of items to his
workshop with some degree of certainty. It was once assumed that the earliest Gutenberg item was a vellum fragment
of a calendar for the year 1448 printed in 1447, but it has
now been established that this calendar actually is a collection of planetary tables for use in compiling horoscopes, and
must have been printed around the middle of the 1450's. The
same applies to a sheet printed in the same type as the calendar, and called the "Weltgericht" because the text deals
with the day of judgement; it is actually a fragment of a Ger-

29.   Type caster pouring lead into the casting matrix.   In
the basket at the left are finished types which will be worked
over with a file before being used.   Wood-cut by Jost Amman
in the book "Beschreybung aller Stände" (1568) with verses by
Hans Sachs.

man poem about the Sybilline oracles. This sheet is preserved in the Gutenberg museum in Mainz. It was considered
the oldest extant example of typography but this theory has
been abandoned. These two items are usually assigned to
Gutenberg's workshop, though there are some who believe
that they were made in another Mainz printing shop by one
of Gutenberg's apprentices. Various Donets, letters of indulgence and other small items, are likewise believed to have
been printed there, along with a small pamphlet "Ein Mahnung" (1454) previously attributed to Gutenberg. The large
Latin Bible mentioned above is the only work that is ascribed
to Gutenberg by general agreement.

Spread of the Art of Printing

When Fust came into possession of part of Gutenberg's
equipment he started a printing business in partnership with
another German, a former scribe and initial-designer named
Peter Schöffer, who undoubtedly had worked for Gutenberg.
As early as 1457 Fust and Schöffer were able to issue a large
Psalter which will be discussed later. It was followed by a
long series of notable works, among them a magnificent Bible
issued in 1462, all of which bear witness to Schöffer's unusual ability and his earlier work as an artist. Without doubt
it was he who was the moving spirit in the undertaking, while
Fust mainly provided the money. After Fust's death, Schöffer
continued the business alone for many years until his own
death in 1502 or 1503. Like the other early book printers,
Schöffer cast his own types; these surpassed even Gutenberg's
in accuracy and appearance -- he did not content himself with
using Gutenberg's type material alone. Some of the latter,
however, appears again in the 1460's in the work of a book
printer of Bamberg, Albrecht Pfister.

There were practitioners of the art of printing in the
various other towns round about in southern Germany in the
1460's. One reason for this was the attack on Mainz during
which a large numer of the inhabitants were exiled or fled.
The journeymen printers also left, Schöffer for instance going
to Frankfurt. Thus, destruction of Mainz contributed to the
rapid spread of the art. First it naturally followed the old
trade route of the Rhine; Strassburg became one of the chief
centers of printing, but Cologne, Augsburg and Nuremberg
soon had printing shops as well, in some instances rather
large establishments. An unusually large enterprise was developed by Anton Koberger in Nuremberg. Around 1470 he
is said to have had 100 men and 24 presses at work. A generation after the discovery of the art more than a score of

30. Printing shop of the 17th century (from wood-cut by Abraham von Werdt). At the left are the composing tables, at the right, the type forms and ink balls, and the printing press itself.

German towns had printing shops. The fact that the majority were in western Germany is not only because the home of the art, Mainz, was in that part of the country, but also because it was here that the largest trade centers of the time were located, since the greater part of the trade went by way of the Mediterranean and the Levant. In general it was the large commercial centers that offered printers the greatest possibilities for continued activity, while in the small towns they found occupation for only brief periods.

An early typographical workshop had the same general appearance as those of later times, until their character was changed by the introduction of power machinery. The dominant feature of the shop was the large oaken presses fastened to the ceiling as well as the floor. In these the platen was pressed down on a sheet of paper laid over the type form; the press was operated by a large wooden screw and considerable manual force was required to provide sufficient pressure. The platen was considerably smaller than the base on which the type form itself lay, and as a rule a whole sheet could not be

printed at one time, but had to be divided into two or more
folds that were printed separately and then put together by
the binder.

The type was set in the same way that hand-setting is
done today. Two leather pillows with handles were used to
ink the type; they were similar to those used for block-print-
ing and were called "ink-balls." A great deal of practice was
required to apply the ink uniformly and at the same time a-
void drawing out any of the separate pieces of type, thus
making the impression uneven.

However, the cutting of the type face (punch-cutting)
and particularly its casting must have been the most difficult
operation for Gutenberg and the other early printers. The
essential part of the casting equipment, the matrices in which
the type was cast, were made of copper or brass (Fig. 29),
and with constant use they became worn so that the types did
not have exactly the same size and were consequently difficult to combine into lines. The types were made of a mixture of lead, antimony and bismuth, the very same mixture
that is used today, and it is amazing that Gutenberg himself
probably hit upon this substance. It melted so readily that
the casting operation could proceed rapidly, and it was hard
enough after cooling to withstand the heavy pressure of the
press.

In other respects as well Gutenberg learned to master
typographical technique surprisingly early. Although the
"Weltgericht" still had uneven letters and lines of different
length, other contemporary printing shows great precision in
the form of the letters and great uniformity in the spacing
between the letters, and all the lines are the same length.
Gutenberg gradually developed a very practical system of
characters that included the abbreviations and ligatures found
in manuscripts, and also a series of letters that did not have
the small hooks and points that characterized the ordinary
type letters. These special letters were used when two letters with hooks in opposing directions came together. One
of them was then replaced by the hookless type and the result was that the space between the two letters was no greater
than usual. It is evident of course that the work of setting
type with such a large number of different characters must
have been very taxing, and also that the casting of the type
must have required great care and patience.

a b c d e î m n o p r u

a b c d e î m n o p r u

ba bo ba pe fi tt tt ffi

ī ā ŕ m̃ m̄ ñ ȯ ō ŕ ū

ʒ ɮ ɔ ʇ 9 ꝯ ꞓ ∴ ⸪ •

31. Ordinary type, type without points, double letters
(ligatures) and abbreviation signs (abbreviatures) from Gutenberg's type material. (After Otto Hupp).

The First Printed Books

Many of the earliest printed books stand very high in
esthetic respects; one reason in particular for this is that
they had the entire manuscript tradition of the Middle Ages
behind them. The first printers quite naturally took these
manuscripts as their models; their letters were made like
those in manuscripts, the general arrangement of the manuscript page was closely followed, and those features that they
could not reproduce by printing -- the initials and other decorations -- were done in the old manner by the hand illuminator with his brushes and paints. To an amazing degree the
entire external appearance of the medieval vellum codex was
thus transferred to the printed book and the resulting products
are no less beautiful than an illuminated manuscript. It needs
only a glance at the Bible printed by Gutenberg in 1456 in two
folio volumes to show that this is true. Until it is examined
closely it might be mistaken for a manuscript. This Bible is
often called the 42-line Bible because most of the pages have
that number of lines in each column, but it is also known as
the Mazarin Bible because the first copy of it was found in

the library of the French cardinal Mazarin. Each page --
there are over 1200 in all -- is divided into two columns
and the letters are those of the Gothic style of writing that is
found in the magnificent liturgical manuscripts of the late-
Gothic period, with their heavy angular shape; black-letter
"text," "missal," and "canon," as the larger forms of it are
called. For headings, initials and borders the printer left
blank spaces where they could be painted in later; in some
copies a few headings are printed in red ink (the red headings were called rubrics from Latin rubrum = red). Forty-
six copies of the Gutenberg Bible are known, twelve of which
are on vellum. The entire edition presumably consisted of
only about 120 copies. On the rare occasion when this Bible
has come on the market it has brought fantastic prices. In
1897 at an auction in London a copy brought the equivalent of
about $12,000, but in 1926 an American purchased the copy
of the Austrian monastery of Melk for $120,000 and presented
it to Yale University, and a few years ago a copy was sold
from an English private library to the U.S. for over $150,000.
Another famous early edition of the Bible, the so-called Schell-
horn Bible from 1459 or 1460, has 36 lines in each column
and only 13 copies of it are known. It was printed in Bamberg, perhaps by Gutenberg, but in any case with the same
type that he used.

Even more beautiful than these Bibles, however, is the
Psalter (David's Psalms) referred to above, printed by Fust
and Schöffer on vellum in 1457, in which early printing reached
its highest level. It is also the first printed book to contain
a notation of when and by whom it was printed; its closing
lines (colophon) can be translated briefly as follows: "This
Psalter has been produced by the ingenious process of printing and forming letters without any writing by hand, and was
completed with diligence for the glory of God by Johann Fust,
a citizen of Mainz, and Peter Schöffer of Gernsheim in the
year 1457, the eve of Ascension Day (i. e. Aug. 14)." There
is much to indicate that Gutenberg had started this work and
that it was merely brought to completion in Fust and Schöffer's
workshop.

The colophon quoted above makes it clear that we have
here a book in which everything is done by printing, including
the unusually beautiful initials in red or in red and blue, which
seem to have been cut in metal rather than in wood. The
Psalter also carries the first printer's mark that we know,
the coats of arms of the two printers hanging from a branch
(Fig. 45). Later, of course, it became general practice for
printers to sign their work with a monogram or an emblem,
some of which were very decorative. Only 10 copies are

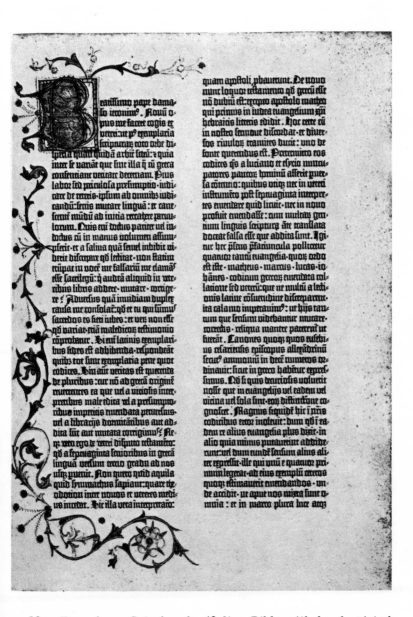

32.   Page from Gutenberg's 42-line Bible with hand-painted
border and initial.

33. Page from the Catholicon of Johannes Balbus (1460) with red hand-painted initials.

34. Wood-cut showing Christ before Pilate, from the
"Speculum humanae salvationis" printed about 1472 by Günther
Zainer and also extant in many medieval manuscripts.

known today of the Mainz Psalter; these are all printed on
vellum, but they represent variant editions.

Another famous work considered by many to have been
executed by Schöffer in 1460 is the Catholicon of Johannes
Balbus, a sort of encyclopedic lexicon, printed in a peculiar
small type. It is certain that Schöffer was responsible for a
later edition of this work, but whether he also printed the
original edition is still a moot question.

The imitation of manuscripts that is characteristic of
the earliest book printing extends also to the absence of a
proper title; the text begins on the very first page with the
introductory word incipit, or hic incipit. An isolated exception to this rule is found in the small work mentioned earlier, "Ein Mahnung der Christenheit wider die Türken" printed
in 1454 and now extant in only one copy (Munich Staatsbiblio-
tek); it was issued in facsimile in Copenhagen, 1902. Here
the title appears, printed by itself, at the top of the first
page. The first true title page, however, did not occur until about 1470. "Ein Mahnung" is in the form of a calendar
and contains exhortations to the Christian countries to resist
the Turks, who had captured Constantinople the year before.

Like several of the other books printed in German in this
initial period, it was a propaganda item intended for the public at large.

The Earliest Illustrated Books

It was not long before printed books began to desert
the manuscript tradition. For example, they soon began to
have pictures printed along with the text instead of having
them drawn in after the printing was completed. The block
books that continued to be widely distributed during the first
decades of printing had illustrations cut into the wood block
along with the text. Quite naturally such illustrations cut in
wood (wood-cuts) were quickly transferred to books printed
with movable type, by incorporating the block in which the
picture was cut as part of the page and printing it together
with the typeset material, or perhaps more likely in a separate printing operation after the text had been printed. At
the beginning, however, it is certain that these illustrations
were considered simply outlines to be filled in with color
later by the artist (Fig. 36).

The first printer known to have used wood-cuts in his
books was Albrecht Pfister of Bamberg, a man who had presumably once made his living painting pictures of saints,
playing cards and similar block-prints, and was consequently
quite familiar with illustrations cut in wood. In 1461 he issued a small popular book with many wood-cuts, the "Edel-
stein" of Ulrich Boner, a collection of fables. This book is
also of interest as the oldest book printed in German -- only
two copies of it remain. Wood-cuts are excellently suited
for combining with type material; the bold black-letter text
and the heavy wood-cut lines form a unity of great decorative effect. However, the purpose of the pictures in Pfister's
books and in those of his contemporaries was not decoration;
the pictures are to be interpreted as actual visualizations of
the contents of the text for the ordinary reader for whom
these books as well as the block books were intended. This
also applies to the pictures with which the Angsburg printer,
Günther Zainer, illustrated the many German devotional and
popular books that he issued, and for which there must have
been a ready sale. Zainer was also the first to use wood-
cut decorative initials on a large scale.

In several of these books from the earliest period of
printing we find the same wood-cut used to illustrate widely
different subjects; the same human figure, for instance, is
often used to represent a whole series of different individuals.

35. Wood-cut by Erhard Reuwich from Breydenbach's journey to the Holy Land, 1486. Bernhard von Breydenbach and the painter Erhard Reuwich made a pilgrimage together in 1483.

Perhaps this was done to save expense; cutting a picture in a block of pear-tree or beech wood was a task that took time even for an experienced hand. It is more likely, however, that the artist was lacking in imagination. In spite of all their shortcomings, however, the wood-cuts in Pfister's and other early illustrated books are by no means to be despised from an artistic standpoint; in fact, they are probably of interest today just because of their original and primitive character. Their connection with the early saints' pictures and block-book illustrations is unmistakable; at the same time they do carry the seed of the highly developed German wood-cutting art of some decades later, whose great names are Dürer and Holbein, and which branched out in new directions in Italy.

One step along the road from the earliest wood-cuts to those of the Dürer period is represented by the Cologne Bible of 1478, probably the most famous of the many illustrated Bibles in the history of the book. Its 125 pictures are drawn by an artist of the first rank, whose name is unknown. In contrast to the books already mentioned, these wood-cuts are

36.   Page from Hartman Schedel's Weltchronik, printed by Anton Koberger in 1493.   The wood-cuts are colored after printing.

not merely outline drawings. They make extensive use of
shading to give the figures a three-dimensional appearance,
and the figures also seem more alive than in earlier pictures. All the illustrations in the Cologne Bible were used
by Anton Koberger of Nuremberg in 1483 and thereby achieved
a still wider distribution and exerted a strong influence on
Bible illustration in later times.

There are several other large illustrated books from
the later decades of the 15th century that represent stages
on the road to the great flowering of the wood-cut art, such
as Bernhard von Breydenbach's very popular travel description of the Holy Land (1846). It is the first book to mention
the name of the artist who drew the pictures (Erhard Reuwich) and these are probably the first pictures to be drawn
from nature and intended to represent the actual features of
the various towns and landscapes. There is also the book a-
bout medicinal herbs issued by Schöffer, "Gart der Gesund-
heit" (1485), in which the plant drawing are likewise ascribed
to Reuwich, and Hartman Schedel's famous Weltchronik,
printed by Koberger in 1493. The latter contains approximately 1,800 wood-cuts and is one of the most profusely illustrated books that has ever been printed; some of the drawings are ascribed to Dürer's teacher Michael Wohlgemuth.
These wood-cuts were still intended to be painted in color,
and this has, in fact, been done in several of the copies. In
the Dürer period, however, this carry-over from the days of
illuminated manuscripts is given up, and black-and-white illustrations become almost universal in books, right up to the
advent of hand-colored copper engravings.

Development of Printing in Italy

After the capture of Mainz it was not long before the
practitioners of the art of book printing made their appearance in other countries. Italy, with her rich literary culture, was quite naturally the country that would attract them,
and in 1465 two pupils of Schöffer, Conrad Sweynheim and
Arnold Pannartz, did start a printing shop at a monastery in
Subiaco near Rome. They used a black-letter (gothic) type
that later became the pattern for one of the type fonts cut by
John Hornby for the Ashendene Press. Sweynheim and Pannartz stayed only two years at the Subiaco monastery; they
had been encouraged to come to Rome, and there in the
course of the next 7 years they issued a long series of books
-- 36 works and a total of 12,475 volumes, by their own figures -- mainly editions of the Latin classics. They used a
new type, the roman (or antiqua) which unlike the black-letter

nihil iis fegetibus : quæ deiceps in eo loco feminari debent:profuturum
fit. Ac de iis quoq; leguminibus:quæ uellunt:Tremelius obeffe maxie
ait folo uirus ciceris & lini:alterum quia fit falfæ:alterum quia fit fer-
uidæ naturæ. Quod etiam Virgilius fignificat dicendo:
Vrit enim lini campum feges:urit auenæ:
Vrūt lætheo perfufa papauera fomno. Neq; enim dubium quin & iis
feminibus infeftetur ager:ficut & milio & panico : fed omni folo quod
prædictorum leguminū fegetibus fatifcit:una præfens medicina eft:ut
ftercore adiuues:& abfumptas uires hoc uelur pabulo refoueas. Nec tā-
tum propter femina quæ fulcis aratri committuntur:uerum etiā ,ppter
arbores & uirgulta : quæ maiorem in modum lætantur eiufmodi ali-
mento. Quare fi eft ut uidetur agricolis utiliffimū:diligentius de eo di-
cendum exiftimo:cum prifcis auctoribus quáuis nõ omiffa res:leui tamen admodum cura fit prodita.

37.   Nicolaus Jenson's roman type.

(gothic) was patterned on the humanistic book hand, which
goes back to the Carolingian minuscule. Since the Carolingian goes back to the Latin cursive, the roman type is a
"Latin" type, and in many respects is reminiscent of the inscriptions on the old Roman monuments. It has rounded shape
without breaks or sharp angles, and hence is both easier to
cut and easier to read than black-letter. It is clear and distinctive in style, but it is also more severe than black-letter
and does not have the fullness and the festive air that characterizes several varieties of black-letter and harmonizes
so well with the heavy wood-cuts.

During the next decades many other German printers
followed the footsteps of Sweynheim and Pannartz to Italy and
settled there, some in Rome (such as Ulrich Han, who in
1467 printed the first book in Italy with wood-cuts) and some
in other large cities. The great trade center of Venice offered the most favorable conditions, and from 1469 on we
find a large colony of book printers there, many of whom
made names for themselves, such as the brothers Johann and
Wendelin of Speyer, who printed one of the first books in I-
talian, Petrarch's sonnets. Then there was the French engraver, Nicolaus Jenson, who had been sent by King Charles
VII to Mainz in 1458 to learn the new art. He later emi-
grated to Italy and may have cut Sweynheim and Pannartz's

38.   Ratdolt initials from the 1480's.   When Ratdolt returned to Augsburg in 1486 he took part of his material with
him.

roman types.   For his own use he cut another roman type,
which brought him fame as one of the most outstanding artists of type design that has ever lived; his type has been
imitated time and again, especially by English and American
book artists in recent times.

Jenson then worked in Venice, where still another German, Erhart Ratdolt from Augsburg, established a printing
shop in 1476; together with Jenson and the brothers Johann
and Wendelin of Speyer, he contributed to giving the city its
position of leadership in the first period of Italian book printing.   Ratdolt's books from the 1470's introduced Venetian
wood-cut art, which developed so prolifically in the ensuing
decades.   His wood-cut borders and initials are the first in
which the Renaissance style is unmistakable; in them are encountered again the classical motifs that are known from
Renaissance manuscripts.   These are not just in the form of
imitations; great artistry has been used in producing them in
their black and white dress, and the result is just as effective as that attained with color in manuscripts.   Even after
Ratdolt left Italy in 1486 his influence continued to be felt;
in the following years there were more and more books whose
opening page, just as in Ratdolt's books, is entirely surrounded by a wide Renaissance border of imaginative and varied
designs: columns and vases, acanthus leaves and vine
branches, strange mythical animals, human heads and masks,
etc.   In addition there are initials of great beauty, white on
black background, with the decoration enclosed in a square
frame of straight lines.   In spite of its excellence the decoration never detracts from the text itself; on the contrary,
there is a definite harmony between the two.   Here, then, on
the soil of Italian humanism, and primarily in Venice, early
German wood-cut art established a fruitful contact with the
esthetic ideals of the Renaissance, and in the course of an
amazingly short time this resulted in the printing of books so
beautiful that they have scarcely been equalled since.   In

spite of the experience of the intervening centuries and in
spite of the much more perfect material at our disposal today, we are still not able to produce works that equal these
Venetian books printed around the year 1500.

The significance of Ratdolt's books is of course primarily in the field of ornamentation, but the art of illustration also made rapid advances in this period of Italian printing.   Ratdolt himself printed several illustrated books and
has earned the honor of being the first book printer -- when
we disregard the two-colored initials in the Mainz Psalter --
who attempted the difficult feat of printing in more than one
color; a few of his pictures are printed in four colors, a
different cut being used for each color.   Among the most
famous of the early Italian illustrated books is also Niccolo
de Malermis' Bible translation of 1490, in which the numerous small fine-lined wood-cuts show the influence of the illustrations in the Cologne Bible.   This work, together with
Ratdolt's books and the illustrated editions of Dante and
Boccaccio, serves to introduce the great period of Italian
book art, the Aldine period.

Development of Printing
in Other Countries

The art of printing came to the countries outside of
Germany and Italy in the years following 1470.   In the Netherlands the first books were presumably printed in Utrecht,
but they carry neither date nor printer's name.   These Dutch
books, like the German, were printed in various forms of
black-letter type; one of these variants, which descended
from Italian manuscript writing (Fig. 39), and was also common in Italian printed books, was characterized by it's
rounded shapes and is hence called round-gothic (rotunda).
The best known of the early Belgian printers was Colard
Mansion in Bruges; he was originally a book dealer and
scribe, but in 1475 he began to print books, using types cut
on the model of Flemish manuscripts.

Netherlands wood-cut art, which developed along with
the extensive production of block books in that country,
flourished vigorously for a brief period.   An illustrated work
of special beauty, "Le Chevalier délibéré," printed in 1486,
deals with Charles the Bold and is assumed to have been
printed by Gotfred van Os in Gouda, who later worked in
Copenhagen under the name of Gotfred of Ghemen.

The first English printer, William Caxton, was orig-

> dibus noſtris peccatorum tenc
> bris: ad veram lucem que chriſ
> tus eſt nos facias pervenire: p̃

39. Round-gothic script (rotunda) in an Italian missal from
the end of the 15th century. This type was developed in
Bologna and spread from there throughout Europe.

inally a merchant, but he also had literary interests and was
a competent translator; he was accordingly led to try his hand
at the printing trade, which he had learned in Cologne and
later also in Colard Mansion's shop in Bruges. In 1486 he
returned to England, settled in Westminster, and there printed
almost a hundred books, some of which were his own translations while others were national literary works like Chaucer's "Canterbury Tales."

It might have been expected that France would be a-
mong the first countries to receive the art of book printing,
but this did not happen until 1470 when two professors in
Paris called in three Germans to set up a typographic shop
at the Sorbonne and had them print a series of Latin texts for
use at the University. Thereafter, however, the new art expanded rapidly in France, and around 1500 Paris had close to
70 printing establishments. Most French printing of the early
period was in black-letter type, but a few books showed the
influence of French manuscripts. This applied, for instance,
to the type used by Jean Dupré whose first book, a missal,
was printed in 1481. He was also responsible for the first
printed Books of Hours; in their general features these imitated the hand-written ones as much as possible. They were
often printed on vellum and supplied with borders and illustrations, which, although printed from wood or metal cuts,
kept very close to the illuminated manuscript tradition, and
were even painted in colors and gilded. Around the end of
the 15th century hundreds of these delightful and popular
prayer-books were printed; the publisher Antoine Vérard alone
issued about 200 editions, including a series of "petites
heures" and a series of "grandes heures" or "heures royales,"
the latter in very elaborate format. From Vérard's establishment also came many illustrated chronicles, tales of knighthood and romances, though to what extent he himself actually
engaged in printing is not known. The same can be said of

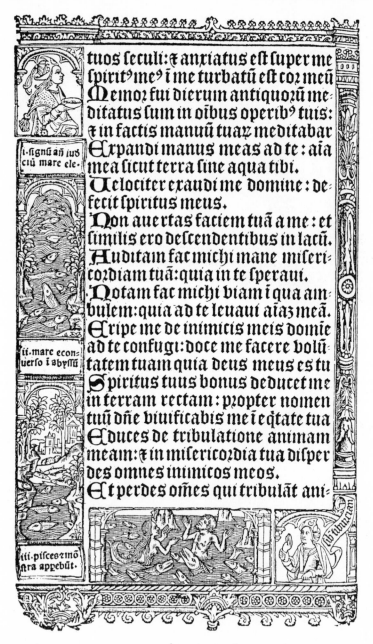

40. Page from a Book of Hours (Heures à l'usage de Rome, 1520) issued by Simon Vostre.

the publisher Simon Vostre, who began using metal cuts in his Books of Hours toward the close of the 15th century; in these cuts the background was punched with small dots to give the picture greater body. In the borders around the prayers for the dead he introduced the picture series known as the "Dance of Death;" in 1485 these pictures were also issued separately by a publisher in Paris and became a great success.

Aside from Paris, only the large commercial city of Lyons could rank as an important printing center. Lyons had Johannes Treschel, who had the learned Jodocus Badius Ascenius in his service as editor; in 1503 the latter established his own printing business in Paris where he issued some 700 works.

About the same time that the Netherlands and France were becoming acquainted with the art of printing it also spread to Spain and finally to North Germany. In this latter region printing found many competent practitioners, some of them working in the flourishing Hanseatic city of Lübeck. The first book printer there was Lucas Brandis; several other members of the Brandis family were also active as printers at various times in Lübeck as well as in Merseburg, Magdeburg and Leipzig. They created a special round-gothic type that spread throughout the whole of North Germany in several variant forms.

In 1483 Lucas Brandis printed a missal ordered for the diocese of Odense in Denmark -- about the same time that Our Lady cathedral in Copenhagen had a missal printed by Schöffer in Mainz. Another Lübeck printer, Johann Snell, became the first book printer in Denmark and also in Sweden. In 1482 he was called to Odense by Bishop Karl Ronnov to print a prayer book for the diocese; a printing shop was set up in the St. Hans monastery of the city and here he worked for a year printing not only the "Breviarium Ottoniense" ordered by the bishop, but also a small book about the seige of Rhodes by the Turks. Thereafter Snell returned to Lübeck, but in 1483-4 he was in Sweden where he printed a small moralizing book "Dialogus Creaturarum" (1483) and a missal for Uppsala diocese (1484). Two years later there was again a Lübeck printer in Sweden, Bartholamäus Ghotan, who printed a missal for Strängnäs diocese (1487), and then later in Lübeck, an illustrated edition of the visions of the holy Birgitta (1492) ordered by Vadstena monastery. His pupil and successor, Johannes Fabri, printed the first book in Swedish in 1495.

41. Page from the first book printed in Denmark, a prayer book for the diocese of Odense (Breviarium Ottoniense) printed in 1482 by Johann Snell.

Jeg willæ ep leggæ meg nogher i mobh
seg effter sith sindh hwer leffue lodh
Thi wore ther mãgæ wthi mit land
som hwerken skøttæ gudh elder mand
The skøttæ or hwerkē loff elder ræth
thi wor bland folket megit wseth
Jeg giorde ep repser bort wthñ lantz
spden seg sik rigz or worde tÿl mantz
Thi fullæ meg tha the ængelskæ fra
som hade mpne forelder i dãmark thæ
Jeffnt i tpwæ or hūdredæ aar
som seg haffuer høøth or scriffuet staar
Danskæ gaff seg for low or sedh
at the skullæ thm mz theres eedh
Om nogher mã setther paa ãnen sagh
or hã will bliffue for hãnñ mz magh
Tha skall hã sweriæ som saghñ ær staar
och lowen hū holdher ordh fraa ordh
The soræ ther hwer en oppaa
ath the willæ hellder i døden gaa
En the willæ mesthe thñ sáme ræth
som thm gaffx och føre wor iæth
Jeg wor ep kõning wthñ tw aar
seg døde aff soth or ep aff saar

Sancte Kanud

t Hz ær hwer mã én hedher swl stoor
at hã holder fast spn hedher or oor
Och spnderlig thñ aff all spn acth
som skpcket ær i kõgeligh macth

42. Page from the first book printed in the Danish language, Den danske Rimkrønike, a history of Denmark in verse, printed in Copenhagen in 1495 by Gotfred of Ghemen. The initial T has not been draw in, but is indicated by the small printed letter.

In Denmark, too, printing was continued by immi-
grants after Johann Snell had left. Steffen Arndes came to
Slesvig in 1486. He had learned printing in Mainz and had
later worked in Italy (Foligno, Perugia) attaining great proficiency in the trade. He now printed the great "Missale
Slesvicense," a beautiful work with its stately missal type,
executed in the familiar German liturgical style. His chief
work, however, was the Low-German Bible issued in 1494
with a series of striking wood-cuts.

Book printing did not come to Copenhagen until about
1489 with the arrival of the Dutch printer Gotfried van Os,
mentioned above, who called himself Gotfred of Ghemen. He
worked in Copenhagen until his death in 1510, printing first
a Donet, and later "Den danske Rimkronike" (1495), the oldest printed book in Danish, besides a great many other popular and devotional books in Danish -- all very good workmanship.

Economic Circumstances of the
Early Book Printers

The history of book printing in the Scandinavian countries provides good examples of the wandering life that many
of the early printers had to lead. The reason for this was
to be found in the circumstance that cathedrals and other ecclesiastical units in towns that were otherwise too small to
support a regular book printer would call in a printer for a
short time to produce some particular liturgical work, as in
the case of Snell and Arndes, for example. Another reason
for their extensive wandering was to be found in the intense
competition that rapidly developed, first between the printers
and the old manuscript dealers, and soon thereafter among
the book printers themselves. The stationers, mentioned
earlier, together with the scribes, illuminators and binders
of manuscript books formed a group, that was not ready to
give up without a struggle. Aided by the universities, they
sought to hold the new competitor down though without success
in the long run.

At first manuscripts did keep the upper hand over
printed books; they enjoyed greater respect, just as in ancient times the papyrus roll had over the new vellum books,
or as hand-set do over machine-set books at the present time.
The printed book, which could be produced in so many identical copies, was looked upon as something more vulgar
than a manuscript, which was still unique no matter how many
other copies might be made of it. Some book collectors in

this transition period were actually hostile toward printed books and would neither own them nor allow them in their collections; one of these was Duke Federigo of Urbino. The fact that the first printers sought to imitate manuscripts so closely is certainly to be explained in part by the higher value that was attached to these.

With amazing speed, however, the printed book gained ground. In a library such as that of Corvinus in Hungary manuscripts were presumably in the majority, but a considerable number of printed books were also included. The church soon made use of printing; in fact, in many monasteries printing shops were gradually installed in place of writing rooms. Even Italian humanism with its great love of manuscripts soon learned to make use of the new art and appreciate the advantages it offered.

With this rapid development of book printing, competition followed within the trade itself, the more so as there were no legal regulations to protect a publisher's right; any book that proved salable could be reprinted by other publishers. The cheap price at which printed books could be sold, from a fifth to an eighth of the price of a corresponding manuscript, had greatly expanded the book market. It is no accident that so many of the products of the earliest period were popular items: chronicles and fables, devotional books, prophecies, etc., printed in the national language and supplied with illustrations to appeal to the common people, who up to that time had been almost completely outside the world of book-buyers. Nevertheless, this new public was not large enough or wealthy enough to take care of the flood of printed books that poured forth, and block-books were still an important competitor. In Italy things went reasonably well, but in other countries most printers did not have a gold mine in their new trade, and they often had to move from one town to another with their equipment. In the period before the year 1500 it is estimated that about 30,000 different books were produced by printing and even though most of these may have been issued in editions of only 100 up to perhaps 1,000 copies, the total production was still quite impressive.

In the beginning the printer was usually also a book dealer; he himself sold the books he printed. But before long the so-called colporteurs travelled about from town to town and offered for sale books that they had bought from the printers. A church festival, trade fair, market or other event that would bring people together, was an opportunity that the colporteur was sure to take advantage of. Available copies of advertising sheets used by these book agents date

as far back as 1470; these sheets announced their arrival in
the town, listed the books they had for sale, and invited the
public to examine the books at some particular inn. The only printers who could make a profitable business of their
trade were those who operated on a large scale and could afford to maintain stocks in the larger cities as Schöffer did
in Frankfurt and Paris. The market for Latin literature was
not, of course, restricted to a single country.

Frankfurt, Cologne and Strassburg became important
centers for the book trade. Among others, Adolph Rusch
was active in the last-mentioned city; he not only printed
books himself but also had other printers for whom he acted
as publisher, paying them double the number of blank sheets
for their products. The greatest of all these printer-publishers was Anton Koberger. His business in Nuremberg
was the most extensive in Germany at that time. In Italy
the dominant individual at the end of the century was Nicolas
Jenson in Venice. When a particularly large work was to be
produced, a printer, a wood-carver and a capitalist would
often go into partnership, the first two contributing their work
and the third the money. Among the printers of the early
period we find several with an extensive literary background,
and the larger printing establishments often had scholars attached to them as editors and proof-readers (castigatores) of
ancient classical texts.

In the large cities just mentioned and also particularly
in Augsburg, Leipzig and Basel a few dealers in the books of
various publishers established themselves as early as the end
of the 15th century; their business was of the same type as
that of the colpoteurs, except that they did not travel about
but were permanently located; they could find enough customers
within the city. Like the travelling book agents they received
a certain discount from the publishers on large works; otherwise they paid the publisher's full price according to the number of sheets in the book, payment usually being in cash or
on six months credit. On the other hand, there were no fixed
retail sale prices; these varied from place to place, being determined only by the demand and the dealer's ability as a
salesman. In general, however, book-selling was not a lucra-
tive business, and the field was too crowded. Book-binders
also engaged in selling.

The Study of Early Printed Books (Incunabula)

The oldest printed books are called incunabula (cradle
books; Lat. cunabula = cradle) since they belong to the earliest

childhood of the art of printing.   The word paleotypes is also
used, but it applies to all old printing, while incunabula are
only those books printed before the year 1501.   In the Scandinavian countries, where printing did not begin until the
1480's, the incunabulum period is extended to 1550.   Incunabula can be of interest because of the texts they contain, especially those that represent the first printed editions of
Medieval manuscripts, but their greatest importance is in the
study of the early history of book printing.   It was not until
the 18th century that there was any interest in incunabula as
typographic productions, and only in the course of the last
three generations has the study of them made significant progress.   Detailed analysis of the form and size of the various
letters has made it possible to determine the place of origin
of many incunabula that do not themselves contain information about when and where they were printed.   The early
type fonts have a great many small variations that are evident on close examination and serve to identify them.   In the
case of manuscripts it is possible to distinguish the peculiarities of different schools of writing, even when the style is
the same; similarly the letters of the earliest printed books
show small divergences that make it possible to tell them a-
part, even though they may represent the same variety of
black-letter or roman type.   In determining the locality of a
printed work there is, however, the difficulty that one printer
often took over another's type material or matrices.   Hence,
for example, Gutenberg can not be credited with all the books
printed with his material, and similar care must be exercised
in many other instances.

Panel-stamped Bindings

With the spread of the art of printing a new era began for the book trade, but the art of bookbinding was also
affected.   It was not until the introduction of printing that
book binding developed into a separately organized trade.
During the first century following the invention of printing it
was quite common for printers to do their own binding; this
was especially true in the larger printing establishments, where
the books were often issued in bound form, but it was usually
a specially trained person who executed the binding.   It is
known that Ratdolt, Caxton, Koberger and others had binders
working for them, either in or outside their establishments.

Since printing had made books more plentiful and
cheaper, binding methods also had to keep step; a type of
binding had to be found that was cheaper to produce than the
blind-stamped bindings used earlier, in which the decoration

was made by the separate application of many small stamps.
In the last third of the 15th century bindings began to be
produced in Holland by engraving the decoration of the entire
cover on a metal plate and pressing this down on the book in
one operation in a screw press.   This was still a blind-stamp
ing or embossing process, the design being cut into the plate,
just as in the earlier small stamps, so that it came out
raised on the leather.   The figures represented were saints,
angels, birds, flowers, grotesque animals, coat-of-arms,
etc. If the binding was too large to be completely covered
by the plate, the impression was repeated two or four times
and any blank space was then filled in with small stamped
borders.

These plate-impressed or panel-stamped bindings
could, of course, be produced more rapidly and hence more
cheaply than those made with the small stamps; consequently
their use spread rapidly through Holland and the Rhineland.
In the rest of Germany, strangely enough, they did not come
into use on a large scale until quite late; here the custom
continued of decorating the central portion of the cover with
diagonal lines and small stamped figures; in the border around
this central section an inscription was often printed, such as
a Biblical quotation or a statement about the binder of the
book.   Bindings of this type were sometimes made in the
monasteries, and some of them were stamped with the name
of the monastery, or its symbol.   But as the art of printing
developed bookbinding was no longer an occupation for monks
alone or for the book-binders attached to universities; it now
became a regular trade, and toward the end of the 15th century in Germany the names of several such independent
craftsmen appeared in the decoration on the books they bound.
In Lübeck there was Heinrich Coster, whose bindings state
the "Hainz Coster bant dit," and in Erfurt, Johann Fogel,
who among other things is known to have bound two copies of
the 42-line Bible.

Panel-stamped bindings were introduced into France
and England from Holland by itinerant journeyman book
binders, many of whom like the printers, also led an unsettled life.   The bindings executed for Caxton's establishment still had their decoration made with small stamps, but
his followers, especially the printers in Cambridge used
panel-stamping almost exclusively, and the process also made
progress in artistic respects in England.

43. Dutch panel-stamped binding from about 1520. (Royal Library, Copenhagen). The same stamp is repeated four times and includes the name of the binder, Joris de Gavere. Between the panels there is a space in the middle of the cover where Mary is shown on the dragon between two chimeras.

Oriental Book-making and its
Influence in Italy

An entirely different and more significant development
took place in contemporary bookbinding in Italy. Through
Venice and the other commercial centers there was active contact with the Orient, and at the close of the 15th century, at
the very time when book-printing was developing and expanding
under the influence of the Renaissance, bookbinders came from
the Orient to Italy.

Thes Oriental bookbinders taught their colleagues in
Italy various special techniques and also gave them new ideas
for decoration. The Orient in this case refers only to the
Islamic part of it. In China and India and the countries adjoining them bookbinding was not used. Chinese books, then
as today, received, at most, a covering of colored paper or
silk, and the narrow palm leaves used for writing in India
were gathered together between two decorated end-pieces of
wood. But in the Mohammedan world leather bindings were
used as in Europe, and the Persians, in particular, were
masters of the art of producing and decorating them.

In general the Persians held a very prominent position
in the field of book-making. In the time of Tamerlane and
his successors calligraphy was practiced with considerable
artistry, and in the 15th century Persian miniature painting
flourished and was continued and further refined throughout the
two succeeding centuries. Not only were the illustrations
painted but the first page of text was adorned with rich and
colorful designs (the so-called ser-i-lauh) consisting of minute
stylized flower and leaf ornaments or the arabesques (also
called mauresques) so characteristic of Islamic art. Closely
connected with the brilliant evolution of Persian miniature
painting was the development of Persian binding. In Persian
bindings the back cover was extended to form a flap that could
be folded over half of the front cover and could be decorated
along with it. The ornamentation on the covers consisted in
the main of an almond-shaped central design and four corner
ornaments -- representing the same principle that is known
so well from Persian rugs. The central design as well as the
corners was filled with small stylized leaves and flowers, arabesques or entwined knots; the whole being pressed down into
the leather and for the most part gilded by painting on gold
leaf or gold dust. In addition the space between the pressed
ornaments was often decorated with leaf and flower designs
in color.

Neither the idea of the flap nor the gilding originated

44. Persian binding from the 16th century. The decoration on the flap forms a unit with that of the cover, which is partly covered by the flap. The binding shown here illustrates the typical decoration seen also in Persian rugs; this is a luxury binding made for a valuable manuscript. Similar decorative patterns are found on Turkish bindings. Besides leather bindings the Persians and Turks also used lacquered paper bindings; the paper was covered with chalk and a thin coating of lacquer on which water colors were painted and then another coating of lacquer applied.

within Islam; they go back to Coptic book binding, and Islamic binding thus represents a further development of the Coptic pattern. The finest Islamic bindings from the 14-15th century showed such a highly developed sense of surface decoration and such a brilliant technique, and they stood far above the level that European binding had reached at that time. The art spread from Persia to the western countries of Islam, including Turkey, and in the 15th century, it began to influence the work of Italian bookbinders and thus turn western binding into entirely new paths. In this connection note should also be taken of the Moorish bindings that were made in Spain.

It was primarily the art of gold tooling that the Italian binders learned from their Islamic teachers. Up until then all decoration on European bindings had been blind-stamped but now this was emphasized by gilding, though not done as in Islam by painting on the gold with a brush but by pressing leaf gold on with hot stamps. This does not mean that they immediately gave up blind stamping entirely; gold tooling was at first used sparingly along with blind-stamped decorations, as in the bindings that belonged to the Hungarian King Corvinus. Some of these must have been made in Budapest in the years 1470-90, but by a binder who had become acquainted with Islamic style from southeastern Europe, for the decoration shows unmistakable Oriental features. They are probably the earliest bindings in Europe on which gold-tooling is found. But it was not used exclusively; only the central field and the corner ornaments were in gold, while the borders along the edges of the covers were blind-stamped.

These Corvinian bindings were the precursors of Italian Renaissance binding, which was to be the mature fruit of the influence from the Orient. An important contribution to this development was made by the great printer and publisher Aldus Manutius, the most famous of the Venetian printers, who had already by the end of the 15th century produced some 150 books.

Aldus Manutius Introduces Italic Type

Aldus Manutius, or as he later called himself, Aldus Pius Manutius, had studied both the Greek and Latin classics and had composed small grammatical textbooks of these languages; he thus had a full humanistic background when he started his printing and publishing business in Venice around 1490 for the purpose, in part, of issuing critical editions of the ancient classical writers. The first book from his press was a 1495 edition of a standard Greek grammar; Greek books

45.   Three famous printers' marks: Fust and Schöffer,
Aldus Manutius and Christophe Plantin.

had been printed before in Italy, imitating the calligraphy of
Greek manuscripts, but Aldus introduced a Greek type cut on
the pattern of contemporary Greek handwriting with its many
abbreviated forms.   The first Latin book from Aldus' press
was Pietro Bembo's dialog about Aetna (1495) printed in a
roman type that became the model for later French types including Garamond's.

At the beginning Aldus gave his books the usual folio
or quarto format, but in a Vergil edition of 1501 he broke
completely with tradition and started printing the classics in
a small octavo format -- almost a pocket format -- with an
entirely new type face (Fig. 47) adapted to the reduced size
of the book page.   This type imitated the humanistic cursive
handwriting, and like Aldus' roman type it was cut by Francesco Griffo of Bologna.   It can best be described as a form
of roman type that slopes slightly to the right, and is called
italic (or cursive); it has continued to the present day, although it is now used mainly for emphasizing individual words
or lines in a roman text.   The term "Aldines" refers particularly to these small classical texts printed in italic, of
which Aldus issued so many over a period of years.   Among
these 28 were editiones principes, that is, first editions
printed directly from hitherto unpublished manuscripts.   At
first he himself did the philological work connected with these
editions, but later as his publishing business grew, he needed
co-workers and in time he had a whole company of scholars --

ALDVS PIVS MANVTIVS.

46. Aldus Manutius, born 1449, died 1515. From a 16th
century engraving. His printer's mark is shown in Fig. 45.
Aldus was the first publisher to issue a catalog giving the
prices of his books.

"Aldi Neacademia" it was called -- in his shop and his home
The more business-like relationship of later times between
publisher and writers was not known then.

          In these small and practical Aldine editions the clas-
sics, and with them the whole of humanistic culture, could
he disseminate more widely than before; in fact, the popularity of Aldines, with their handsome printers mark, a·dol-
phin twined about an anchor (Fig. 45) on the title page, became so great that they soon found imitators; in Lyons, in
particular, a large number of counterfeit "Aldines" were produced, being more or less successful copies, including even
the printer's mark. Aldines were used a great deal by students, and so many copies were worn out that some editions
are now very great rarities. Their fame was not due to their
format and the new italic type or to good paper and excellent
workmanship alone, but also to the care that was taken to
provide a correct version of the text, and the scholarship
that was expended on them. A scholarly production on a gran
scale was the edition of Aristotles works that Aldus published
in five folio volumes in 1495-98; it was the first complete edition in Greek.

          The italic type face was not Aldus' only contribution to
book printing. The term Aldine period is used because he wa

IVNII IVVENALIS AQVINA
TIS SATYRA PRIMA.

EMPER EGO AVDITOR
tantum?nunquám ne reponem
S   V exatus toties raucí thefeide
Codri ?
I mpune ergo mihireatauerit ille
togatus?
H ic elegos?impune diem confumpferit ingens
T elephus?aut summi plena iam margine libri
S criptus, et in tergo nec dum finitus, Orestes?
N ota magis nulli domus est sua, quam mihi lucus
M artis, et æoliis uicinum rupibus antrum
V ulcani · Quid agant uenti, quas torqueat umbras
A eacus, unde alius furtiuæ deuehat aurum
P elliculæ, quantas iaculetur Monychus ornos,
F rontonis platani, conuulsáq; marmora clamant
S emper, et affiduo ruptæ lectore columnæ ·
E xpectes eadem a summo, minimóq; poeta ·
E t nos ergo manum ferulæ subduximus, et nos
C onfilium dedimus Syllæ, priuatus ut altum
D ormiret· stulta est clementia, cum tot ubique
V atibus occurras, perituræ parcere chartæ ·
C ur tamen hoc libeat potius decurrere campo,
P er quem magnus equos Auruncæ flexit alumnus,
S i uacat, et placidi rationem admittitis, edam.
C um tener uxorem ducat spado, Meuia thuscum·
F igat aprum, et nuda teneat uenabula mamma,
P atricios omnes opibus cum prouocat unus,
A ii

47.   Page from Aldus' edition of Virgil, 1501, printed in
italic type.   Space has been left for painting in the initial S.

48.   Venetian initials in the Aldine style.

particularly successful in giving a classical character -- different from that of Ratdolt's books -- to the initials, borders
and friezes with which he, always in judiscious moderation,
decorated his books. While Ratdolt's ornaments were mainly
executed in white on a black background, those in Aldus'
books were all line drawing without any filling in of the background, giving a facile and bright appearance that is equally
well suited to the italic type and the Greek letters. Whether
preference is given to one or the other will be mainly a matter of taste, but it is certain that every single one of Aldus'
friezes and initials is a small masterpiece in itself, whether
it is made up entirely of entwined plants or grotesque masks
and other classical features or whether it shows Oriental influence in its interlaced bands and ribbons. Aldus reached

49.   Headpiece from Aldus' edition of Aristotle, 1497.

his highest point in 1499 when he issued the allegorical romance of Francesco Colonna, entitled "Hypnerotomachia Poliphili" and depicting in dream visions the realm of classical
art. The book contains some 70 illustrations, mostly pure
line drawings, done in true classical style similar to that of
Mantegna's paintings but still with their own special character.
However graceful and poetic these pictures and the accompany-
ing friezes and vignettes are in themselves, it is especially
the balance between them and the text that places this book
so high; there are many persons today who consider it to be
the most perfect book that has ever come off a printing press.

Aldus' establishment also included a bindery, so that
his books could be issued in bound form. These Aldine publisher bindings, which in large part are done in "maroquin"
or morocco leather (goatskin) from North Africa, were among
the first that showed definite traces of the influence of Islamic
book-binding, and through their wide distribution they aided in
spreading the knowledge of gold tooling. It is quite true that
at first Aldus used only blind stamping, but later on he added
gilded arabesques or flowing lines around the central panel
where the title of the book was stamped in gilded roman letters. The decoration, however, always shows the same moderation that is found in the use of friezes and vignettes inside
the book.

Aldine bindings show Oriental influence in one respect;
instead of the usual wooden core for the covers of the binding
Aldus followed the Oriental practice of using cardboard, which
was of course not as solid as a wooden board, but was much
lighter and more practical particularly for the small formats
that he used. Wooden boards did not disappear entirely from
book binding until the 18th century; as late as the 15-16th
century there were many bindings in which the wooden boards
were only partly covered with leather -- presumably to save
material. Gradually cardboard came more and more into
use. Often spoiled sheets, pages from discarded books and
other rejected material, as well as pieces of old vellum
manuscripts were pasted together and used; fragments of otherwise unknown texts have sometimes been found inside the covers
of books.

Grolier and his Contemporaries

Of greater importance, however, than Aldus' trade
bindings were the luxury bindings that he had made for rich
book collectors who were not content with the ordinary books
but required special copies printed on vellum or large paper,

Hora quale animale che per la dolce efca, lo occulto dolo non perpen
de, poftponendo el naturale bifogno, retro ad quella inhumana nota fen
cia mora cum uehementia feftinante la uia, io andai. Alla quale quando
effere uenuto ragioneuolmente arbitraua, in altra parte la udiua. Oue &
quando a quello loco properante era giunto, altronde apparea effere affir
mata. Et cufi como gli lochi mutaua, fimilmente piu fuaue & delecteuo,
le uoce mutaua cum cœlefti concenti. Dunque per quefta inane fatica,
& tanto cum molefta fete corfo hauendo, me debilitai tanto, che apena
poteua io el laffo corpo fuftentare. Et gli affannati fpiriti habili non effen
do el corpo grauemente affaticato hogi mai foftenire, fi per el tranfacto pa
uore, fi per la urgente fete, quale per el longo peruagabondo indagare,
& etiam per le graue anxietate, & per la calda hora, difefo, & relicto
dalle proprie uirtute, altro unquantulo defiderando ne appetendo, fe
non ad le debilitate membra quieto ripofo. Mirabondo dellaccidente
cafo, ftupido della melliflua uoce, & molto piu per ritrouarme in regio-
ne incognita & inculta, ma affai amœno paefe. Oltra de quefto, forte
me doleua, che el liquente fonte laboriofamente trouato, & cum tanto
folerte inquifito fuffe fublato & perdito da gliochii mei. Per le quale tu-
te cofe, io ftetti cum lanimo intricato de ambiguitate, & molto tra pen-
fofo. Finalmente per tanta laffitudine correpto, tutto el corpo frigefcen-

50. Page from the Hypherotomachia Poliphili of Francesco
    Colonna, 1499.

and in fine bindings. From 1512 on he had dealings with the most famous of these collectors, Jean Grolier. Grolier was born in Lyons in 1479 but between 1510 and 1537 he was in Italy most of the time as a French legate, and thereafter became government treasurer and lived in Paris until his death in 1565.

Through his connection with Grolier, Aldus presumably had considerable influence on the execution of the highly treasured Grolier bindings, which represent the culmination of Italian Renaissance binding. These represent the development of a special style which some have thought could be traced to the gold embroidery work done in Venice in the Middle Ages. Gold tooling became predominant, and the entire cover of the book was filled with geometric figures or other designs made by a band or ribbon of two lines enclosing a central space that contains the title of the book on the front cover and Grolier's motto on the back. At the bottom of the front cover there was also the inscription: Jo. Grolierii et amicorum, the book belongs "to Grolier and his friends." In some of the later bindings the entwining ribbon or strapwork that forms the basis of the decoration was often emphasized by being lacquered in color or stained black, and the designs it formed were more arabesque-like and had branch and leaf ornaments added within the convolutions. (Fig. 53). On a number of bindings the leaves and arabesques were done with hatched or shaded stamps (fers azurés) discovered in Lyons. The spine of the book, which had earlier been left bare, was also decorated in some Grolier bindings; the inner faces of the covers were covered with vellum and there are several extra pages at the front and back, some of vellum. Extraordinary imagination, but always with artistic restraint, was exhibited in the variations of the design on Grolier bindings. Only a small number of them were made at the Aldine press or at other places in Italy; the majority of them, including the most artistic, were certainly made in Paris by binders who had learned the trade in Italy. Grolier's library was sold and widely scattered in the 17th century; only some 400 Grolier bindings are known today. These extraordinarily beautiful calf-skin and morocco bindings with their characteristic decoration and inscription are highly prized by collectors; an ordinary Grolier binding, irrespective of the text it covers, will bring over a thousand dollars.

Some similarity to Grolier's bindings is seen in certain bindings executed for his younger contemporary, Thomas Mahieu (Maiolu) who was secretary to Catherine de Medici in 1549-60. A special feature of his bindings was the braided work made up of rolled leaves. Mahieu also used an inscrip-

51.   Grolier binding (National Library, Vienna) with his motto in the center.   This binding is from Grolier's later years; it is in red morocco and the decoration is suggestive of the later fanfare style.   A more typical Grolier binding is seen in Fig. 53.

tion on his bindings stating that they belonged to him and his friends, the same as Grolier. These two men were the first real bibliophiles in the modern sense, they were possessed of the same passion for beautiful books in beautiful bindings that is characteristic of bibliophiles today.

A third collector who, often named along with Grolier and Mahieu, was Demetrio Canevari, a physician to the Pope, to whom, wrongly as it has been shown, have been ascribed certain morocco bindings of the Aldine type made in Rome in the 1540's. In the center of the front cover they were embellished with an oval relief showing Apollo driving his chariot against a mountain, a design that resembles the earlier cameos (Fig. 54). It is now definitely established that these cameo bindings belonged to the Farnese family and were probably made for cardinal Alessandro Farnese (later Pope under the name of Paul III). Together with other contemporary cameo bindings they form a special group within Italian Renaissance binding. Like several other types of binding in particular demand by present-day collectors, the Farnese bindings have been the object of a number of disappointing imitations.

Aldus died in 1515; his press was continued, but it did not play any major role after the founder's death. On the other hand, his work was imitated in many respects by another family of printers the Giunta (Junta), whose members were active up into the 17th century in Italy, Spain and France. From the establishment of Filippo Giunta in Florence came numerous small editions of the classics printed in italic, and Aldus' publisher bindings were also imitated here, perhaps by the same craftsmen that had worked for Aldus. The Giunta's trade bindings can be seen on many books in libraries around Europe today, also in Copenhagen, indicating the wide distribution they had in their time. Florence had also developed a flourishing wood-cut art that could compete with the Venetian in artistic value; of special fame were the dramatic illustrations for various writings of Savanarola. Venice, however, continued to maintain its position of leadership in book printing; one of its prominent printers in the second half of the 16th century was Gabriel de Ferrari, who issued about 850 books, many with beautiful wood-cut illustrations, ornaments and initials, the latter often containing scenes from classical mythology.

52. Binding made for Thomas Mahieu. Formerly owned
by Robert Hoe and sold at the auction of his books in 1912
for $3,200.

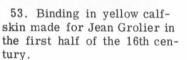

53. Binding in yellow calf-
skin made for Jean Grolier in
the first half of the 16th century.

54. Italian cameo binding
from about 1550, showing A-
pollo driving his chariot against
a mountain-side.

German Wood-Cut Illustrations

The rise of the golden age of wood-cut illustration in
southern Germany came at the time that Italian book-making
was celebrating the great triumphs of the Venetian and Flor-
entian printers of the first two decades of the 16th century.
It was here that wood-cuts had first been used for illustration purposes, and the development that began to culminate
in the last years of the incunabula period was introduced by
such works as Breydenbach's pilgrim book and Schedel's
Weltchronik. In 1498 Albrecht Dürer's "Apocalypse" appeared
in Nuremberg. Its 15 large wood-cuts represent one of the
epoch-making works of graphic art, for in them the black-
and-white picture evolves without any consideration for color;
here the brilliant artistic effect is attained by the interplay of
light and shadow alone, through the contrast of the black lines
against the white paper. In these wood-cuts and in other series in which Dürer depicted the story of the life and suffering
of the Virgin Mary his deep religious feeling found its full artistic expression. It is obvious that it was the hand of a

master that cut these illustrations from the wood block.

The course of events in Germany paralleled that in
Italy. Within a surprisingly short span of years the wood-
cut art developed to full maturity, then it became an item
of fashion and finally was choked by overfeeding. The great
center of this art, which has set its mark on several thousand German books, was not Dürer's own city of Nuremberg,
but three other cities: Strassburg, where some of the great
botanical works (Kräuterbücher) were produced, and then
Augsburg and Basel. The last of these had early attained
fame as the literary center of German Switzerland and was
also the place where one of the most popular books of the
time was issued in 1494: Sebastian Brant's satire "Narren-
schiff," with it brilliant wood-cuts (among them the famous
"book fool") that some have considered a youthful work of
Dürer. Book production in Basel was closely connected with
that of South Germany, but at the same time, presumably
because of the great church meetings that were held there
in 1431-49, Basel was one of the towns through which the
Germanic world first came into contact with the Italian Renaissance. At the time of the great wood-cut period Basel
became the principal seat of German humanism. Erasmus
of Rotterdam issued his famous editions of the classics and
the church fathers, which outshone even the Aldines in philological scholarship, in Basel. Conditions were especially
favorable for the evolution of the book-arts of the time.
Basel was the home of one of the greatest artists in this
field, Hans Holbein the younger. He worked with a wood-
carver of the first rank, Hans Lützelburger, and a no less
outstanding printer, Johan Froben (Frobenius), in whose house
Erasmus lived for several years as an active adviser and
helper, and where he also issued the New Testament in
Greek (1516).

Each one of these was among the greatest in his field
and together they were able to create works that attained
fame throughout Europe. Froben was responsible for the
typography, aided by his large stock of roman and italic type
fonts. He used italic not only for small octavo editions, but
also for marginal notes in quartos and folios. Holbein's and
Lützelburger's contributions were the handsome title borders
and initials cut in metal plates, in which a host of small
happy children tumble around in a framework of antique columns and arches or other Renaissance ornaments. Holbein's
illustrations for the Old Testament, which first appeared in
1538 in a book issued in Lyons, and his depiction of the old
Dance of Death motif, also first issued in Lyons in 1538 were
among his most outstanding work. He used a clear and simpl

55. Wood-cut drawn by Hans Holbein the younger showing
Erasmus of Rotterdam with his hand on a bust of Hermes as
a symbol of his literary work.   This wood-cut, which is extant in only a few copies, was probably intended for an edition of Erasmus' works, but was never used. (Copper-engraving collection, Copenhagen).

Nach inhalt gesprochner vrteyl
    Nam der nachrichter an das sayl
  Furwittig den vast armen Man
  Fürt In hinaus für das thor/an
    Die stat/daran man die armen lewt
  Vmb Ir missetat riche noch hewt
  Als Furwittig kein rettung sach
  Fieng Er an vnnd offenlich sprach   N iiii

56.   Page from Teuerdank, 1517.   The type is a forerunner of "fraktur" type.

wood-cut line, which looks as though it were made to suit
the slender roman or italic type, and hence there was harmony between the text page and the illustrations as there was
in the "Hypnerotomachi," however different the style of these
books in other respects.

The Emperor Maximilian's Books

Augsburg became the second main seat of German Renaissance book-making. Through its active trade connections
with Venice this city had also been stimulated by the Renaissance movement south of the Alps, and through the initiative
of the Emperor Maximilian I this movement soon set its mark
on the books produced in Augsburg and brought new life to an
art that had hitherto been dominated by the gothic style. In
his eagerness to glorify his own regime and strengthen his
people's national consciousness Maximilian had a number of
historical works undertaken, the best known of which is the
one entitled "Teuerdank" (Fig. 56), recounting in allegorical
form the emperor's own adventures on his courtship journey
to Burgundy. The fame of this great folio work is due to its
illustrations and to the charming lines of its type, in which
the scrolls and flourishes used in the handwriting of the imperial documents are transferred to printed black-letter type.
This "Teuerdank type" is a sort of forerunner of the so-
called "fraktur" (Latin fractum = broken, bent), a type-face
that appeared in 1524 and is recognizable by its "elephant's
trunks," or the scrolls that are added to the capital letters.
Fraktur type was originally made by the Nuremberg type-
cutter Hieronymus Andreä and from his and other fraktur
types developed the form that came into general use in Germany and the countries under her influence during the following centuries and has continued down to the present day. In
Denmark its use was not given up entirely until the last generation. Fraktur type was thus an off-shoot of the black-
letter or gothic types of the incunabula period and later superseded these entirely.

Another somewhat earlier offshoot was the so-called
Schwabacher type (the origin of the name is uncertain) (Fig.
58); it also came from Nuremberg. In it the sharp features
of black-letter type were more or less rounded off, so that
it constituted a German variant of the Italian rounded-gothic
type; its lines are too heavy for ordinary use, though in the
Reformation period it was used extensively throughout all Germany.

The Teuerdank work was published for the first time

Dem Durchleuchtigen Hochge-
bornen Fürsten vnd Herrn/ Herrn Ferdinan-
den/ Ertzhertzogen zu Osterreich/ Hertzogen zu Bur-
gundi/ꝛc. Graffen zu Tyrol/ꝛc. Meinem gne-
digen Fürsten vnd Herrn.

Vrchleuchtiger hoch
geborner Fürst/ Gnediger Herr/
Euwer Fürstlichen Durchleuchtig-
keyt seyen meine vnterthenige gehor-
same dienst jeder zeyt zuvor/ Gnediger Herr. Der Großmechtig Keyser
Heinrich/ dieses Namens der Erste/ zugenannt der Vog-
ler/ seliger vñ hochlöblicher gedechtnuß/ nach dem er mehr

57.   Fraktur type as used by Sigismund Feuerabend in
Frankfort, 1566.

in 1517, printed by the imperial court printer, Hans Schön-
sperger. Like the other works planned by the Emperor Maximilian but only partly completed, it is famous for the many
large illustrations that almost make it a picture book with
supplemental text rather than an illustrated text.   Albrecht
Dürer, Lucas Cranach the elder, Hans Burgkmair, Daniel
Hopfer and many other excellent artists worked for Maximilian. Dürer, for instance, worked on the magnificent prayer
book for the Knights of St. George, which was to have been
used as propaganda for the Crusades but, because of the
Emperor's early death, was never finished.

Just as the Grolier bindings and the other luxury bindings were of great significance in the history of art but did
not reach beyond the circle of the wealthy, so the wood-cut
masterpieces, although produced in rather large numbers,
were still only individual high points rising above the ordinary level of book production.

Other books that distinguished themselves were many

Silla der römisch ratther hat nach vil tatté in dem Jugurthinische krieg geübet die ere vnd glori eins keysers von dem römischen rat erlangt. S daū wider Mithridatem geschickt in Achaia vnd afia obsiget.diser was auß dem alten vnd hohberümbten geslecht der Scipioner geporn vñ all sein tag von iugent auff in vbung schentlicher lesterlicher henndel gestanden. bis er vnder Mario wider Jugurtham zu dem rentmaister ambt geordnet wardt in demselben ambt verwādelt er sein leben gantz.daū er hat Jngurtham geket tent. Mitridatem geschwaigt.die betrübnus des gesellischen kriegs nyderge drugckt.die herrschung Cinne zerbrochen vnd Marium in das ellend gezwū gen.Er was in kriechyscher vnd lateinischer schrift gar wol erfarn.gesprech. paldsahig.geschickt.eregirig.milt vnnd großmüetig. also das man zweyfeln mocht ob er stercker oder glückfaliger wer.Als er nw zu einem dictator vnnd

58. Schwabacher type as used by Anton Koberger in Nuremberg, 1493.

of the missals, choir books, breviaries, psalters and other large liturgical works that the church had produced in such large numbers, and some of which have already been mentioned. The figures given for the various liturgical works printed in the period 1457-1525 for Germany alone are between 550 and 600. A variety of large and small type-faces were used to indicate the various divisions of the liturgical text and there was a continual interchange of red and black ink, which gave these folios a very decorative appearance. Many large presses made a specialty of liturgical books, and cities like Mainz, Leipzig, Speier, Cologne, Magdeburg, Basel and Geneva, Paris, Lyons and Venice were the seats of the greatest activity in this field. Outstanding artists also made their contribution to these books.

The same is true to some extent of the small French livres d'heures that have been mentioned, as well as the corresponding German devotional books, Seelengärtlein (Garden of the soul), where an artist like Hans Springinklee is seen, and the so-called "Heiltumsbücher," or "guides" for the towns to which pilgrims travelled, containing descriptions of outstanding features, etc.; Lucas Cranach worked on one of the most successful of the latter. Many of these small devotional books show indications of the tendency to overcrowding that brought on the decline of the wood-cut art in Italy, France and Germany in that half of the century.

Books of the Reformation Period

Most of the literature occasioned by the Reformation definitely belongs in the class of commonplace book-making. When Luther began his fight against the Church of Rome in 1517 the signal was given for great revolutionary development that also left deep traces on the history of the book. Floods of pamphlets covered Germany and the neighboring countries in the ensuing years as one of the most effective weapons of the new movement. Not entirely without justification has it been said that the rapid triumph of the Reformation had its basis in the invention of printing. However, in these countless German Reformation items, with their provocative titles, there was usually no thought of putting more work on the physical features of the book than absolutely necessary; this was ephemeral literature and had to be sold cheaply in order to fulfill its mission. Poor quality paper was used; Schwabacher and especially fraktur type in anything but flawless form took the place of the older black-letter type; the same worn-out wood-cuts were used in one publication after another and the workmanship became more and more routine so that the products acquired an almost factory-like appearance. This is the general impression of the enormous literary production of the Reformation period, if the printed Bibles and a few other exceptions are disregarded. On the other hand, the Reformation brought with it a hitherto unknown democratization of the book, the effect of which can scarcely be over-estimated. Our present-day efforts at popular enlightenment can with some justification be said to have originated in the interest that Lutheranism showed in the spiritual life of the ordinary man.

North Germany, which unlike the southern part of the country, did not know the close connection between book printers and wood-cutters, came to the forefront. Wittenberg, with its newly founded university, suddenly became an important center in the book world. Here a great deal of Luther's enormous production of sermons, devotional and polemic writings was printed, especially at the press of Melchior Lotter the younger. Lotter also printed the famous first edition of Luther's translation of the New Testament (September and December 1522). The first complete Bible translation, beautifully illustrated, was printed in 1534 by another Wittenberg printer, Hans Lufft. Two of Lucas Cranach's sons made the borders and initials for many of the Luther items. In spite of Luther's protests many of his works including the Bibles, were reprinted on a large scale, even by respectable printers, in the towns that accepted the new teaching, such as Basel, Augsburg, Nuremberg and Strassburg.

The itinerant book-sellers experienced greater activity in their business than they had ever known; in addition to the Bible they now had hymn books in German editions which they sold from booths by and even in the churches.   Luther's cate-chism was also a large-selling item.   One of Luther's pam-phlets sold 4,000 copies in 5 days, and the more than 100 editions of the New Testament that were issued in the years 1519-34 sold a total of about 20,000 copies.   The whole of Germany, both town and country, was overrun by book agents selling the numerous pamphlets that were issued by both the Lutherans and the Catholics.

But along with these travelling book-sellers the regu-lar book dealers, many of whom were both publishers and booksellers, also handled a good deal of the new literature, particularly the larger works.   Twice a year, in the spring and in the fall, they met at the fair in Frankfurt and traded books among themselves sheet for sheet.   Greater and more varied activity developed here than ever before, and the book trade of Germany as well as of other countries was repre-sented.   Later, however, the fair in Leipzig took precedence over the Frankfurt fair and Leipzig has continued until re-cently to be the center of the German book trade.   In 1564 catalogs were first printed of the books on sale at the fair, and from these fair catalogs developed the excellent semi-annual German trade catalogs of later times.

Destruction of Monastery Libraries

The Reformation gave rise to flourishing literary ac-tivity, but it also became the occasion for the destruction of many books already in existence.   In its fight against the Church of Rome it turned against the entire Catholic (Papist) literature, and in this struggle many old monastery manu-scripts and incunabula suffered a sad fate.   During the peasant uprisings in Germany in 1524-25 German monastic libraries suffered very great losses, just as French monastic libraries did later during the Hugenot wars.

Nevertheless, it is unjust to generalize so as to lay the chief blame for the fact that so little of the great book treasures of the Middle Ages have been preserved to the fol-lowers of the Reformation.   A great deal had been destroyed during the Middle Ages by the many fires that ravaged churches and monasteries and, in the later period, by the monks' own carelessness.   A great deal has also been de-stroyed by fire and wars in more recent times.

It should not be forgotten that after the first excitement of the Reformation, the Lutheran church was not without appreciation of the value of Medieval manuscripts. In Denmark, for example, a specific order issued at the church conference in Odense in 1577 said, "the old books of the church, missals, graduals, hymn books and Bibles, whether on vellum or paper, must not be thrown away or used as binding for other books." And finally, it must be pointed out that Luther himself in his letter to the leaders of the German states in 1524 specifies that neither money nor effort is to be spared to establish "gute Libareyen odder Bücherheuser," especially in the larger towns. The result of this was the establishment of many new "Stadtbibliotheken" and church and school libraries round about in Germany. Luther's friend, the Wittenberg pastor Johann Bugenhagen was especially zealous in carrying out this order of the master. To a large extent these libraries were based on already existing collections from the Catholic period.

However, only a few of these new institutions had any great importance at the beginning, at least not in comparison with the importance of monastery libraries in their great period. In fact the influence of the Reformation on the history of libraries was more indirect in nature. When the governments began to confiscate church and monastery property (to secularize it, as it was called) their book collections came into the possession of the state, and often the old books received no gentle treatment. The situation was at its worst in England since secularization came very soon after the triumph of the Reformation, when the destructive desire was still in the blood of those in power. In the course of the first two or three decades following the secession from the Church of Rome the larger part of the 1,000 or so monastery and church libraries throughout the land were secularized, and in many instances their books fared badly. It might have been expected that in England, with her well-known attachment to everything old and honorable, conservative forces would have made themselves felt, but this occurred only in a very limited degree. Henry VIII's librarian, John Leland, did make a trip around the country in 1536-42 and was able to save some of the most valuable of these book treasures from destruction and bring them back to the royal library. On the other hand, the famous library in Oxford which went back to the 14th century was plundered in 1550 by Edward VI's men, who burned some of the books and sold others; six years later the empty shelves were also sold. Not until half a century thereafter, in 1602, was the library reestablished, through the efforts of one of Queen Elizabeth's statesmen, Thomas Bodley (hence the name that it still carries today: The Bodlei

an Library); it has gradually developed to become the second
largest library in England (Fig. 114).

In Denmark the situation was somewhat better. King
Christian III commissioned a German teacher to travel around
to churches and monasteries and collect books for the Library of the University of Copenhagen, which had been founded
in 1482; a large number of books was collected in this manner. In adding books to its collection -- 50 rix-dollars were
available annually for book purchases -- the library followed
the procedure recommended by Luther himself: first the
missing works of the church fathers were acquired, then
Latin and Greek authors, and finally books on legal, medical
and natural science. A similar development took place in
Luther's own country where both the existing and the newly
established university libraries, such as those at Marburg,
Königsberg, and Jena, acquired many books from the monasteries.

Later in the century the University of Copenhagen Library likewise received additions from the old monastery and
church collections and the royal historiographers also obtained some source material from them. What was left after
that was usually destroyed. Local officials or their scribes,
however, both in Denmark and in Norway, had no respect
for the order from the Odense conference. They cut up
great numbers of the old vellum manuscripts and used them
as covers for their own accounts and tax lists, or cut them
into strips to strengthen the backs of bindings; pages of old
Saxo Grammaticus manuscripts have, for instance been found
as covers on Kronborg Castle's court rolls for 1627-28. The
custom of using vellum as covers for books or as inlays for
bindings was so general that by the middle of the 17th century there was very little of it left. The old books of the
monasteries were also made to serve other purposes; in 1634
many of them took part in celebrating the wedding of the heir
to the throne, Prince Christian, where they were used as
cartridge paper for the great fireworks spectacle.

In those countries that remained faithful to the Church
of Rome the old Catholic libraries, after a brief period of
disorder, continued to exist as before; new collections were
also established, especially where the Jesuits were in control.
In these countries, that is, in Southern Germany and Austria,
France and Italy, it was not until along in the 18th and 19th
centuries that the civil governments took over the Medieval
book collections.

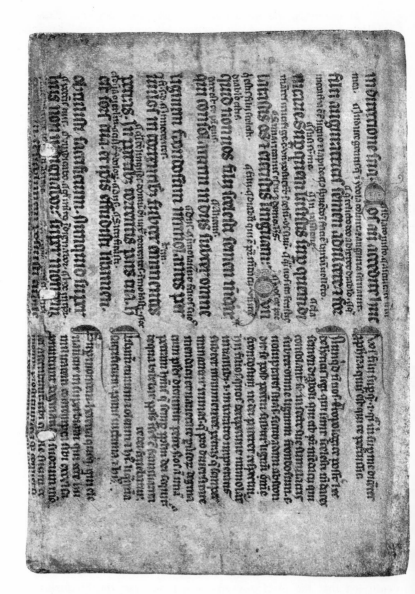

59. Binding for a 15th century book made from a parchment manuscript sheet. (Royal Library, Copenhagen).

Book Printing and Binding in Denmark
during the Reformation

Just as the Protestant church excluded from its services the brilliant colors and the beautiful music with which the Catholic church seeks to arouse and stimulate religious feeling, so it also pushed artistic decoration of books into the background in favor of the text itself. Protestant liturgical books cannot come up to those of the previous period. Neither can Lutheran illustrated Bibles stand comparison with the Catholic. If for instance, a book like the oldest complete Danish Bible translation, Christian III's Bible, which was issued in Copenhagen in 1550 in 3,000 copies, is placed alongside the great German works of the Dürer period, it will not appear to advantage, although its wood-cuts have many good points. This Bible is typical of its time. With respect to book printing Denmark was at that time only a province of North Germany, and Christian III's Bible was printed by a German printer, Ludwig Dietz, who had been called to Denmark for that purpose. In its general appearance it is simply a copy of a Low-German Bible that Dietz had made earlier; its many wood-cuts were also made by a German artist.

During the conflicts of the Reformation period many book printers were drawn into the battle between the old and the new and had to take sides. In Denmark Paul Raeff - the first Danish-born printer -- worked in the service of the Catholics and printed such things as Poul Helgesen's writings, while an immigrant German, Hans Vingaard, issued a number of Protestant pamphlets from his press in Viborg and later in Copenhagen worked for Peder Palladius. Malmö was one of the chief printing centers of the Danish Reformation. Here the earliest preserved Danish editions of Luther's Catechism were issued. From 1533-35 Christiern Pederson, who had returned after many years abroad brining with him a large stock of type and a Dutch typographer, worked in Malmö. In 1514 he had had the first edition of Saxo's great Denmark Chronicle printed by the famous printer Ascenius in Paris. This imposing work which is not excessively rare has title borders in Renaissance style, and its initials carry Pedersen's own signature. In his Malmö editions he also used Renaissance ornaments, and he was the first to use italic type in Denmark. Roman type appears for the first time in 1538 in the work of a Roskilde printer, Hans Barth, in a Latin work by Melanchthon.

Denmark was also subsidiary to Germany in matters of binding. The names of a number of Swedish book binders

60. Binding made for Tycho Brahe, with his portrait plate-
stamped in gold while the decoration is blind-stamped with
roulettes. (Röhsska Museum, Gothenburg).

of the 16th century are known but very little is known about
Danish book-binding of this period.   One Danish binder was
Niels Poulsen, who became court binder in 1559 at an annual
salary of 100 Danish marks, and the initials of a few others
are known from their bindings.   It can safely be assumed
that a large number of Danish bindings were, like many of
the Swedish, made in German shops or by Germans who had
immigrated from Germany or had learned their trade there.
When Christian III had his great Bible translation bound for
use in churches, he did call in both a French and a German
binder.   But this was an exception; on the whole, Danish
binding was still under the German aegis at that time.

Roller-stamped Bindings

In Germany panel-stamped bindings had gradually been
adopted and were the prevailing type throughout the 16th century even though decoration was not entirely stamped from
plates.   As early as 1469 a new tool, the roller or roulette,
appeared in German binderies.   The design was engraved a-
long the edge of a narrow wheel, and as this was pushed a-
long over the moistened leather under heavy pressure a continuous frame or border was produced, in which the design
kept repeating itself.   This new instrument meant a great
saving of effort and time for the binder, and accordingly its
use spread rapidly and has continued down to the present.
The designs engraved on the roulettes were either small religious pictures (figures or Christ or Biblical scenes), allegorical representations of the Christian virtues, or portraits
of princes and rulers.   No attention was paid to the fact
that on the horizontal parts of the border the figures were
lying down.   Rollers were also often used for the central
field, though here panel-stamping predominated.   At the time
of the Reformation pictures of Luther and Melanchthon, either
busts or full figures, were often used on the front and back
covers respectively.   There are some bindings for which
Lucas Cranach the younger drew portraits of these two principle personages of the Reformation.   But portraits of princes
and other persons of noble rank or of classical authors were
also common, and many of these binding portraits indicate
that they were made in a country where the art of wood and
metal carving had reached a high stage of development.

The type of binding that is most frequently encountered
in Germany and the Scandinavian countries during the century
of the Reformation and long afterwards was stereotyped in
appearance.   It was made of calfskin, parchment or bleached

pigskin with two or three rolled borders within one another
enclosing a relatively small panel-stamped central field.
This was often divided horizontally so that the owner's initials were given in the upper part and the year of binding below, while the center section was taken up by a picture or
by the owner's coat of arms -- the whole being blind-
stamped. There was no decoration on the spine, but the
heavy cording of vellum or hemp bulged out under the leather
and divided the spine into several sections.

The smooth spines that became common later did appear on a few 16th century bindings. In these the cording
was set down into slots cut across the backs of the pages.
After the middle of the century gold stamping became more
and more common in this type of binding. Some of the best
gold-tooled bindings were those made for Count Otto Heinrich for his library in Heidelberg. The arabesques and interlaced ribbons known from Italian bindings began appearing
more and more frequently in the decoration.

Jakob Krause Bindings

It is only in exceptional instances, however, that any
considerable influence from Italy in Germany may be de-
tected. On the other hand, it is found very clearly in a
number of bindings made at the court of Saxony. Together
with the Palatinate, Saxony became the center for German
book binding at that time and the Electors of Saxony, like
the Count Palatine had many gold-tooled bindings of the type
described above. But under the connoisseur of art and books,
the Elector August, who ruled 1553-86, the development took
a definite oriental-Italian turn. Together with his Danish-
born queen, Anna the daughter of Christian III, he collected
a large library in which the bindings were made by Jakob
Krause between 1566 and 1585, and after 1574 also by Caspar
Meuser, both outstanding men in their craft. Krause had
been apprenticed at Augsburg to Antoni Ludwig, who had o-
riginally worked as a book binder in Venice, and it is really
because of him that so many of the Elector's bindings exhibit the characteristics of Venetian Renaissance binding;
namely, paper inlay, gold-tooling, the standard oriental ornamental designs, the arabesques and intertwined bands of
the Grolier style, spine decoration, etc. Krause mastered
all this and was able to combine these decorative elements
in a multitude of different ways. Some covers were filled
with vines or leaves and flowers in the French style. The
designs are gilded, and sometimes tooled and painted. Even
though the Krause bindings were mainly imitations and were

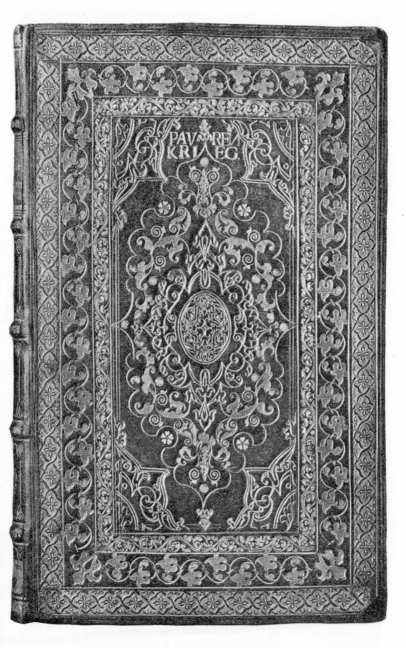

61. Binding by Jakob Krause in brown calf-skin with gold tooling. (Landesbibliothek, Dresden).

not always free of a tendency to overcrowding, they still are
entitled to a place of honor in the annals of artistic book binding; their brilliant technical execution alone would justify this.
A number of Krause bindings are still preserved, but the
greatest collection of them, comprising over 800 items, was
for the most part destroyed when the Sächsische Landesbibliothek was demolished during the second World War.

It is strange that the gem bindings of the Middle Ages
should experience a sort of revival in the 16th century in Germany. The twenty silver bindings that have been preserved
from the collection of Duke Albrecht of Prussia are especially
famous; they were made by a silversmith in Königsberg, where
they are now one of the principal treasures of the University
library.

French Renaissance Book Making

The Grolier style of binding played a significant role at
only one single place in Germany, but in France it was adopte
and continued with increasing enthusiasm. With the return of
Grolier to his native land in 1537 the influence of the Italian
Renaissance began to assert itself in French binderies as
shown by the bindings made in Lyons and bindings made for
King Francis I. Francis I was the first to introduce compul-
sory deposit of books. In 1537 he ordered all French presses
to deliver a copy of everything they printed to the Royal library. Several of his bindings, which were usually in black
calfskin, have typical Grolier ornaments. In the central panel
on the cover there were the French coat-of-arms and the
king's own seal, a salamander in flames. Others of Francis
I's bindings were decorated with rows of fleur-de-lis alter-
nating with his initial F; these fleur-de-lis bindings continued
in use for a long time as a very popular style of French book
binding.

A contemporary of Francis I was the great book artist
Geofroy Tory, who in 1530 became the first "royal printer" in
Paris. The gothic style was still dominant in French books at
that time, though Italian influence had begun to make itself felt
and the roman type had found its way into not a few French
books. It was used, for instance, by Jodocus Badius Ascenius, who printed numerous works of Erasmus and other great
humanists of the period. However, when the learned Tory in
the years following 1520 turned from scholarship to art and
developed his remarkable talents as a designer and stamp-
cutter, the roman type and Renaissance book decoration experienced their real, though rather late, flowering in France.

Outstanding among Tory's work is a series of Books of Hours
which he decorated with illustrations and single-lined borders
that harmonized well with the roman type of the text.   The
most famous of his works, however, is the one entitled
Champfleury that he issued in 1529 -- a book that concerns
itself with the question of orthography and the esthetics of
typography.   In designing his type Tory drew the letters within a square that was re-divided into smaller squares.   Among
those who followed him were Simon de Colines, who also published small editions of the classics, patterned after those of
Aldus and printed in three italic type faces cut by himself,
and Robert Granjon, who was active in Lyons from 1557 on
not only as printer but also as type cutter.   Granjon supplied
large quantities of type to famous European presses, and created his "civilité" type from an expanded italic.   This type
gained wide acceptance and Granjon's composite flower and
leaf ornaments also became standard equipment in printing
shops.

The most famous of the Renaissance presses that broke
with the gothic tradition was that of the Étienne family in
Paris, whose most prominent member was Robert Étienne (or
in Latinized form, Robertus Stephanus).   Like Aldus, Froben,
Tory and several other great printers he was a scholar; in
1532, for instance, he issued a great Latin lexicon compiled
by himself.   Like Tory he was appointed "royal printer" by
Francis I, but he was in continuous struggle with the theolo-
gians of the University of Paris who attacked him because of
the sympathy for the reform movement that he exhibited in
his editions of the Bible.   Finally, in spite of the royal protection, he was forced to leave the country and settle in
Geneva.   Étienne also used Hebrew and Greek characters; the
latter were cut by one of Tory's pupils, Claude Garamond
(Garamont).   Garamond also cut a roman type in several variations, somewhat like that of Nicolaus Jenson but with a lighter
and finer line; it has become recognized as one of the best
proportioned types ever created.   Modern Garamond type faces
made for linotype use have gained acceptance in the presses
of several countries.   Robert Étienne's son, Henri, continued
to operate the press and was also in contact with the great
Augsburg merchant family Fugger, several members of which
were book collectors on a scale that was very uncommon in
middle class circles in Germany at that time.   One of the
family, Johann Jakob Fugger, had some of his bindings made
in Paris and some by Antoni Ludwig in Augsburg.

On certain fine bindings made for Étienne, Groler ornaments occur again, and the same is true of several bindings
made for Henry II, who was an even greater friend and pro-

62.   Final page of Geoffroy Tory's Champfleury (Paris,
1529) with his mark and a decorative border.   Tory's mark
(a broken vase, pot cassé) is an imitation of a wood-cut in
"Hypnerotomachia Poliphili."

miſerables conditions d'adminiſtre, & regir ſes citez &
prouinces, eſquelles diligence eſt pleine de rancune, negligen-
ce & blaſme & meſpris : eſquelles ſeuerité eſt dangereuſe, libe-
ralité non aggreable, ſe parlee plain d'embuches, flaterie per-
nicieuſe, le front familier à tous, l'eſprit de pluſieurs plain d'in-
dignation, courroux ſecrete, et flaterie ouuertee : toutes leſ-
quelles choſes attendent les pretures ſenant en poſſeſſion de
leure dignitez, elles ſeruent à eux quand ils ſom, preſens, et les
delaiſſent lors quils s'en vom.

63.   Robert Granjon's "Caractères de civilité," designed
from an expanded gothic type and used by Plantin and others.

Olympius Iupiter: eius autem quod in Pythiis fit certaminis, Apollo. Prin-
cipium igitur huiuſmodi orationis, quæcumq; fuerit, laus dei nobis ſit, tam-
quam vultus ſeu perſona quædam ſplendida, in ſermonis initio poſita atque
conſtituta. Laudandi autem exordium, ab iis quæ deo inſunt, eique attri-
buuntur, prout res copiam ſuppeditent, ſumes. Si quidem Iupiter fuerit, ad-
ducendum erit, deorum regem, rerumque omnium opificem eſſe: Si vero
Apollo, muſices inuétorem exſtitiſſe, & eundem eſſe cum ſole: Solem autem
omnium omnibus bonorum auctorem. Præterea ſi Hercules erit, Iouis eſſe
filium: & ea quæ mortalium vitæ præbuit, cónumerabis. Et locus ferme có-
plebitur ex ijs quæ quilibet aut inuenerit, aut hominibus tradiderit. Verum
hæc breuibus narrabis; ne præcedens oratio ſequenti maior euadere videa-
tur. Deinceps vrbis laudes, in qua publicus conuentus celebratur, vel a ſitu,

64.   Garamond's roman, designed from Nicolaus Jenson's
15th century type, which was also the model for Aldus' and
many other roman types.

65. Binding made for Henry II and Diana of Poitiers. (Royal Library, Copenhagen).

66. Fanfare binding with J. A. de Thou's coat-of-arms in the center, from about 1575. Some fanfare bindings have the spirals set even more closely together so that they almost completely cover the surface.

tector of books than his predecessor Francis I. Henry II's
reign (1547-59) came when Italy had already begun to recede
into the background with respect to book making. Her art
was exhibiting more and more of that coarsening which is a
sure indication of degeneration. Signs of this same degeneration were also beginning to appear in contemporary French
book illustration, mainly in some of the small Books of Hours
issued as luxury items.

It was at this very time, however, that fine book binding in France reached its most magnificent form. The bindings that Henry II had made for himself, for his Queen Catherine of Medici and for his mistress Diana of Poitiers, and
which were imitated by other book collectors at the court and
among the nobility, were at least in technical respects, a-
mong the best that have ever been produced in France. With
their characteristic monograms, an H intertwined with a C or
a D, and often with halfmoons and the bow-and-arrow symbol
of Diana, goddess of the hunt, they show that French book
binders had not only completely adopted the spirit of the Grolier style but had learned to manifest it in an independent
manner.

Fine book binding flourished under both Charles IX and
Henry III. Henry III, in particular, was passionately fond of
fine bindings and had as his royal binder (relieur du Roy)
Nicolas Ève, who was also engaged in book selling and publishing in Paris. In some of Ève's bindings the entire cover
is filled with the French fleur-de-lis, but he was especially
known for his "fanfare" style, which has the greater part of
the cover closely filled with spiralling flower plants, palms
and laurel branches. Decoration of this type could only develop in a country where the art of gold tooling had been completely mastered, for the golden threads that cover the sides
and back of the binding in graceful swirls are made with a
great many small stamps put together with unusual craftsmanship. The name "fanfare," was probably not used until the
19th century when the book-collector Nodier had one of his
books entitled "Les fanfares" bound in a similar style.

After the deaths of Henry III and Nicolas Ève the style
continued in use and there are many examples of it in the
great collections of the French nobility. An example was the
collection of the great statesman and historian, Jacques Auguste de Thou, whose father had been Grolier's friend and
whose library finally numbered some 8,000 printed volumes
and about 1,000 manuscripts. De Thou's books were easy to
recognize because the bindings carry his coat-of-arms with
the three wasps and the monogram IADT; his books were

scattered when they were sold by one of his descendents in
1788.

French trade bindings and other ordinary bindings of
the 16th century were very little influenced by the fine bindings described above. They were made of calf or pigskin or
vellum, and their designs were either panel-stamped, blind
or gilded, or were made up of blind designs applied with
roller stamps.

English Roller-stamped and
Embroidered Bindings

The roller had been accepted in France, and its use
became even more general in England. The artisans in Cambridge gradually began using the rollers in preference to other
stamps. In fact, many of their bindings were made entirely
with rollers, the central field being filled out with rolled borders. The designs on the rollers used in England were quite
different from those in Germany; they included dancing figures
and strange animal forms, or S-shaped flower branches and
leaves. Along toward the middle of the century, however,
the Italian Renaissance binding styles came to England and
with them also gold-tooling. The English court and nobles
were interested in books, although not to the same extent or
in such an elaborate style as we found among the French nobility. Both Henry VII and Henry VIII, as well as Edward
VI and not least Queen Elizabeth, collected books and had
them bound in fine bindings in the French or Italian manner.
Henry VIII and Edward VI's book-binders were French and
successfully imitated the Aldine and Grolier styles. One of
the many collectors among the nobility, Thomas Wotton, has
been called "the English Grolier" because he imitated the
great French book collector even to the extent of having his
bindings inscribed "Thomae Wottoni et amicorun." Queen
Elizabeth was very fond of velvet and silk bindings on which
the decoration was embroidered in gold or silver thread or
colored silk thread, sometimes also using pearls -- a style
of binding that was used by the English royal house all through
the 16th and 17th centuries. But like the earlier gem bindings
these textile bindings were atypical of the book-binding art.

Plantin. Final Flowering of
German Wood-cut Art

The great Belgian book-maker Christopher Plantin was
French and originally a book-binder. But it was as printer

and publisher that he made his name one of the greatest in
the history of typography. His shop was in the flourishing
city of Antwerp, where over half of all the presses of the
Netherlands were located in the first half of the 16th century.
He issued over 1,600 works, some of them quite large, in
the course of the 40 years or so that he worked there before
his death in 1589. His stock of type was so extensive that
he was able to print books in all languages then known in
Europe; his Polyglot Bible in eight volumes gave the text in
four different languages (Fig. 68). Few printer-publishers
have had as wide a market as he; his publications were sold
in Germany and Scandinavia, in France, Spain and England,
and he had branch establishments in Leyden and Paris. He
printed scientific works on philology, law, mathematics, etc.,
as well as many classical authors, French literature and theological works; and a series of large liturgical works. His
mark was a hand with a pair of dividers and his motto "labore
et constantia" (Fig. 45).

   Plantin's broad, heavy roman type, cut by the type designer Granjon and other French artisans, was scarcely inferior to Étienne's, and his italic almost surpassed that of
Aldus. Like his predecessors, he had scholars in his service
and his son-in-law, Frans Raphelengius, who inherited the
press in Antwerp, was himself a learned man. Two other
sons-in-law also took over branches; a son of one of these,
Balthasar Moretus, later became known for his collaboration
with Rubens. Plantin's great business brought together a
whole colony of printers, type-casters, punch-cutters, illustrators and book-binders, and their activity continued until
1876 when the Belgian government purchased the beautiful
ancestral house in Antwerp which had been the headquarters
of the establishment and made it into a museum (Musée
Plantin-Moretus). The old work-rooms are still preserved
as one of the sights of the town, a very instructive presenta-
tion of the typographic methods and working conditions of an
earlier period. Unfortunately it did not escape damage in
the bombardments of World War II.

   Plantin provided his books generously with wood-cuts,
but at this period the art of wood-carving was on the decline;
hence Plantin also made considerable use of the new process
of copper-plate engraving. Around the middle of the 16th century wood-carving experienced an Indian summer revival in
Germany. The great publisher Sigismund Feyerabend in Frankfort brought together a group of artists among whom the best
known are Hans Sebald Beham, Jost Amman (Amann), Virgil
Solis and Tobias Stimmer, who collaborated on a number of
large Bibles and editions of the classics. An especially popu-

67. Christophe Plantin. Painting by Rubens, after Plantin's death in 1589.

lar work was the wood-cut book prepared by Jost Amman in
1568 and entitled: "Beschreybung aller Stande auff Erden."
The illustrations in this book have been reproduced again and
again as the oldest known and most accurate representations
of the crafts and workshops of the past; among them are some
of the earliest pictures of a type-casting shop (Fig. 29), a
printing press, a book bindery and a paper-making plant.
Tobias Stimmer collaborated on some of the large portrait
works so highly prized in those days (Icones or Effigies).

While the familiar classical designs, acanthus leaves,
vine branches, columns, playful cupids, etc., had been almost
completely dominant in high-Renaissance book decoration, ara-
besque ornaments came more and more into use at the middle
of the 16th century for vignettes and head-pieces in French
books, and then spread to other countries. At the same time
more and more frequent use was made of the cartouche for
title and picture borders; it was the favorite of the time in
all types of decorative art; even into the 17th century it maintained a prominent place in book decoration.

Introduction of Copper Engraving

By the middle of the 16th century in Denmark the Renaissance style, which had been introduced by Christiern Peder
sen, had begun to set its mark on book printing. At the same
time scholarship and literature flourished as is shown by the
fact that while there are only 226 Danish books preserved
from the period 1482-1550 there are some 1400 from 1550-
1600. Fortunately Denmark had a competent person to direct
the development of book-making, namely Lorenz (Lauritz)
Benedicht; he was presumably German-born, and worked in
Copenhagen from about 1560 to 1601. He was the first in
Denmark to use fraktur as his main type, but the thing that
gave his books their special character and distinction was the
excellent proportioning of the text page and the ornamentation.
Benedicht was a wood-carver himself and his title borders,
initials and illustrations rank with the best German work of
the time. Among his famous printed products were Hans
Thomeson's Hymnal (1569) and Nils Jesperson's "Gradual"
(1573), which introduced the printing of music to Denmark
(Fig. 69), and the book he printed in 1578 in one single copy
for his royal patron, King Frederick II, a work on warfare
with numerous large hand-colored wood-cuts. Frederik II's

Interp.ex Græc. lxx. CAP. I.   ΗΣΑΙΑΣ. *μθ᾽ ἑρμηνέυσις τῶν ὅ.*

ESAIAS. CAPVT I.

VISIO quã vidit Esaias fi-
lius Amos , quam vidit contra Judæam & contra Jeru-
salem in regno Oziæ, et Joa-
tham, Achaz et Ezechiæ, qui
regnauerunt in Judæa.

[2] *Audi cælum, et auribus percipe terra, quia*
Dominus locutus est : Filios genui & exaltaui;
ipsi autê me spreuerunt. [3] *Cognouit bos possessorê,*
& asinus præsepe domini sui ; Israel autem me
non cognouit, & populus me non intellexit.

[4] *Væ gens peccatrix, popule plene peccatis, se-*
men nequam, filij iniqui dereliquistis Dominũ,
& ad iracundiam concitastis sanctum Israel :
alienati sunt in retro.

[5] *Quid vltrà percutiemini addentes iniqui-*
tatem? Omne caput in laborem, & omne cor in
tristitiam. [6] *A pedibus vsque ad caput non*
est in eo sanitas: vulnus, liuor, plaga tumens;non
est maligna imponere, neque oleum neque alli-
gaturas. [7] *Terra vestra deserta, ciuitates*
vestræ succensæ igni:regionem vestram coram
vobis alieni deuorant eam; & desolata est sub-
uersà à populis alienis.

[8] *Derelinquetur filia Sion sicut tentorium*
in vinea, et sicut pomorum custodia in cucume-
rario,sicut ciuitas obsessa. [9] *Et nisi Dominus*
Sabaoth reliquisset nobis semen , quasi Sodoma
vtique facti fuissemus,& quasi Gomorra vtiq;
assimilati essemus. [10] *Audite verbum Domini*
principes Sodomorum, attendite legê Dei nostri
populus Gomorræ. [11] *Quid mihi multitudo vi-*
ctimarum vestrarum, dicit Dominus? plenus
sum holocaustis arietum,& adipem agnorum,&
sanguinem taurorum & hircorum non volo.

[12] *Neque veneritis apparere mihi. quis enim*
quæsiuit hæc de manibus vestris? calcare atrium
meum. [13] *Non apponetis, si obtuleritis siliginem;*
vanum: incensum abominatio mihi est. Neome-
nias vestras & sabbata, & diem magnum non
feram:ieiunium & ocium;

ΗΣΑΙΑΣ. κεφ. α´.

Ὅρασις ἣν εἶδεν ἡσαίας υἱὸς ἀμώς,ἣν εἶδεν
κ᾽ τ᾽ ιουδαίας, κỳ κ᾽ ἱερȣσαλὴμ ἐν
βασιλεία ὀζίȣ κỳ ιώαθαμ κỳ ἄχαζ
ᵓ εζεκίȣ,οἱ ἐβασίλϵυσαν τῆς ιουδαίας.

[2] ἄκȣϵ ȣρανὲ κỳ ἐνωτίζȣ γῆ,ὅτι κύ-
ρι⊙ ἐλάλησϵν. υἱȣς ἐγέννησα κỳ ὕψωσα,αὐτοὶ δέ μϵ
ἠθέτησαν. [3] ἔγνω βȣς τὸν κτησάμϵνον , κỳ ὄν⊙ τὴν
φάτνην τ κυρίȣ αὐτȣ , ἰσραὴλ δέ μϵ ȣκ ἔγνω, κỳ ὁ
λαός μϵ ȣ συνῆκϵν. [4] Ȣαὶ ἔθν⊙ ἁμαρτωλόν, λαὸς
πλήρης ἁμαρτιῶν, σπέρμα πονηρόν, υἱοὶ ἄνομοι ἐγκατϵ-
λίπϵτϵ τὸν κύριον, κỳ παρωργίσατϵ τὸν ἅγιον τ ισραὴλ,
ἀπηλλοτριώθητϵ εἰς τὰ ὀπίσω.

[5] τί ἔτι πληγῆτϵ προστιθέντϵς ἀνομίαν; πᾶσα κεφα-
λὴ εἰς πόνον, κỳ πᾶσα καρδία εἰς λύπην.
[6] ἀπὸ ποδῶν ἕως κϵφαλῆς ȣκ ἔστιν ἐν αὐτῷ ὁλοκληρία,
τραῦμα μώλωψ πληγὴ φλϵγμαίνȣσα, ȣκ ἔστι μά-
λαγμα ἐπιθῆναι ȣτϵ ἔλαιον ȣτϵ καταδέσμȣς.

[7] ἡ γῆ ὑμῶν ἔρημ⊙, αἱ πόλϵις ὑμῶν πυρίκαυσοι,τὴν
χώραν ὑμῶν ἐνώπιον ὑμῶν ἀλλότριοι κατϵσθίȣσιν αὐτὴν,
κỳ ἠρήμωται κατϵστραμμένη ὑπὸ λαῶν ἀλλοτρίων.

[8] ἐγκαταλϵιφθήσϵται ἡ θυγάτηρ σιῶν ὡς σκηνὴ ἐν ἀμ-
πϵλῶνι καὶ ὡς ὀπωροφυλάκιον ἐν σικυηρατίῳ, ὡς πόλις
πολιορκȣμένη. [9] καὶ ϵἰ μὴ κύρι⊙ σαβαὼθ ἐγκατέλιπϵν
ἡμῖν σπέρμα, ὡς σόδομα ἂν ἐγϵνήθημϵν, κỳ ὡς γό-
μορρα ἂν ὡμοιώθημϵν.

[10] ἀκȣσατϵ λόγον κυρίȣ ἄρχοντϵς σοδόμων, προσέχϵ-
τϵ νόμον θϵȣ ὑμῶν λαὸς γομόρρας.

[11] τί μοι πλῆθ⊙ τῶν θυσιῶν ὑμῶν, λέγϵι κύρι⊙; πλήρης ϵἰμὶ ὁλοκαυτωμάτων κριῶν, κỳ στέαρ ἀρνῶν,ᵓ αἷμα
ταύρων ᵓ τράγων ȣ βȣλομαι.

[12] ȣδ᾽ ἂν ἔρχησθϵ ὀφθῆναί μοι· τίς γὰρ ἐξϵζήτησϵ ταῦτα
ἐκ τῶν χϵιρῶν ὑμῶν, πατϵῖν τὴν αὐλήν μȣ.

[13] ȣ προσθήσϵσθϵ. ἐὰν φέρητϵ σϵμίδαλιν, μάταιον·
θυμίαμα βδέλυγμά μοι ἐστί. τὰς νȣμηνίας ὑμῶν κỳ
τὰ σάββατα ᵓ ἡμέραν μϵγάλην ȣκ ἀνέχομαι. νηστείαν
κỳ ἀργίαν·

INTERPRETATIO LATINA TRANSLATIONIS CHALDAICAE IN ESAIAM.

Ex Complutensi Bibliotheca, ad Hebraicam & Chaldaicam veritatem à B. Aria Montano correcta.

PROPHETIA Esaiæ filij Amos, quam prophetauit super viros Iuda,& habitatores Ierusalê in diebus Oziæ, Iotham,Achaz,Eze-
chiæ,regum domus Iuda. [2] Audite cæli,qui commoti estis,quando dedi legem meam populo meo; & auscultā terra,quæ conte-
muisti à facie Verbi mei,quoniā Dñs locutus est:Populus meus domus Israel,quos vocaui filios,& dilexi eos,& honorificaui eos,
& ipsi rebellauerunt in verbum meum. [3] Cognouit bos emptorem suum, & asinus præsepe domini sui, Israel autem non didicit
vt sciret timorem mei:populus meus non intellexit vt conuerteretur ad timorem mei. [4] Væ tibi qui vocati sunt populus sān-
ctus,& peccauerunt; congregatio electa, & multiplicauerunt delicta. Cogominati sunt semen electum, & malè egerunt;& dicti sunt filij
dilecti; & corruperunt vias suas; dereliquerunt cultum Domini , detestati sunt timorem Sancti Israel, & propter opera eorum praua auersi
sunt, & facti sunt retrorsum. [5] Non animaduerterunt, dicentes:Propter quid percussi sumus? adhuc addunt peccare, nec dicunt : Quare
omne caput languidū,& omne cor mœrens? [6] A reliquo pedis vsque ad principem,non est in eis qui sit perfectus fit in timore mei: omnes
sunt cōtumaces, & rebelles;coin quinati sunt in peccatis suis,sicut plaga vlcerosa,nō dimittunt superbias suas,nec desiderant agere pœniten-
tiam, neque sunt in eis iustitia quibus protegantur. [7] Terra vestra deserta, ciuitates vestræ succensæ igni:terrā vestram coram vobis populi
possident eam,& propter peccata vestra deserta est terra, & translata est ad alienos. [8] Et relinquetur cœtus Sion,sicut vmbraculū in vinea,
postquam vindemiarunt eam,sicut tugurium manens in cucumerario postquam legerunt cucumeres ab eo; sicut ciuitas quæ obsidetur.

[9] Nisi superexcedens bonitas Domini exercituum reliquisset nobis redemptionem in miserationibus suis;peccata funt in nobis propter
quæ quasi viri Sodomæ perissemus, & quasi habitatores Gomorræ consumpti essemus. [10] Suscipite verbum Domini principes,quorū opera sunt mala,sicut principum Sodomæ:auscultate legem Dei nostri populi quorum opera similia sunt populo Gomorræ. [11] Non est beneplacitum coram me in multitudine victimarum vestrarum, dicit Dominus:satiatus sum abundantia holocaustorum arietum, & adipe pin-
guium, & sanguine taurorum, & agnorum, & hircorum; quia in eis non est beneplacitum coram me. [12] Cùm venitis vt appareatis in con-
spectu meo,quis quæsiuit hoc de manibus vestris, vt veniatis ad conculcandā atria mea? [13] Non addatis vltrà offerre oblationem ex rapi-
na;sacrificium abominabile est coram me, & neomenia & sabbatha cœtus congregationis vestræ , quoniam non relinquitis peccata vestra,
vt exaudiatur oratio vestra in tempore congregationis vestræ.   A 3

---

68. Page from Plantin's Polyglot Bible, printed in 1569-
72 for Philip II of Spain. The earliest polyglot Bible was
issued in Spain in 1502-17.

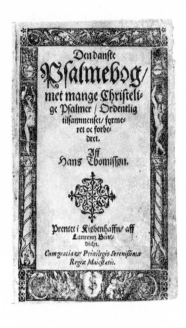

69. Title-page and text page from Hans Thomeson's hymn-
nal of 1569, printed by Lorenz Benedicht. The title-page has
wood-cut borders and the text includes musical notation, the
first ever printed in Denmark.

Bible, which appeared in 1589 and was also illustrated, was
not printed by Benedicht but by another capable printer in
the capital city, Mads Vingaard. Benedicht is known to have
printed some 350 different works in all, but over 100 of them
have disappeared completely. Presumably his actual production was greater than the above figure; it extended from ephemeral pamphlets to large scientific works, the latter including
Tycho Brahe's book about the new star (1573).

Later Tycho Brahe set up his own printing press and
bindery on the island Hven and also had his own paper mill.
Most of his works bear the imprint Uraniburgum. Even when
he lived as an exile in Wandsbeck in Holstein at the home of
the learned humanist, Henrik Rantzan, himself an ardent book
collector, Tycho Brahe had his own press with him. Most of
his products were printed in large varieties of roman and
italic, which gave them a stately appearance. Those of his
bindings that are preserved are in keeping with this style;

usually they are of vellum or satin and have his picture
stamped in gold on the front cover and his coat-of-arms on
the back (Fig. 60).

One of Tycho Brahe's books printed in Holstein was
the monumental work "Astronomiae instauratae mechanica,"
now quite scarce, with both wood-cuts and copper engravings.

Toward the end of the 16th century the art of wood-
carving declined more and more; the excessive use that was
made of it led to factory-like methods of production; most of
the designs had become stereotyped, whether cast in metal or
cut in wood, and the late Renaissance taste for luxuriance in
a high degree led to profusion and overcrowding at the expense of artistic talent.

However, it is not only in the matter of decoration
that there was evidence of decline, it was apparent in the
typography as well. The flourishing scholarly literature of
the 16th century made greater and greater demands on the
printer in the way of complicated type-setting, elaborate dedications, involved musical notation, etc. The printer had no
models to follow, and in his hesitation before this typographical task he was tempted into stylized overextension. It was
unfortunate that type casting had become a separate trade as
early as 1530, as the result of a number of workers' dis-
putes, and the intimate relationship between printing and type
production was gradually lost.

THE 17th CENTURY

Ascendancy of Copper-Plate Engraving

The first book in which copper-plate engravings were used was issued in Florence in 1477. During the next hundred years copper engravings were used only occasionally for illustrations, and in several instances books that had originally had copper engravings were reissued with wood-cuts. Copper engraving met with resistance at first from printers because, in contrast to wood-cuts, they could not be printed in one operation with the text. In a wood-cut the block is carved so that the outlines of the drawing stand out in relief, and as in ordinary type it is then these raised portions that take the ink and make the impression. This is called relief or letterpress printing. In a copper engraving, on the other hand, the lines of the drawing are traced on the copper plate and cut down into it, and these depressions are then filled with ink for printing, i.e. intaglio printing. In principle, copper engravings are not suited to use in books, and it is rather difficult to understand why for some two hundred years they provided the dominant method for printing book illustrations. In cases where illustrations or plates are printed separately and then bound in with the book, copper-plate engraving has a natural place, and it was in this form that it was used at the beginning. Engraved "frontispieces" were introduced and inserted before the regular letterpress title page; these frontispieces contained the title of the book set against a background of allegorical figures or imaginative representations of the contents of the book, or they might contain a portrait of the author to precede the title page. Engraved plates were extensively used in the large illustrated works that were becoming more and more fashionable, and also in scientific works where the illustrations were of special importance, as in book on geography, natural history, history of art and archeology. Large books containing reproductions of paintings or illustrations of architecture and sculpture or of archeological finds were produced in large numbers at the end of the 16th century and all through the 17th century, and production of travel accounts and topographic works with maps and drawings of landscapes, cities and buildings was also extensive. Some famous examples are Theodor de Bry's voluminous work on India

(1590-1625), Georg Braun's "Theatrum urbium," a description of certain towns published in 1572, Martin Zeiller's enormous geographical work with over 200 maps and views, and finally a large collection of illustrations issued in periodical form under the title of "Theatrum Europaeum" and describing contemporary historical events.   Many of the so-called "architectural works" are famous.   Their illustrations were intended to serve as models for builders.   Archeological works included those of the papal antiquarian Pietro Santo Bartoli on the ancient monuments of Rome, and among works on the history of art there were Pietro Aguila's reproductions of famous contemporary paintings.

Copper-plate printing was especially suited for the reproduction of paintings, since it could imitate the fine shades of color and the general artistic effect.   Hence it is no accident that its greatest advance came in a period when the art of painting was developing so rapidly.   The copper-plate engraver, however, made less of an independent artistic contribution in his work than did the wood-carver in his wood-cuts. In the case of copper engravings for the large works just mentioned it was a question of representing an original as accurately as possible whether by transferring the colors of a painting to black-and-white form, or presenting a picture of a building, a work of sculpture, an animal or a plant.   In the field of archeology, art history and natural history copper engraving became an invaluable aid for accurate representation until photographic methods came into use in the 19th century and made possible even greater accuracy.   The better copper-plate engravings did also show artistic ability as well as good craftsmanship; the Swiss engraver Matthäus Merian, for instance, who collaborated with his sons and his daughter, Maria Sibylla, on some of the works mentioned above, attained considerable fame as an artist.

Baroque Style in Book Arts

The baroque style next became dominant in the field of book-making.   The insatiable desire for grandiose effects found expression in large folio formats and large type faces, but it was manifested especially in a overwhelming profusion on the frontispieces with which ordinary and otherwise unillustrated books were provided.   In a travel account the frontispiece would often represent a foreign scene with all sorts of exotic humans and animals scattered about; in archeological works the frontispieces were filled with classical figures in deep meditation among picturesque ruins, etc.; and everywhere there were the allegorical figures that symbolize Wisdom,

Love, Justice, the State, Religion, etc. Many, perhaps most, of these frontispiece title pages, on which there was scarcely room enough for the title itself, cannot be compared with the better productions of 16th century book-making, but there were a few that stand far above the general level. That was especially true of the frontispieces that were sketched by Rubens in the years that he worked with the Galle family of copper engravers for Balthasar Moretus of the Plantin establishment. Rubens' and his pupils' engravings still showed a predilection for allegorical figures, but the artist's genius asserted itself. In spite of their profusion and other faults these engravings showed an artistic restraint that was uncommon in the book decoration of the time. In many instances Rubens made only a rough outline for the design (Rubens invenit) while someone else completed the drawing (delineavit) and a third engraved it in copper (sculpsit).

Plantin's printing business in Antwerp came to have great significance for the application of copper engraving to book illustration. Even after his death, and all through the 17th century it was Belgium and especially Holland that took the lead in most aspects of book production in Europe. This was due partly to the powerful political position that the Netherlands had attained at that time, and partly to the liberal form of government that left the artist free of the strict censorship that prevailed in absolute states. In addition the Netherlands also held a position of leadership in the scientific and scholarly world. Students came from all countries to the famous University of Leyden.

The Elzevirs. The Blaeu Family

Toward the close of the 16th century a book-binder and porter named Lodewijk Elzevir (Elsevier) was appointed at the University of Leyden. He obtained permission to sell books to the students and gradually worked up a book business of considerable size. His field of activity extended far beyond the borders of that town and of the country; he maintained a regular stock of books in Frankfurt, and throughout Southern Germany people bought their foreign literature from him.

Lodewijk Elzevir was the first of the great family of printers and publishers who established themselves in several towns in Holland during the 17th century and made the name Elzevir famous throughout Europe. The most outstanding members of the family were Lodewijk's son Bonaventura and his grandsons, Isaac, Lodewijk the younger, and Abraham, and the period in which their activity fell, 1625-64, was the great

70. Copper-engraved title-page of a book published by Balthasar Moretus in 1623; drawn by Rubens.

period of the Elzevirs.   Just as Aldus in his time had distributed small editions of the classics in italic type from
Venice across Europe, a multitude of very similar duodecime
editions were distributed from the Elzevirs' press.   At a
time when large folios were in vogue these small books were
something quite unusual and like the Aldines, something more
democratic.   They rapidly became popular because of their
practical format and low price; the editions of Caesar, Pliny,
Terence and Vergil were in particular demand.   While they
could not compare with the Aldines in philological accuracy,
the general effect of their clear roman type was quite impressive, although somewhat monotonous.   The type was cut
by Christofel van Dyck on the model of Garaamond's type, an
it was also used in England after Bishop John Fell introduced
it at the Oxford University Press in 1670.

Besides these editions of the classics the Elzevirs
published many other books; in 1626 they were granted a license to issue a series of statistical and topographical descriptions of various countries, the so-called "Republics,"
which enjoyed considerable success.   Many of the greatest
literary figures of the time belonged to the Elzevir circle:
Descartes, Molière, Calvin, Bacon, Hobbes, Galilei and especially the great Dutch jurist Hugo Grotius, whose famous
work on the freedom of the seas was issued in 1609 by the
older Lodewijk.   Other well-known Elzevir books are an edition of St. Augustine dated 1675, an edition of Corneille's
translation of Thomas a Kempis' "Imitation of Christ" (1652),
a folio edition of Roman Law (1663) and editions of Molière,
Corneille, Pascal and other great French writers.   The total
of Elzevir editions and authentic Elzevir imprints -- for,
like the Aldines, they had many imitators -- amounts to a-
round 2,200, besides some 3,000 university publications.   In
the 18th and especially the 19th century Elzevir publications
were greatly sought after by book collectors, and that afflic-
tion has persisted, appearing mainly in wealthy American collectors.   Great value has been attached to copies that have
been trimmed as little as possible, and a special Elzevir
scale has been adopted for measuring the width of the margins
Well-preserved Elzevir books from the family's best period
have risen to fantastic values, even when the editions cannot
be called rare.   One example of the rise in price of Elzevir
books is that experienced by the little French book on pastry
making, "Le pastissier francois."   The Elzevirs reprinted
this book in 1655 from the French original and in one of their
catalogs they listed it at a price of slightly over half a gulden
In the course of time the book became scarce, and in the latter half of the 19th century good copies brought as high as
10,000 francs.   One of the largest and finest Elzevir collec-

P. VIRGILII MARONIS

BVCOLICA.

TITYRVS, ECLOGA I.

ARGVMENTVM.

Virgilius fub perfona Tityri paftoru , quo arietem
majorem , aut hircum fignificari ajunt , ut evi-
dentius fortunam fuam,beneficiaque Cæfaru ex-
plicaret, ex adverfo Melibæum,id eft,qui curam
agit boum , introducit , à patria, adempto agro,
pulfum.

MELIBOEVS, TITYRVS.

M. Ityre, tu patulæ recubans fub tegmi-
ne fagi,
Silvéftrem tenui Mufam meditaris
avena
Nos patriæ fineis , & dulcia linquimus arva,
Nos patriam fugimus : tu Tityre lentus in umbra
Formofam refonare doces Amaryllida filvas.
T. O Melibœe, deus nobis hæc otia fecit.
Namque erit ille mihi femper deus: illius aram
Sæpe tener noftris ab ovilibus imbuet agnus.
Ille meas errare boves, ut cernis, & ipfum
Ludere quæ vellem calamo permifit agrefti.
M. Non equidem invideo : miror magis: undique
totis
Vfque adeo turbatur agris. en ipfe capellas
Protenus æger ago: hanc etiam vix Tityre duco.
Heic inter denfas corulos modo namq; gemellos,
Spem

71.   Page from an Elzivir edition of Virgil in duodecimo.
In the octavo format the sheet is folded three times, while
in the duodecimo it is folded to make 12 sheets or 24 pages
Duodecimo is abbreviated 12 mo.

tions is the Berghman collection in the Royal Library at Stockholm.

Part of the Elzevirs' type was taken over in the 18th
century by another famous printing dynasty, the Enschedé
family in Haarlem, whose firm was founded in 1703 by Izaak
Enschedé; it is still in existence and possesses a greater variety of type face from different periods than any other European press; it also acquired the type of the famous Berlin
printer J. F. Unger.

As booksellers the Elzevirs outdistanced all others of the time; none had such wide-spread trade connections as they did. The younger Lodewijk even came to Copenhagen on one of his trips and founded a branch at Børsen, which was later also used by another Dutch printer, Johannes Janssonius, the greatest reprint publisher of the 17th century. Through his and the Elzevirs' reprints of French works, con temporary French literature was given a wider distribution than it would otherwise have had. Dutch book dealers did a considerable business with England; all England's book connections with the continent at that time went through Holland and here again the Elzevirs were in the lead.

Like other large publishers they issued many of their books in bound form; they had the Magnus family of bookbinders working for them, imitating the French bindings of the time. This family also found employment at several othe Dutch printing establishments, such as the Blaeu firm which was active from 1618 to 1672 and attained renown for its large geographical atlases.

Cartography had reached a high stage of development in the seafaring Dutch nation, and the founder of the firm, Willem Janszoon Blaeu, had become acquainted with Tycho Brahe on a trip to Denmark and had acquired a basic knowledge of astronomy and cartography. As "globen- en kaartenmaker" in Amsterdam he issued several large editions of marine charts that surpassed all earlier ones in accuracy and attractiveness. His main work was the "Novus Atlas," but the family attained its greatest fame from the work by the founder's son Johann, entitled "Atlas major," which was first published in 1662 in 11 folio volumes. Here the art of coppe engraving came into its own, not only in the hand-colored maps but also in the titles and ornaments. In spite of its size and cost the "Atlas major" was very much in demand. It is said that the Archduchess of Tuscany paid 30,000 gulden for a particularly beautiful copy, and the work is still valued highly today. The financing of this and so many of the other monumental literary enterprises of that time, seems miraculous. Part of the answer undoubtedly lay in the low-paid labor that was available. But in many instances financial support from patrons among royalty and the nobility, in return for dedications and eulogies in prose and verse at the beginning of the printed work must have been part of the financing. Without this support these large scholarly works would have had just as little chance of publication then as they would have today without grants from the government or from private foundations.

The First Book Auctions

The early years of the 17th century marked the beginning of a new form of book trade in which books are put up
at auction for sale to the highest bidder.   The first book auctions were held in Leyden.   The initiative was presumably
taken by the older Lodewijk Elzevir, and it soon became apparent that this procedure had advantages for both the buyer
and the seller.

The seller obtained maximum financial return and the
buyer was offered collections that did not have the miscellaneous composition of the ordinary bookseller's stock.   Quite early, however, there were complaints that the book dealers who
arranged the auctions used them to get rid of the less desirable
books in their stock by mixing them with those to be put up
at auction.   Printed catalogs were sent out in advance, usually listing the books by size; octavos, quartos and folios.

These Dutch book auctions soon attracted attention in
other countries, and acquired increasing international significance.   An English clergyman, Joseph Hill, who had spent
some time in Holland, introduced the custom into London in
1676 when he proposed that the library of a deceased parson
be sold at auction, and thereafter the idea spread rapidly in
England.   It had reached America in 1622.   The spirit of excitement that pervades any auction was present at book auctions, and when important rarities were put under the ham-
mer episodes of a truly dramatic nature often occurred.   The
practice of holding book auctions had spread in France and
Germany during the second half of the 17th century -- German dealers tried in vain to fight it -- and in Denmark the
first book auction was held in Copenhagen in the 1650's (the
oldest preserved auction catalog is dated 1654).

French Book Collectors

Holland assumed the leading position in the European
book world of the 17th century.   France -- despite her brilliant literary production -- had to take a secondary position,
and French literature was largely disseminated through books
reprinted in Holland.   In the field of book-collecting, however, the French were in the front rank; French bibliophiles
had continued the Grolier tradition and preserved the luxury
aspects that distinguished it throughout Europe.   The more
the power of the French royal house increased, the greater
and more luxurious was the display at court.   The king and
the other royal book collectors were surrounded by noble

lords and ladies who took part in the competition for fine
books that was under way in the reign of Louis XIV and gathered speed under his successors, Louis XV and XVI. It
would be a considerable exaggeration, however, to ascribe
any abiding interest in literature to these kings and nobles;
it is much more likely that this paralleled the collection of
fine books by wealthy Romans during the Empire; and Seneca's
judgement of them could equally well be applied to many
French collectors of the 17th and 18th centuries.

This does not mean that we do not find educated and
well-read men who collected books for other reasons than to
satisfy their personal vanity. There was, for instance, the
learned Nicolas Claude de Peiresc, whose special interest was
Coptic manuscripts and printed books with marginal notations
by their previous owners. True interest in books must also
be ascribed to the great statesmen Richelieu, Mazarin and
Colbert. Richelieu's literary interests were evidenced by his
establishment of a royal press in the Louvre, an institution
that later had great influence on typography in France. Colbert made a considerable contribution to Louis XIV's library,
which grew to 40,000 volumes and 10,000 manuscripts. Mazarin had had a special passion for books ever since his early
youth.

Richelieu and Mazarin received considerable assistance
from their librarian Gabriel Naudé. His name is known in
the history of books through the work that he issued in 1627
entitled "Advis pour dresser une bibliothèque." This can be
called the earliest attempt at writing a guide to library work.
Naudé showed great energy and financial sense in searching
through the stocks of dealers throught Europe and gradually
built the Mazarin library up to 45,000 volumes.

In his book Naudé placed particular emphasis on the
importance of making a library accessible to everyone. It
was also the cardinal's ambition to become France's Asinius
Pollio, and his collections were opened in 1643 to scientists
and literary scholars for six hours each day. But a few years
thereafter Mazarin was banished and during the wars of the
Fronde the magnificent library was sold and scattered to the
winds. Deeply sorrowed by this misfortune Naudé answered
a call to Sweden as librarian to Queen Christina. When Mazarin again came to power and began to collect books once
more he summoned back his old librarian, but Naudé died on
the journey and did not live to see the growth of the second
Bibliothèque Mazarine, which was opened to the public in 1691.
It is still one of the most important libraries in the Department of the Seine.

Die Kayserliche Bibliothek in Vienna

72.   Interior of hall in the Imperial Library in Vienna in the 17th century. The Emperor is paying a visit to the library. (From Edward Brown: Account of some travels, 1685).

The St. Victor library of the Augustinian order was made accessible to scholars at the middle of the century, while the old and wealthy Benedictive monastery, Saint-Germain-des-Prés only reluctantly opened its doors and the Abbey of Sainte-Geneviève did not make its library public until the 18th century. The latter was the only library that survived the ravages of the Revolution, and today it still holds a prominent place among the public libraries of France.

Library Architecture

The outer form of libraries had changed gradually. Throughout the greater part of the 16th century the medieval custom of keeping the books on desks persisted. Library quarters gradually took the form of a large room or hall with the books arranged on shelves along the walls; often these shelves extended up to the ceiling so that a gallery had to be installed to reach them. This type of library construction found its first full realization in the magnificent building that was erected in the latter half of the 16th century for the Escorial Library in Madrid. It soon became the prevailing

style and was not superseded by more practical forms until
about the middle of the 19th century.   In these large library
halls the architect would give free play to his imagination,
and there is often great artistic merit in the domes, columns,
friezes and ceiling decorations that were used.   It cannot be
denied that the architectural splendor of the structure itself
almost overshadowed the books.   The frame, so to speak,
took precedence over the picture, but in the baroque period
with its tendency toward the grandiose this was scarcely considered a defect.   It was intended that a library should have
the appearance of a museum, and this effect was still further
emphasized by placing globes of the heavens and the earth in
the center of the hall, and all sorts of art objects on pedes-
tals round about.   The reason for this lies partly in the fact
that many of the great book collectors were also collectors
of art; the French minister, Pierre Séguier, had collected
over 20, 000 volumes, but in the library rooms in his palace
the display of porcelain almost outshone the books themselves.

One of the most magnificent examples of a library hall
was the famous domed room built in the 18th century for the
Court Library in Vienna.

Ordinary Book Binding

This architectural magnificence found its counterpart in
the elegance of bindings.   Nevertheless, in the 17th century,
as in earlier periods, the greater part of the books were in
more ordinary bindings.   We still have many French calf and
sheepskin bindings of that period that are marbled to give a
tortoise-shell appearance or simply stained black, with no
decoration except on the spine.   A still more Spartan effect
is presented by the English bindings in brown sheepskin, whose
plain appearance is further emphasized by the fact that the inside of the covers do not even have paper pasted over the
gray cardboard filling.   The ordinary Dutch "horn bindings"
were made of hard white vellum polished smooth, with very
little decoration, and the title was written in India ink at the
top of the spine.   On Italian and Spanish vellum bindings,
however, the title was stamped down along the spine, and
there was no cardboard insert in the covers at all, but these
were soft and flexible like the small suede leather bindings
of today.

But the wealthy collectors were not satisfied with the
plainer types of binding alone, and in France, in particular,
the art of fine book binding continued to be cultivated as in
the time of Francis I and Henry II.   At the beginning of the

73. The great hall in the Imperial Library (now the
Austrian National Library) in Vienna, built by J. B. Fischer
von Erlach and completed in 1726.

17th century the fanfare style with its conventional laurel
branches was still dominant, but in the later years of Louis
XIII's reign an entirely new style of decoration made its appearance when stamps with dotted lines (fers pointillés) began to be used; the fine curved or spiral lines are broken up
into a series of small dots and are arranged to form a web
or network over the entire cover or around the central panel
containing the owner's coat-of-arms. In this type of decoration, strangely enough, there were faint traces of baroque
ornaments. The dotted stamps were also used on the back
of books and even on the inside of the covers, which in fine
bindings were often covered with leather or silk. The end-
papers which had usually been of plain white paper were often
marbled, as were the edges of the book.

    The originator of the dotted-line (or "pinhead") style

74.   Red morocco binding in the Gascon style, from the
beginning of the 17th century.

is considered to be the bookbinder Le Gascon, about whom
very little is actually known.   It is not even certain whether
Le Gascon was his real name or merely an appellation to indicate his home district.   Some have tried, without justification, to identify him with another book binder, Florimond
Badier, who made bindings in the same style and put his signature on them.   It is certain that Le Gascon or pupils of
his worked for the great collectors of the time, Mazarin,
Seguier and the learned Nicolas de Peiresc, just as it is certain that his style was soon imitated throughout France and in
the neighboring countries.   Dotted lines were easier to exe-
cute than solid lines, so that the introduction of the Gascon
style meant some simplification.   A still further simplification occurred when the bookbinder Macé Ruette introduced the
practice of replacing the numerous small stamps with larger
stamps that combined the dotted ornaments into larger units
placed inside and around a line border.   In the latter half of

75. Binding by Florimond Badier (his name is seen at
lower left), decorated in the pointillé style.

76. Binding by Samuel
Maerne in the "all-over" style
with crescent designs stamped
in the borders surrounding the
three central panels.

77. English binding in the
Harleian style, 1702. (British
Museum).

the century many of these larger stamps were made in the
shape of a crescent or rocker with the ends turned back, or
they were kidney-shaped; these variations of the Gascon style
achieved wide distribution.

In Holland the Gascon style was imitated by the Magnus family of book-binders. They used the dotted stamps on
Elzevir trade bindings, which were usually executed in green
morocco, while in France and other countries red was the
preferred color. In England, where the nobility and the
higher clergy included many bibliophiles, the Gascon style
was also adopted. A special variation of it was used by
Charles II's court binder, Samuel Mearne, who combined the
dotted stamps with solid crescents, conventional tulips, car-
nations and other flowers. On some of his bindings of the
"all-over" type the crescent stamps are predominant, but he
also made the so-called "cottage bindings" in which the top
and bottom lines of the central panel gave the appearance of
an English cottage.

An entirely different kind of binding was made for
Louis XIV and his court by the royal binder Antoine Ruette.
These had practically no decoration, and the effect was produced by the dark-colored leather alone. This ascetic style
contrasts strangely with the usual elaborate style of the time.
At the beginning of the 18th century it was called Jansenist
binding after the strict religious sect of the Jansenists.   The
books of some other French bibliophiles also showed a minimum of decoration, this being limited to a border along the
edge, a few corner ornaments, a coat-of-arms or a monogram in the center, with additional decoration only on the
spine. By way of compensation, however, only the highest
quality of goatskin was used, and it may be that appreciation
of the beauty of the material itself caused a reaction against
excessive gold tooling.

The original Gascon stamps were gradually supplemented by new variants (including the so-called Duseuil
stamps) that were put on the market by die-cutters along with
patterns and designs drawn by artists for the bookbinder to
follow. Stamps in the form of rosettes on fans (fers à l'-
évantail) were especially in demand in Italy, where the bindings generally featured large heraldic designs. They were
also accepted in Germany, but only the Heidelberg book-
binders, who had maintained the tradition from the days of
Otto Heinrich, succeeded in bringing their work up to the
level of the French model.

The Thirty Years' War

In Germany the period following the 1620's was for
the most part one of stagnation or of decline. The battles of
the Thirty Years' War destroyed the power of the country
both politically and economically, and this impoverization was
followed by a cultural decline that was slow to abate. It was
this situation that had given the book-makers and book-sellers
of Holland their opportunity. The products of 17th century
Germany in the field of illustrative art were mainly an echo
of Dutch or French copper-plate engraving. The level of
typography in the 17th century was generally below that of the
preceding centuries, but German book printing was the worst
of all. Large numbers of books were issued in Germany,
many of a devotional character, but their typographical appearance was usually quite inferior, and any advance in the printing arts was prevented by the rigid guild regulations that continued in force right down to the beginning of the 19th century.
The German book trade also suffered greatly from the practice of unrestricted reprinting that made the publisher's rights

illusory; efforts to control the practice were ineffective since the regulations could not be enforced in a country so divided as Germany. Danish printers also suffered. Not only was Danish literature reprinted within Denmark, but the printers of North Germany, especially those of Lübeck, also copied Danish editions, so that many books of that time that bear a Copenhagen imprint were actually printed in Germany. The Germans continued the book-binding tradition of the 16th century, but the fine craftsmanship that had been evident in many of the older bindings became less apparent. The work of the Heidelberg binders in the new French styles was one of the exceptions to the general rule.

While the ravages of religious wars and the other conditions had a repressive effect on German book-making, the results of the wars were even more fateful for the libraries of the country. The oldest of the German university libraries and one of the most outstanding of the time, Heidelberg's famous Bibliotheca Palatina, was presented to the Pope by the great Catholic leader, Emperor Maximilian of Bavaria, when the town was captured by Tilly's troops in 1623. The books were incorporated into the Vatican Library. But the Protestants had their revenge later. When Gustavus Adolphus organized Protestant resistance and repelled the Catholics' advances he confiscated all libraries wherever he came, especially those in the Jesuit colleges, and the countries into which he carried his campaigns saw one library after another pass to Sweden as the spoils of war. The University of Uppsala had been founded in 1620 and to it Gustavus Adolphus presented many of the collections that he took from Riga and Prussia, and South-German libraries.

The period of greatness in the history of Swedish libraries that was thus introduced continued after the death of Gustavus Adolphus, for the Swedish nobles who acted as officers in the army or held administrative positions during the war were adept at turning their successes in battle to their own advantage. Since ancient times it had been the practice in every large war for the victorious troops to carry off books and libraries, but not until the last World War had this been done with such thoroughness as during the period of Sweden's greatness. Moreover, what the Swedes once acquired they did not again give up, although in later wars book collections acquired in this way were usually returned after the conclusion of a peace treaty.

During the latter part of the Thirty Years' War the monastery libraries of Bohemia and Moravia suffered especially. When the Swedes stormed Prague in 1648 they

took a rich booty in books, especially from the magnificent
collection of the Bohemian kings at Hradschin, which contained what is probably the largest extant vellum manuscript,
the Devil's Bible (gigas librorum).   Along with the rest of
the Bohemian royal library it was brought to Stockholm and
incorporated in Queen Christina's library.   A large part of
this she took with her when she left Sweden -- most of the
manuscripts, for instance, are now in the Vatican -- but the
part that remained still forms the main body of the Royal Library in Stockholm; it was supplemented by the booty taken
during Charles Gustavus' (Charles X) wars in Poland and
Denmark.   Many libraries of the Swedish nobility were also
stocked by these victorious expeditions.   Several of the great
statesmen, Axel and Erik Oxenstierna, Schering Rosenhane,
Claes Rålamb, and not least the king's brother-in-law and
chancellor, Magnus Gabriel de la Gardie, were educated men
with literary interests.   De la Gardie made considerable book
acquisitions in Denmark; he purchased the collection of the
royal historiographer, Prof. Stephan Hansen Stephanius, which
contained important source material for Danish history and a
famous manuscript of the Younger Edda, and as war spoil
he also took Gunde Rosenkrantz' library which included a part
of Anders Sørensen Vedel's collection.   Under Charles XI,
De la Gardie's possessions, like those of the other nobility,
were taken over by the crown, and after his death they were
presented to the historical archives and to the University Library at Uppsala, which thereby came into possession of the
Gothic Bible of Bishop Ulfilas (Codex argenteus); it had been
taken from Prague and purchased by De la Gardie.

While the collections of De la Gardie, including their
Danish portions, are still preserved, another large Danish
private library that came into the possession of the Swedes
did not fare so well.   The high-court judge at Ringsted monastery, Jørgen Seefeldt, possessed over 25,000 volumes, including Old Norse-Icelandic manuscripts and many rare printed
books; this entire collection was given to Corfitz Ulfeld to
take to Malmø in appreciation of his collaboration.   Later
however, both these and Ulfeld's own books were confiscated
by the Swedish government and incorporated into the Royal
Library at Stockholm.   When the greater part of this went
up in flames in the palace fire of 1697, the story of Seefeldt's collection came to an end.   A very small part, however, including some of the many editions of the Bible, had
by a devious route come into the possession of the Swedish
envoy, Peter Julius Coyet, and when his possessions were
taken over by Danish soldiers in 1710 these books were brought
back to Seefeldt's homeland.

Even though Jørgen Seefeldt was by far the greatest
collector in Denmark in the 17th century, there are several
others that deserve to be mentioned. The well-known author
of the great topographical work, Resens Danske Atlas, Professor Peder Hansen Resen, collected a library that was
strong in Scandinavian literature and jurisprudence, and in
1675 he presented it to the University Library in Copenhagen.
In the course of time the University library had grown through
numerous gifts; King Christian IV had given it the major part
of the royal family's books in 1605, and it had also received
the books left by the royal historians, the latter including
numerous medieval manuscripts and other source material for
the history of Denmark and Norway. But its growth had been
very irregular, and Resen's collection filled important gaps,
especially since he had emphasized Scandinavian literature.

An even more distinctly national collector was Anne
Gjøe; she willed her books to her relative Karen Brahe, who
was partial to German as well as Danish literature, and she
in turn presented the library to the aristocratic nunnery that
she founded in Odense. Here the collection gradually deteri-
rated and it was not till the beginning of the 19th century
that it was rescued from oblivion. It is now in the regional
archives at Odense and represents the only independent collection that has been preserved from the 17th century in Denmark; it contains several Danish books that are extant in no
other copies, and among the manuscripts there is a famous
one of folk songs, known as "Karen Brahe's folio."

The Age of the Polyhistors

In the Scandinavian countries at that time there was
scarcely anyone to equal Resen and the two noble Danish ladies in their appreciation of Danish national literature. Book
collections in Denmark as well as elsewhere in Europe usually
had a cosmopolitan character; scholarly literature was for the
most part written in Latin, and in the field of devotional and
other literature Danish collectors were mainly concerned with
the popular French, Italian and Spanish authors of the time,
and to some extent also Dutch, German and English writers.
Besides the international character of book collections in respect to language, they also covered a wide range of subjects.
It was the age of the polyhistors, when knowledge had a universal basis and specialization was still unknown. Scholars
were familiar with practically all fields of knowledge -- time
and again we find a professor lecturing now in one field and
now in another, presumably mastering them all equally well.
The encyclopedic character of this age, and of the 18th cen-

tury as well, showed itself in the libraries and the people
who worked with them. A typical polyhistor was the Italian
eccentric, Antonio Maggliabecchi, about whose remarkable
memory just as many strange anecdotes were circulated as
about the unbelievable disorder in which he lived among his
stacks of books.

The Origin of National Libraries

Maggliabecchi was librarian to Archduke Cosimo III of
Florence, whose collection developed into the present Italian
National Library. Several other national libraries of the
present day had their origin in libraries of the aristocracy of
the 17th century, or were considerably increased in size at
that period. Even in war-ravaged Germany there were examples of this. In 1659 the Elector Palatine, Frederick
William, signed a document in his camp at Viborg making
the palace library in Berlin accessible to the public -- "public" to be taken in much more limited sense than today --
and thereby laid the foundation for the later Prussian Staatsbibliothek. In the early years of the century Duke August of
Braunschweig-Lüneburg had started assembling a library,
which at his death was rated one of the largest in Europe,
and of which he himself had compiled a catalog of nearly
4,000 pages. It was this library that later came under the
zealous care of the great polyhistor and philosopher Leib-
nitz, and as the Wolfenbüttel Library it is still a gem among
Germany's libraries.

Danish Book-Binding and Printing

For binding his books Frederik III called in binders
from France, and thereby the new French Gascon style of
dotted-line decorations finally came to Denmark. In general,
however, Danish book-binding followed in Germany's footsteps as before, and it was not until toward the end of the
17th century that the dotted spirals, fans and crescents became common.

At the middle of the century the number of book-binders
in Copenhagen had become so large that the need for a trade
organization was felt; in 1646 a book-binders association was
then formed under the leadership of Jørgen Holst, book-binder
to the University and former book dealer and author. Within
this association there developed, after the German pattern,
those peculiar trade practices, some of which are still found
in trade unions of today, and which can in part be traced

back to the ceremonies of the medieval guilds. The binders'
association worked against those who established themselves
as master book-binders without proper training and thereby
lowered the prestige of the craft.

The journeymen who travelled from Denmark through
Germany had to be well versed in all the practices of the
craft in order to take their place among foreign workers;
they strengthened still further the ties that had connected
Denmark and Germany from early times in the field of book
making, especially printing. Printers did not have a separate organization but followed German trade practices more
or less of their own accord, including the "Artickeln und
Satzungen" that had been laid down by various German au-
thorities in 1573. King Frederik III outlawed these, but they
still continued in use till around 1800.

Two of the greatest Danish printers of the first half
of the 17th century were Henrich Waldkirch and Melchior
Martzan. Like many of their predecessors they were German-born, and like many of their German colleagues they
were also book dealers, doing business in one of the chapels
of Our Lady's Cathedral in Copenhagen. German influence
is seen very clearly in their work, as it was in that of many
other Danish printers, by the growing excess of ornamentation, often composed of very tasteless rosettes and head-
pieces; the old wood-cut material from the 16th century was
still being used, no matter how worn it had become. Even
after copper engraving began to be used, as in the folio
Bible that Martzan printed for Christian IV in 1633, the old
material was still not discarded; in one and the same book a
peculiar mixture of old and new can be found; wood-cut Renaissance ornaments along with copper-plate frontispieces in
baroque style.

The oldest work with copper-engraved illustrations produced in Denmark was one on fencing written by Christian
IV's Italian fencing master and printed by Waldkirch in 1606.
It is almost the only Danish work in reasonably pure baroque
style that remains from the 17th century. The plates were
made by a Dutch engraver, and most of the other engravings
in Danish books of the period were also made by Dutch or
German artisans. The first engraver who may possibly have
been born in Denmark and can be compared with foreign engravers was Albert Haelweg; his work included the charming
frontispiece to Simon Paulli's "Flora Danica" (1648), the portrait of Arild Huitfeldt in the folio edition of the latter's History of Denmark (1652), and the portrait of Birgitte Thott in
her translation of Seneca issued in Sorø in 1658. Not until

the final decades of the 17th century do Danish books entirely
in the baroque style appear, such as Holger Jacobaeus' large
folio work of 1696 on the royal art gallery, "Museum regium."
In it the headpieces, initials and vignettes, as well as the
plates, were printed from copper engravings.

The fact that Danish printers held so firmly to the old
style is not due to any particular conservative attitude on their
part, but rather to the poor economic conditions under which
they worked, and which forced them to make maximum use of
the old material. The difficult economic position of the
country as a whole did not permit that indulgence in luxury
which might otherwise have been quite natural with the establishment of the absolute monarchy. The printers suffered
under this situation and from the reprinting practices mentioned earlier, and in addition there was the strict political
censorship that accompanied the establishment of the absolute
monarchy and resulted in fines and punishment for many authors as well as printers. Under such conditions most printers
had to make their living by producing small popular works, devotional literature, funeral sermons, etc. The newspaper
"privilege" was much sought after -- it was granted for the
first time to the printer Martzan and the book dealer Joachim
Moltke, and gave them the right to issue the small sheets
("Relationer") containing accounts in German and Danish of important happenings abroad. Those printers who were fortunate enough to obtain this privilege or the sole license to
print school text-books and almanacs, or who became royal
printers with the right to print official documents, or became
printers to the University, could count on a good income.
That was true of men like Henrik Gøde and Johan Philip
Bockenhoffer. Most of the other printers, like the majority
of the book-binders, made only a modest living. This stagnation of Danish book printing lasted far into the 18th century,
the century which was elsewhere a great period in the history
of the book, after the ground had been prepared by such great
French illustrators as Jacques Callot and his pupil Sebastien
Leclerc in the course of the 17th century.

The 18th Century

Rococo Vignette Art

The heavy baroque style that still dominated art, and
hence also the art of book-making, in the early days of Louis
XV's reign, did not suit the way of life and the philosophy
that was typical of the upper classes in the 18th century. The
undercurrent of social forces that gradually gathered strength
and finally culminated in the Revolution at the end of the century was still quite weak and did not show on the surface;
everything seemed calm and quiet, with the Court setting the
tone and the common people looking on from without, dazzled
by the splendor. For the upper classes life was only worth
living when it formed a continuous chain of amusements and
festivities. Never before had amorous intrigue characterized
an entire age to the same extent -- the little winged cupid
with his bow and arrows was the symbol of the time. In literature pastoral poetry was one of the most popular forms,
in art love was the constantly recurring theme, and even in
political life the tender passion made its influence felt through
the intrigues of the royal mistresses for or against the leading statesmen of the day.

This philosophy of life found artistic expression in the
rococo style with its light, festive and elegant tone in place
of the heavy and grandiose. In books the large folios were
more and more superseded by smaller formats, and cooper-
plate engraving became even more prevalent and was used
more extensively for decorative purposes than ever before.
Books were not only provided with illustrations as such, but
small vignettes were scattered liberally throughout the pages
in the form of headpieces (fleurons, en-tetes) at the beginning of each chapter and tail-pieces (culs de lampe) at the
end. Flying cupids encircled by rose garlands were a frequent subject for these vignettes (the word means literally
"vine branch"), and rococo ornaments with their C- and S-
shaped lines are prominent features of the surrounding borders. Rococo ornamentation thus freed itself from the rigid
symmetry that had previously prevailed; its characteristic
designs -- shells, palm branches, bouquets and festoons of
flowers and fruit -- were all arranged in more or less un-

180

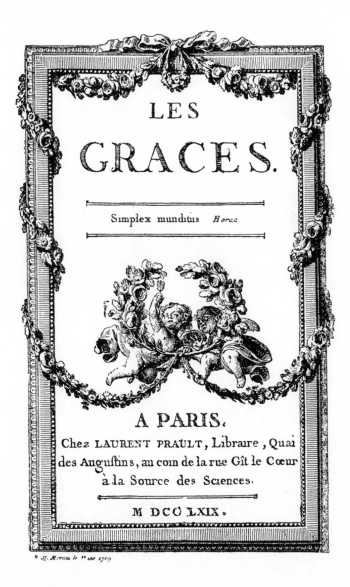

78.   Typical rococo title-page from 1769, drawn by Moreau
le jeune.

79. Vignette by Charles Eisen in Claude Joseph Dorat's
Les baisers, The Hague, 1770.

symmetrical fashion.

        A group of French artists and painters soon brought
the rococo style in books to perfection, and even the Flemish, Swiss, German and English artists who worked in great
numbers in Paris, adopted the French style completely. In
graceful lines that were so well suited to the nature of copper engraving and to their subjects, these artists created
pictures that accurately expressed the gay and refined taste
of the time, and some of the most characteristic of these
are found in the vignette books. However, as was the case
in many Renaissance books, there is often a lack of balance
between the illustrations and the text; the former stand out
at the expense of the latter, since nearly all the care and
attention is devoted to the illustrations and the decoration.
There were also many books consisting entirely of pictures
in the rococo as well as the baroque period; books of architectural drawings, furniture and ornamental designs, archeological, botanical and zoological works, picture books of
travels in foreign countries, etc., and for these the larger
formats were still used. Most of the typical rococo books,
however, were in octavo or duodecimo format.

80. Copper-engraving drawn by Moreau le jeune for J.J.
Rousseau, Oeuvres, vol. 4, 1784.

One of the earliest examples of this new type of book
was the edition of "Daphnis and Chloë" by the Greek writer
Longus that was issued in Paris in 1718, illustrated with
copper-plate engravings from paintings by Duke Philip of
Orléans, who directed the government during the minority of
Louis XV. The real flowering of vignette art, however, began in 1734 with an edition of Molière containing over 200
vignettes by the famous painter Boucher. In these the artist
succeeded, by clever use of light and shadow and also of
perspective, in producing a greater three-dimensional effect
than should have been thought possible in such small pictures.
This effect was also achieved more or less by the other artists who devoted themselves to book illustration: Cochin le
jeune, Choffard, Eisen, Marillier, and above all Gravelot
and the younger Moreau. Charles Nicolas Cochin le jeune
introduced the copper-engraved title page with the title set
in extended type and a grayish color. He was a brilliant artist and showed great decorative talent in his numerous vignettes. Pierre Philippe Choffard was responsible for a large
number of vignette head-pieces and tail-pieces, as seen in the
edition of La Fontaine's fables issued in 1762 by the Farmers-
general. The other illustrations in this book were due to
Charles Eisen, a Flemish artist who attained great fame for
his skill in composition. Eisen was particularly successful
in illustrating books with amorous themes such as Monte-
squieu's "Le temple de Gnide" (1772) or the sentimental
verses "Les baisers" (1770) of the mediocre poet Dorat (Fig.
79), to which his slightly affected style was so well suited.
Pierre Clément Marillier was known for his more than 200
clever vignettes for Dorat's fables (1775); Hubert Francois
Gravelot used a more rigid but also more forceful style in
illustrating works like Marmontel's moralizing tales (1765)
and Voltaire's edition of Corneille (1764). He was an outstanding artist and engraver and knew how to depict the man-
ners and modes of the aristocracy.

The most highly gifted of all, however, was Jean Michel Moreau (called Moreau le jeune). In contrast to the
others he placed great emphasis on making his drawings from
life and nature, and hence there was a greater freshness a-
bout them than was found in other vignettes of the rococo period. It cannot be denied that many of the others had a slight
air of pruriency, however great the artistry they display.
Authors like Boccaccio and Aretino might of course easily
tempt the artist to overstep the bounds of good taste, but that
occurred even in editions of Horace and Ovid. Moreau's pictures had none of this boudoir atmosphere about them; they
have a natural charm that diffused what might otherwise seem
too bold and made it pleasing. Moreau was a worshipper of

nature and no one but he could better give visual expression
to the spirit of Rousseau, as he did in the edition of 1782-
90. His major works were in the 24 large pages that he
executed for "Monument du costume" (1775-83), a book of
illustrations representing the daily life of the upper classes,
which became famous for their almost impressionistic composition and their daring treatment of light and shadow. Another of Moreau's masterpieces were the illustrations for the
Kehl edition of Voltaire's works (1784-89).

One characteristic of all the artists above was that
they had no interest in the psychology of their characters --
faces are usually devoid of expression. The emphasis was
on physical form, setting and costumes. They associated
with the aristocracy, for their social position was not that of
the craftsmen as it had been earlier; they were themselves
considered part of the upper class and worked in close contact with the great bibliophiles and the famous authors and
publishers of the time.

A few of the vignette books are executed entirely by
copper-plate engraving, even the text being drawn by hand
and engraved, but in the majority the text was printed in
letterpress. The types that were used were descendent from
Garamond's roman types, but modernized in form. At the
royal press in the Louvre, where several of the best vignette
books were produced, much use was made of a type-face designed by Philippe Grandjean and called "roman du roi," the
king's roman type; it can be recognized by the fact that the
letter l has a small protuberance at the left. It was an imposing type-face, but could not measure up to Garamond's type.
Somewhat nearer to Garamond's, though still not up to its
level, was a roman type face designed by Pierre Simon
Fournier. At the middle of the century he was Europe's
most famous type caster, and his composite ornamental designs enjoyed tremendous popularity. Another type-face of
the rococo period was one with very narrow letters, called
"poétique" because of its special suitability for printing poetry.

French Bibliophiles

Along with the new developments in book arts during
the rococo period in France there was a flowering of bibliophilism. It had been fashionable for the upper classes to collect books before, but the practice came into much greater
vogue and appeared in more refined form during the reigns
of Louis XV and Louis XVI. This interest in book-collecting
or bibliophilism caused the great demand for vignette books.

Without it these expensive works would certainly never have
found so ready a sale, nor would so many artists and copper
plate engravers have been able to make a livelihood at their
trade -- as it was, they all had plenty to do.

It was not only for contemporary books, however, that
money was spent; the wealthy French collectors also prized
the literature of the preceding century: "les grands écrivain
the monumental works on art and natural history, travel accounts and atlases and the great editions of the Greek and
Latin classics.   One much sought-after item was the edition
in 64 volumes of a series of classical authors that Louis XIV
had commissioned (1674-1730) for the use of the Dauphin
("in usum Delphini") and in which all objectionable passages
were deleted.

This large group of book collectors provided support
for the numerous book auctions that were held in Paris during that period and the prices of desirable items rose.   It
was also a good time for the outdoor booksellers who had
established themselves on Pont Neuf and along the banks of
the Seine -- scarce and beautiful books might be found in
their stalls among a great deal of trash.   The government
did not look favorably on these "outsiders" because -- not
entirely without reason -- they were suspected of selling wor
that had been prohibited by the ecclesiastical and political cen
sors.   The regular book dealers, who had long been well organized in France, also sought to have them supressed.   In
spite of all this these "bouquinists," as they were called from
the Dutch word boekin (little book), continued their business.

The greatest, at least quantitatively, among the many
French collectors of the 18th century was Duke Louis de la
Vallière, who started his collecting in 1738 at the great auction of the library of Count Karl Heinrich von Hoym, the
Saxon ambassador to Paris.   The Duke acquired many unusua
books in expensive bindings, and at subsequent auctions he
made extensive additions to his collection, so that on three
occasions he himself held auctions to dispose of his duplicates.   Among the unusual items in his collection was the
only extant copy of an illustrated work entitled "Tableaux des
moeurs du temps" with somewhat free depictions of the gallar
life that nearly caused its extermination.   La Vallière's collection became known throughout Europe and when it was sold
in 1784, following the Duke's death, it brought book collector
to Paris from all corners of Europe.   The auction lasted 181
days and the sales amounted to about 465, 000 francs.   "Tableaux des moeurs" has been on the auction block several time
since; in 1894 it sold for 25, 000 francs.

Part of La Vallière's collection, however, was not included in the auction but was sold privately to the Marquis
of Paulmy, whose books were later taken over by Charles X
and formed the basis for one of the public libraries of Paris,
the Arsenal Library.   Among the institutions that acquired
books at the La Vallière auction was the French Royal library, bibliothèque du roi.   This library benefited from the general interest in book collection, and on many occasions   it
received books by gift or purchase of private collections or
parts of them.   Many book treasures were brought from the
Orient to Paris and the French ambassadors to other countries, among them Count de Plélo in Copenhagen, often sent
back valuable materials.   The royal library included a collection of copper-plate engravings and of coins and was widely
recognized as the largest and wealthiest book treasury of the
civilized world, while Paris was the city that had the most
and best libraries in 18th century Europe.   Since many of
these libraries were made more or less accessible to the
public, scholars from all countries came to Paris to work.

Lace Patterns in Book-Binding

In the time of Louis XV the royal household and several of the bibliophiles among the nobility employed the book-
binder Antoine Michel Padeloup.   Some of the bindings made
for Louis XV's queen, Maria Leszcinska, and for his mistress, Madame de Pompadour, are signed by Padeloup, as
are also some bindings from Count von Hoym's collection.
He bound, for the king, in uniform red morocco a great many
of the works printed at the royal press recounting and extoll-
ing the festivities of the royal house.   Like another famous
binder of that time, Le Monnier, Padeloup used a technique
that later became very popular, namely mosaic work in
leather, using differently colored pieces to form a tapestry-
like pattern.   He was also the originator of the lace-work
pattern (fers à la dentelle) or at least brought it to a high
stage of development.   Lace was widely used in the costumes
of the period and it was natural to transfer its patterns to
binding designs.   Lace-work bindings soon came to have a
prominent place in the French collector's rococo bookcase.
As a rule, the decoration consisted of a wide laced edge with
projections extending in toward the middle of the cover,
where space was left for the owner's mark, or his superex-
libris, as it is called.   This type of decoration was used in
many variations on a great number of bindings.   The spine
of the book was also decorated, often with a conventional
flower in each of the panels and small ornaments in the
corners of each panel.   The designs were gilded but not often

tooled, as on 17th century bindings. The lace pattern was treated with special grace and virtuosity on the bindings made by Jacques Antoine Deromes and his son Nicolas Denis Deromes (Fig. 81); some of these had the special feature of a small bird with outspread wings set in the corners of the decoration. Two other famous names of this period were those of the binders to the Duke of Orléans, Du Seuil and Pierre Paul Dubuisson.

An air of elegance pervaded these French rococo bindings, and this effect was further increased by the red color of the leather, but they exhibited only faint traces of the characteristic rococo ornamentation. The true C- and S-shaped rococo lines appear only in rare instances on 18th century bindings; most of the bindings with rococo ornaments belong to the later neo-rococo period. On the other hand, the characteristic rococo features in the exlibris that collectors had made for their books to indicate ownership occurred frequently. This custom had already appeared in the 15th and 16th centuries, the ownership marks of that time being printed from wood-cuts, but in the 17th and 18th centuries the use of exlibris spread with the increasing fashion of book-collecting, and they were printed from copper engravings.

The exlibris was a label of varying size pasted on the inner side of the cover, stating who was the owner of the book, either by giving his initials or his full name or by showing his coat-of-arms framed in a cartouche. Heraldic emblems were quite common, even when the exlibris was in the form of a small picture. These pictures might be symbolic, they might represent the interior of the owner's own library or a small landscape vignette. A charming example of the latter is an exlibris made by one of the best Danish artists in this field, O. H. Delode, showing a young man reading a book at the foot of a tree; it bears no name, but the initial letters of its motto; Fallitur hora legendo (reading passes the time) are assumed to stand for Friderici Hornii liber, referring to the lawyer Frederik Horn (Fig. 82). Many other exlibris contained the owner's motto. Most of the great French illustrators of the rococo period designed exlibris, and many of these were small masterpieces in themselves.

The name exlibris for the ownership label came from the fact that they often contained the words "ex libris" (or "ex museo" or "ex bibliotheca") before the name of the owner. At the beginning of the 19th century decadence occurred in the exlibris art, but at the middle of the century it blossomed

81.   Binding in red morocco with lace-work designs by
Nicolas Denis Derome.   Five of Derome's characteristic
bird figures are seen here.

Fallitur Hora Legendo.

82.   Left, exlibris of Frederik Horn with landscape; right,
exlibris of Laurids de Thurah with heraldic design.

anew and today it is again coming into vogue among book
collectors.

English Book Collectors

In the 18th century France set the tone for book collecting among the upper classes throughout Europe.   Even
though none of these countries could match the luxury that
existed in France, they did more or less consciously imitate the life at the court of the French "Roi Soleil" and his
successors.   The English noblemen who gathered at the court
of George I were strongly influenced by French fashions.
There were many bibliophiles among the English nobility, and,
as in France, private collecting was influential in the development of public libraries.   In England, however, the
king's personal library did not develop into the national library, as was the case in most other countries; the national
library of Britain came into being in 1753 when Parliament
decided to purchase the collection of books and manuscripts
that had been left by the physician Hans Sloane.   Two other
important manuscript collections were added to this, those
of Bruce Cotton and Edward Harley, and thus the foundation
was laid for the world-famous British Museum.   A few years
later George II presented the Museum with the library of the
royal house, and along with it the right to receive deposit
copies of all books issued in England.   The new institution
was opened to the public in 1859 with a staff of 48 members,
half of whom were appointed by the government.

Harley, Earl of Oxford, whom we have just mentioned, had inherited an outstanding collection of books and manuscripts from his father, Robert Harley, and this he increased to such an extent that at his death it numbered 7,600 manuscripts, 40,000 letters and documents and 50,000 printed books, besides 400,000 pamphlets and smaller items -- a worthy counterpart to the La Vallière collection in France. Harley's collection included a considerable number of books printed by the first English printer, William Caxton, and his immediate successors, and also gave evidence of an interest in incunabula that was by no means common at that time. The bishop of Ely, John Moore, a book collector whose books had been purchased by George I in 1715 and donated to the University Library of Cambridge, had also paid special attention to these early English black-letter books, but it was not until the final decades of the 18th century that collectors of incunabula began to increase in number, and English collectors have maintained a leading position in this field down to the present.

In the history of English book-binding the bindings that were made for Harley resulted in a "Harleian style". Harley's bindings featured a small central field surrounded by a very wide border and a peculiar combination of lace designs and realistic flowers. These bindings (Fig. 77) became the pattern for the book-binding of that time, but today the style seems severe and heavy, and these bindings cannot measure up to those that were made in Scotland in Harley's time -- the latter were decorated with a central stalk that had long serrated leaves unfolding to both sides.

Books in Germany

While it is true that French bibliophilism was the model for the development of book collecting in England, the latter was no servile imitation of the former. The same is true in the case of Germany, where French influence was generally more diffuse as a natural consequence of the heterogeneous composition of Germany itself. Voltaire's friend Frederick the Great was a zealous admirer of French culture and philosophy; he was also a competent general and a fanatic reader of books, besides being an extensive writer himself. The 25 volume edition of his works that was published in 1787-89 was one of the most impressive typographical productions of 18th century Germany. Frederick the Great had large collections of books at Sans-Souci and in Potsdam, and even carried a library with him on his campaigns. The French rationalists and French literature in general were his favorite reading, and he preferred octavo and duodecimo formats to such an extent that he actually avoided quartos and folios. He shared the French preference for red morocco bindings with gold tooling.

Contrary to what might be expected it was mainly in northern Germany, in the Baltic provinces and in the Hanseatic cities, that French influence made itself felt. It apparently reached there in part by way of England through the extensive trade that existed; and it was also felt in Saxony, which since the days of the Elector August had never entirely lost its connections with the French tradition. Dresden was the home of many large private libraries in the 18th century, and here as in Paris it was considered fashionable to collect books; one of those who led in this respect was Count Heinrich von Brühl, whose collection of 62,000 volumes finally ended in the library of the Saxon court (the present Landesbibliothek).

This library was opened to the public at the very close of the century, but in general there was very little internal organization in the libraries of the aristocracy or of the universities. In the latter group the position of librarian was usually held as an extra responsibility by one of the professors, and it was only rarely that he felt obliged to do more with the library than was absolutely necessary. In many universities the conditions were such as to recall the situation in monastery libraries at the close of the Middle Ages. The University of Copenhagen Library was no exception in this respect; a student was appointed assistant to the librarian at a meagre compensation, and it was undoubtedly he who did most of the work. Since students did not have the right to use the library before 1788 and no serious cataloging work was done, the duties could not have been very taxing.

In Germany, however, there was one university, Göttingen, whose library became the model for all of Europe. At Göttingen a serious effort was made to build up the book collection along definite lines and make it useful and accessible to scholars. Under the direction of Christian Gottlieb Heyne, the library followed a development that did not become effective elsewhere until the 19th century, and Göttingen became the first research library in Europe in the modern sense.

In 1769 the Göttingen library received a valuable addition in the books of Johann Fredrich von Uffenbach, which he had for the most part collected on a long book-buying journey with his brother Zacharias Conrad, who was even more enthusiastic about books. These two had provided themselves with a complete list of the books they wanted to acquire and had then travelled through Germany, Holland and England, filling their diaries with a wealth of bibliographical information. The greatest number of book acquisitions were made in Holland, whose copious stock supplied English, German and Scandinavian collectors.

In Germany books and literature were more of a middle-class phenomenon than in England and France; interest in reading had spread to larger and larger segments of the population and resulted in the formation of reading circles. Later, in the Age of Enlightenment, cultural and general educational literature made hitherto unheard of advances. The ideas of the Enlightenment, which spread from England to France and then developed into the general European intellectual movement of rationalism, also became important for the evolution of science. The modern research library, of which Göttingen was the first example, can rightly be called one of the fruits of the Enlightenment. There was, however, a background of organization of scientific activity in the larger countries going back to the 17th century. It was then that the first scientific academies were founded and the first scientific journals made their appearance -- "Journal des savants" in Paris, the "Philological Transactions" in London, both still alive today, and "Acta eruditorum in Leipzig. Large encyclopedic works presenting the knowledge of all time in convenient form were prepared by the scholars of the 18th century -- Diderot, d'Alembert and their circle compiled the famous French Encyklopaedi, and in Germany the Leipzig publisher Zedler issued his "Universal-Lexikon" in 64 heavy volumes, a work that is still of value. Gradually an increasing volume of critical and literary journals appeared, and the interesting almanacs and pocket books also became very popular. These started in France around the middle of the 18th century and benefited from the current vignette art, especially the theater almanacs, fashion almanacs and those devoted to amorous subjects. Some attention also began to be paid to children's literature, and Campe's adaptation of Defoe's Robinson Crusoe is one of the best children's books ever written.

Small pocket editions of literary works and calendars were especially popular in Germany, where they were provided with copper-engraved vignettes in which German artists more or less successfully imitated the French masters. Only one of these, Daniel Chodowiecki, made an independent approach by adopting German middle-class or even petty-bour-

geois features in his work. This made Chodowiecki the most
nationalistic of the German vignette artists and made his
small-scale representations of daily life very popular among
the common people. A book that was already popular, Gel-
lert's collection of fables, was made even more popular by
Chodowiecki's work, and his charming vignettes for Goethe's
writings also became famous, especially those for "Hermann
und Dorthea" which appeared in a ladies' almanace for 1799.

The growing interest in reading presented new possibilities to the book trade, and with Leipzig as a center it be
gan to develop rapidly. The old method of book exchange,
which consisted in trading sheet for sheet or book for book,
was being given up; the publisher-dealers had separated them
selves more and more from the miscellaneous booksellers
and their business had taken on a more stable character with
a definite price on each item. The other booksellers received so little discount that they often had to exceed the established sale price. The fight against the abuses of reprint
ing was waged with increasing vigor in Germany, but for a
long time in vain. Not until toward the end of the century
was protection obtained for the rights of authors and publishe
that had been provided in England by the Copyright Act of 170

As the dissemination of literature increased, the issu-
ance of multiple printings of the same book became common,
and a method was sought for keeping the type matter in a
form from which duplicate printings could be made as desire
A Scotch goldsmith, William Ged, was the first to experimen
with stereotyping; he made his experiments in the 1720's but
they were not very successful. Stereotyping did not come into practical use until the process had been improved at the
beginning of the 19th century by Charles, 3rd Earl of Stanhope, who printed stereotyped Bibles at the Cambridge University Press. In 1800 this same Lord Stanhope built the fir
iron press to replace the wooden presses that had been in use
ever since Gutenberg's days.

Book-making in Denmark

In Denmark the development follows that in Germany
in many respects. Printing was done in a mixture of styles
and was generally poor. German "fraktur" type in more or
less crude variations constituted the bulk of a Danish printer'
type stock, with old worn-out wood-cuts for illustrations and
decoration. In the more elaborate books German baroque
style was dominant, especially in the many funeral sermons
for noblemen, which had grown to folio size. Along toward

83.   Copper-engraved frontispiece by Daniel Chodowiecki
for Goethe's Works, vol. 1, Leipzig, 1787.

the middle of the century the rococo style began to make its
appearance, at first only in the form of scattered vignettes
in otherwise definitely baroque books.

French style gradually found its way into Danish books.
Two of the most imposing books ever printed in Denmark indicate the advance of the French style.   One contained Fr.
L. Norden's account in French of his travels to Egypt and
Nubia and some 150 copper-engraved plates besides many
headpieces and vignettes (Fig. 85).   Two of the best Danish
vignette artists, the German Marcus Tuscher and the Danish
painter Peter Cramer, worked on this publication, which was

Cap. I.
Handler om Kiøbenhavn i Almindelighed.

Chap. I.
Traité de la Ville de Copenhague en général.

Cap. I.
Handelt von Copenhagen überhaupt.

Mit Forsæt er ey, at anføre noget i denne Beskrivelse om Kiøbenhavns gamle og første Oprindelse, hvorledes den, siden den blev udvalt til Kongernes ordentlige Boe-Sæde, og derudover, og formedelst dens ypperlige Beliggenhed til Handel, med adskillige Herlagtige Friheder af een og anden Konge er bleven beskienket, Tid efter anden har tiltaget i Størelse, Magt, Anseelse og Herlighed, indtil den har naaet den Fuldkommenhed, hvorudi den i disse vore Tider viser sig; thi sligt er saavel i den Danske Vitruvio nogenledes forklaret, som ved adskillige berømmelige Mænds Pen, baade gamle og nyere, noye og omstændelig beskrevet.

Ce n'est pas mon dessein, de m'étendre en la description de Copenhague sur son ancienne & premiere origine, ni d'etaler, de quelle façon elle s'est agrandie de tems en tems, après qu'elle fut choisie pour la demeure, ou Residence ordinaire des Rois, & que par cette raison, & à cause de sa situation excellente pour le negoce, elle fut gratifiée par differens Rois de plusieurs privileges avantageux, & de quelle maniere elle s'est augmentée depuis, en grandeur, en puissance, en splendeur & en majesté, jusqu'à ce qu'elle soit parvenue à la perfection, où elle se présente de nos jours; tout cela étant en quelque façon expliqué dans le Vitruve Danois, & traité amplement & circonstantiellement par plusieurs celebres Savans, tant anciens que modernes.

Mein Vorsatz ist gar nicht, in dieser Beschreibung von dem alten und ersten Ursprunge der Stadt Copenhagen etwas anzuführen, wie selbige, seitdem sie zur ordentlichen Residenz der Könige ausersehen, und dahero, und wegen ihrer vortreflichen Lage zum Handel, von einem und dem andern Könige mit verschiedenen vortheilhaften Freyheiten beschenket worden, von Zeit zu Zeit an Grösse, Macht, Ansehen und Herrlichkeit zugenommen, bis sie endlich zu der Vollkommenheit gelanget, darinnen sie sich zu unsern Zeiten zeiget; denn solches ist sowohl in dem Dänischen Vitruvio einigermassen erkläret, als durch verschiedener, sowohl alter als neuerer, gelehrter Leute Federn genau und umständlich beschrieben.

84.   Page from Laurids de Thurah's "Hafnia hodierna" (1748), a description of Copenhagen with 110 copper engravings. Thurah also published two volumes of "The Danish Vitruvius," an important source-book for the history of Danish architecture.

printed at one of Copenhagen's largest and best presses,
Vajsenhuset. The other was the unfinished treatise on shells
by the German engraver Frantz Michael Regenfuss. The first
volume, which appeared in 1758, was printed by Höpffner's
stepson, Andreas Hartvig Godiche, who was active from 1735
to 1769, and whose business was then continued by his widow,
the Madam Godiche known from Johannes Ewald's epigram.
Many well-made and artistically produced books came from
the Godiche press, including Pontoppidan's Danish Atlas and
the first volumes of Langebeks great collection of medieval
sources for Danish history, "Scriptores rerum Danicarum."
Several of the later volumes of this work were printed by
Nicolaus Møller, who became printer at the royal court in
1765 and was considered the best of his time.

Some publishing work of high artistic quality was undertaken by a group of literarily interested persons under the
leadership of Bolle Luxdorph. At his estate in Naerum high
public officials like Suhm, Langebek, Henrik Hielmstierne and
others, including Luxdorph's librarian Lavrids Skov, came together to talk about books; for these men French typography
and vignette art were the models to be followed. The most
famous of the works that this group had printed was entirely
French in character; Holberg's "Peder Paars," printed in
quarto by Godiche, with engravings from drawings by the
sculptor Wiedewelt.

By and large, Germany formed the connecting link between the French rococo style and Denmark. Most Danish
books from the second half of the 18th century show the same
coarsening of the original French style that characterized
German rococo books, and the same monotony and mediocrity
that was so foreign to the rococo spirit. In addition there is
the fact that the wood-cut ornamental material, initials, vignettes, rosettes, etc., used by Danish printers, although it
might be in the rococo style, was usually of poor quality.

In the field of book-binding, French influence in Denmark goes back to the 17th century, but later there was also
a gradually increasing influence from England. The Gascon-
style stamps were taken over from France, great preference
being shown for a stylized flower with its lines broken up into small dots, and the crescent-shaped tool so extensively
used by the English was widely adopted in various variations.
English patterns may also have been responsible for the evolution of the so-called "mirror bindings" which became the
outstanding feature of book-binding in Denmark in the 18th century. In any case the English used the same principle of
decoration used in the mirror bindings, namely, a central

PRÉFACE.

es Egyptiens ſe vantent d'être un des Peuples les plus anciens de l'Univers. Peu de Nations en effet pourroient leur diſputer cette prérogative. Leurs prétenſions à cet egard ſe fondent ſur une multitude de Monumens marqués au coin de l'antiquité la plus reculée; titres d'autant plus reſpectables, que les Auteurs de tous les ſiècles en ont parlé avec admiration.

Un Pays rendu fameux par tant de merveilles de l'Antiquité n'a pu que s'attirer l'attention des Curieux & dévenir.

a

85. First page of the preface to F. L. Norden's Voyage d'Égypte et de Nubie. Vignette drawn by J. M. Preisler and engraved by I. Haas in 1755.

panel devoid of decoration, surrounded by a gilded border.
Danish book-binders developed this idea in an original manner, so it can actually be called a national type. It has also
been called "Holberg binding" because it began to flourish in
the 1720's, the time of Holberg's comedies. Danish mirror
bindings are made in calf or sheepskin. The dark rectangular panel in the middle of the cover -- the "mirror" -- was
surrounded by a lighter-colored frame and outside this the
leather was again darker. The mirror panel and the light-
colored frame were set off by blind-stamped borders made
with roller stamps and consisting of small flowered designs;
both borders, or only the outer one continued out to the corners of the cover where they ended in somewhat larger ornaments. Along the outer edge of the binding there was usually
a fine gold line. In contrast to this modest decoration on the
covers, there was a profusion of gilded decoration in the small
panels on the spine; the top panel often contained the owner's
mark, or super-exlibris, which on other bindings was usually on the sides.

In the second half of the century mirror bindings became more and more common in Denmark, and blind-stamp-
ing of the borders was partly replaced by gold tooling. Rococo patterns appeared both in the borders and on the spine
of the book, and the mirror panel was accentuated by dark
spots applied with a sponge or sprinkled on with a brush.
The designs were rarely gilded, but were usually colored
red or bluish green, sometimes marbled or speckled; the
end papers were also colored and often marbled in striking
patterns -- stripes spirals, etc. The book-binders of that
time -- men like Andreas Lyman and his sons, Johann Bop-
penhausen and his sons, and the court binder G. J. Liebe --
showed great imagination in their adaptations of this type of
binding; among the thousands of mirror bindings that are preserved in Danish libraries there are few in which the borders
are exactly alike.

Danish Book Collectors and Libraries

This flourishing growth of book arts in Denmark, especially in the second half of the century, was as in France
partly due to increased interest in fine books and book collecting. A man like the Icelander Arne Magnusson cannot
be called a bibliophile in the usual sense of the word, though
he certainly was a collector, and it is to his everlasting
credit that he rescued what was still left of the Old Norse-
Icelandic vellum manuscripts of the Middle Ages.

86.   Mirror binding in calf-skin.   The "mirror" is the
dark marbled central panel; surrounding it is a gold-tooled
frame and outside this a lighter area that is again surrounded
by a blind-stamped line.   The spine is heavily decorated with
gold stamping.

The day in October, 1728, when fire ravaged Copenhagen was a dark day in the history of books in Denmark. The University Library, which at that time was mainly housed in the loft above Trinity Church, was destroyed and Arne Magnusson's book collection as well as several other private collections together with seven of the city's nine printing presses suffered the same fate. By good fortune nearly all of Magnusson's manuscripts were saved, and when Trinity Church was rebuilt in 1731 and a new University Library created, the old Icelandic manuscripts, having been willed to the University, were included in it as a separate collection (the Arnamagnean collection), and the library was rebuilt by gifts and purchases from many sources.

Swedish and Norwegian Collectors

In Sweden the 18th century was likewise a great period for bibliophiles, and it is not surprising that French literature and taste played a still greater role in Sweden than in Denmark -- Gustav III probably went farthest of all the princes of Europe in copying the court life of his French counterpart. The tone for the many Swedish castle and manor libraries that grew up in the second half of the century was set by Carl Gustaf Tessin; he had an extensive knowledge of books and was a bibliophile and art collector after the French pattern. First-rate book-binders, with Kristoffer Schneidler in the lead, raised their craft out of stagnation, and created bindings that clearly showed French influence. One collector whose work has meant much for the preservation of early Swedish literature was the learned court councilor, Carl Gustaf Warmholtz. His own library provided the basis on which he compiled the great work on Swedish history that has preserved his name to the present time.

Norway had no class of land-owners that could follow in the steps of the Danish and Swedish nobility, but the country did not lack important book collectors, like Gerhard Schøning, whose books in large part came from the poet Benjamin Dass and at Schøning's death became part of the library of the Norwegian Academy of Sciences in Trondheim. There was also Bishop B. Deichman, whose library was sold in Copenhagen in 1732, and his son Carl Deichman, whose collection formed the basis of the present municipal library of Oslo, the Deighmanske Library. Several members of the Anker family, especially Carsten Anker of Eidsvold, also built up valuable book collections.

87.   Four great Danish book collectors. Upper left, P. F.
Suhm; upper right, Otto Thott; lower left, B. W. Luxdorph;
lower right, Henrik Hielmstierne.

Neo-classicism in Book Arts

By the time that the rococo style had gained acceptance in Scandinavia it was losing ground in its homeland. During the reign of Louis XVI artists began turning away from it, and the ensuing reaction could scarcely have been stronger; the gay and festive rococo lines were replaced by an imitation of the firm lines of classical antiquity and informality gave way to order. The excavations at Pompeii and Herculaneum had revived interest in Roman art, and motifs from the wall-paintings of the excavated cities came into fashion in both Italy and France; meander borders, acanthus leaves, laurel festoons, vases and candelabra were repeated over and over again as decorative elements. In short classical antiquity was again enthroned as it had been in the Renaissance, though some of the rococo spirit was retained in this new classicism. Symmetry and the straight line again came into prominence, though not in the heavy and rigid form of the baroque style; naturalness and elegance were still the artist's guiding stars. Vignette art was also affected by this change in taste; several of the great illustrators of the rococo period, including Marillier, Cochin and Moreau le jeune, came under its influence when they visited Italy later in life. In Denmark neo-classicism showed in illustrations by the artist Nic. Abildgaard for the famous edition of "Nils Klim" in 1789, and were engraved in copper by Johan Frederik Clemens; most of the other copper engravers who worked in Denmark in the 18th century were merely competent craftsmen, but Clemens was a true artist. He was in fact finally appointed professor at the national Art Academy.

The roman types that came into being in this period likewise indicated a tendency to reproduce the dignity and regularity of the classical style, to such a degree that even the best of them had a certain air of inflexibility and dullness. In Paris the famous Didot family of printers created some of the most popular type faces of the time. One of the greatest members of this family was François Ambroise Didot, who not only attained fame for a roman type that gave the effect of having been engraved in copper, but became even more famous through his introduction of a new system of measuring type. In Didot's system type fonts were classified in accordance with a unit of "point" of which there were 2,660 to a meter; this French system gradually superseded the German system that had been in use earlier. The Didot press was taken over in 1789 by François' son Pierre who was responsible for a number of the most successful neo-classical roman types; his great folio edition of Vergil and Horace, and his illustrated edition of Racine were judged

dono puro di Dio e felicità di natu-
ra, benchè spesso provenga da lunga
esercitazione e abitudine, che le più
difficili cose agevola a segno che in
fine senza più pur pensarvi riescono
ottimamente fatte. Che però la gra-

88. Bodoni's roman type, from the preface to his Manuale
tipografico (Parma, 1818).

ODE I.

AD VENEREM.

Intermissa, Venus, diu
Rursus bella moves. Parce, precor, precor!
Non sum qualis eram bonæ
Sub regno Cinaræ. Desine, dulcium
Mater sæva Cupidinum,
Circa lustra decem flectere mollibus
Iam durum imperiis. Abi
Quo blandæ iuvenum te revocant preces.

89. Firmin Didot's roman type from the beginning of the
19th century. As in Bodoni's types the difference between
the light and heavy lines is quite pronounced. Bodoni's and
Didot's types are both typical of the Empire style.

ME. Hac te nos fragili donabimus ante cicuta.
Hæc nos, Formoſum Corydon ardebat Alexin :
Hæc eadem docuit, Cujum pecus? an Melibœi?
MO. At tu ſume pedum, quod, me quum ſæpe rogaret,
Non tulit Antigenes, (et erat tum dignus amari)
Formoſum paribus nodis atque ære, Menalca.

90. Baskerville's roman, from his edition of Virgil (Birmingham, 1757).

in Paris to be the greatest typographical works in the world, though this judgement is not valid if we also compare them with similar monumental works of the preceding centuries. A brother of Pierre, the scholarly Firmin Didot, became known for his small and inexpensive but beautifully stereotyped editions of the classics. These became as important as those issued by the Elzevirs in the 17th century.

At the time of the elder Didots there was a printer in Italy, Giambattista Bodoni, working for the Duke of Parma; he cut a roman type in no less than 143 different forms and sizes, and, at the behest of the Pope, printed the Lord's Prayer in 155 languages. Bodoni's types attained wide fame and were adopted by various European printers; like other types of this period they are very regular, but one of their characteristics is the strongly emphasized contrast between light and heavy lines in the individual letters.

Neither Didot's nor Bodoni's types, however, have been of lasting significance. Much greater vitality was found in some of the types of the English printer John Baskerville. Even in his own time Baskerville's types were very successful, although they also met with criticism. They show some connection with the French "roman du roi" type mentioned earlier, but at the same time they had calligraphic features -- very likely because Baskerville had originally been a teacher of handwriting.

Actually, however, a superior type is that attributed to one of Baskerville's predecessors, William Caslon. Like Baskerville's, Caslon's type was a transition form between

*Q*uou**ſ**que tandem abutere,
Catilina, patientia no**ſ**tra? qu
Quouſque tandem abutere, Ca-
tilina, patientia noſtra? quam-

91.   Caslon's roman and italic, from his book of type
samples (1763), the first such book issued in England.

the Renaissance type of Aldus and Garamond and the new roman of Didot and Bodoni.   Caslon designed his type on the
basis of the Dutch types that had been widely used in England since the time of the Elzervirs -- it was a roman
type, vigorous and free of all artificial stiffness.   It did not
immediately attain the success that it deserved, but since
its revival in 1844 it has maintained a strong position, and
alongside Nicolaus Jenson's, Garamond's and Baskerville's,
Caslon's roman is the one in widest use today.   England has
thus, with the more recent aid of American type designers,
set her mark on the development of roman type.   The many
private presses in England have been a significant factor in
this development.   One of the first of these was established
by the great collector of books and art, Horace Walpole, for
printing his own as well as other writings.

Baskerville's type was purchased by a French author
and printer, Pierre Augustin de Beamarchais, who had
formed a society to publish a monumental edition of Voltaire.
When this undertaking was opposed by the church the society
moved its press to the small town of Kehl near Strassburg
and issued the famous 70-volume edition of the works of
Voltaire in 1785 as well as an edition of Rousseau.

Roman type faces had never really been accepted in
Germany except for use in scientific works.   Almost down
to the present their principal type has been the black-letter
"fraktur."   At one time there was a rather strong movement
in favor of roman type, but the famous Leipzig printer, J.G.
Immanuel Breitkopf, the founder of the music publishing
house, came out very forcibly in favor of fraktur as the na-

Nachricht des Verlegers.

Mein erster Versuch neuer deutscher
Druckschrift, den ich in der Oster=
messe 1793 bekannt machte, fand Bei=
fall, wurde aber auch hie und da geta=
delt. Männer ohne Vorurtheil gegen
Neuerungen, und denen guter Geschmack
wohl schwerlich abgesprochen werden
kann, munterten mich zu ferner Ver=
vollkommnung auf, und nun wartete
ich nur noch die öffentlichen Urtheile
darüber ab. Diese sind jezt wohl
größtentheils erschienen, und lauten
dafür und dawider. Einer findet
die neuen Lettern den schon vorhanden
gewesenen ähnlich, mit welchen die groß=
octav Bibel in Halle gedruckt ist. Ich
verglich sie, und fand, so wie mehrere
Personen, nicht die geringste Ähnlich=

92. J. F. Unger's type of 1794, a fraktur type which under
the influence of Bodoni's and Didot's Empire types he tried to
bring closer to the roman form by rounding off the letters
somewhat. Unger, who was a printer, type-founder and publisher in Berlin, originally used roman type; in 1790 he purchased the matrices for Didot's types. He had previously
tried to get Didot to cut a fraktur type that would be easily
read by those accustomed to roman type, but in this he was
unsuccessful. In 1794, however, he himself designed the
type-face illustrated here; it was well-suited to the open style
of type-setting with large spaces between the letters, which
was in fashion at the time. Unger's fraktur type is still in
use today. He himself used it even in his editions of the
classics, a field in which he and the Cotta and Göschen publishing firms were specialists.

tional type face of Germany, which should be preserved --
and his position prevailed.   But the new movement did have
its effect on the development of fraktur type.   The type introduced by Johan Fr. Unger, with broad and somewhat
rounded shapes, was an attempt to create something between
roman and fraktur.   It was a product of neo-classicism;
Unger worked with Didot and sought to introduce the latter's
types into Germany, and hence has been called "the German
Didot."

The new tendency in art also made it appearance in
book-binding.   Even in some bindings of the 1770's the lace
pattern had given way to straight lines, meander borders,
acanthus leaves and the other classical elements, and decoration was confined to a narrow border while the rest of the
cover was plain.   Even the super-exlibris in the middle of
the cover gradually disappeared.   A special touch was given
to this style by the English book-binder Roger Payne, a peculiar individual who usually did all his work himself without assistants; in spite of the many expensive bindings that
he completed and the detailed bills that he made to his customers he continued to be poor throughout his lifetime.   His
masterpieces, for which he usually used olive-colored or
blue long-grained morocco or Russia leather were decorated
with neo-classical or oriental-style patterns, while on some
of his bindings the decoration was limited to a narrow border
of fine thin lines or small ornaments along the edtes with a
small rosette in each corner; these simple bindings were a-
mong his best.

The Effect of the French Revolution

Gradually the neo-classical style in book decoration
followed classical forms more closely; the elegance that had
characterized it at first, when there was still interplay between it and the rococo style, disappeared and left only a
simplicity of the sort found in some of the neo-classical roman type faces.   The cause of this lies in the violent reaction of the French Revolution to the refinement of the 18th
century; the stern Roman spirit was now exalted in place of
the effeminacy of the earlier generation, and all aspects of
Roman republican civilization were slavishly imitated.   Profuse illustrations disappeared from books, leaving only the
typography and a few vignettes of a symbolic nature to produce the esthetic effect.   The bindings were dominated by
warlike emblems from Roman times along with the ornaments
mentioned earlier; even a master craftsman from the high
period of laced patterns like Derome submitted to the demands

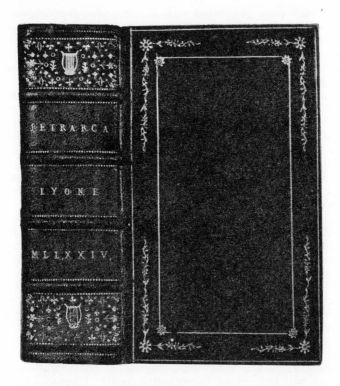

93.   Binding by Roger Payne in olive-colored morocco.
(Royal Library, Copenhagen).

of the new movement.   In Denmark the development was the
same though slower, and in Sweden there were first-rate
binders working along the same lines.

The Revolution was the fateful hour not only for French
book-making but also for French book collecting.   In Novem-
ber of 1789 all church and monastery libraries were de-
clared the property of the state and in 1792 the book collections of the emigrés were confiscated.   The various governments that followed one another in rapid succession in those
years had great library plans; libraries were to become public in the full sense of the word.   But the unsettled conditions were not favorable for realization of these plans, and
were responsible for the destruction of many of the eight
million or so books that are said to have been transferred
from private to public ownership at that time.   Just how
many were destroyed is impossible to say.   During the first
period of the Revolution the libraries of the church and the

aristocracy were plundered with a fanaticism reminiscent of
the destruction of Catholic libraries during the Reformation.
The books that escaped destruction were in large part brought
to the "literary depots" that had been established at various
places throughout the country.   In Paris alone there were
nine of these.   Here all sorts of books and manuscripts were
thrown together in enormous piles.   From these depots the
books were then sent to the various libraries that were already public to some extent; the Arsenal library, the Bibliothèque Mazarine, and others, but above all the Royal Library
which was now named "Bibliothèque Nationale."   No less than
300,000 volumes and numerous manuscripts, including 9,000
from the famous monastery of St. Germain-des-Prés, were
added to the national library, and the French library system
was centralized as never before.   It was a gigantic task to
bring order into these heaps of books and fit them into the
existing framework; it took the Bibliothèque Nationale some
hundred years to assimilate and in some degree catalog these
accessions of the Revolutionary period.

Books that were not destroyed or added to the public
collections were put on the auction block by the government,
but these auctions were held under very unfavorable circum-
stances.   The demand was much less than the supply and
often real rarities had to be sold at ridiculously low prices.
For a relatively small sum a book dealer of that time could
acquire a stock which he might dispose of later, when times
were quieter and prices better, at a profit of several hundred
percent.   The stalls of the bouquinists along the Seine bulged
with books confiscated from the libraries of the nobility.

The 19th and the Beginning
of the 20th Century

The disruptive effect of the French Revolution in the world of books extended to Germany and during the Napoleonic Wars to large parts of the rest of Europe. Napoleon was a book collector, and like Frederick the Great he carried a small library with him on his campaigns. It was his desire that his nation should hold not only political but also cultural leadership in Europe. During the years 1802-05 he had the former Benedictine monk, Jean Baptiste Maugérard, travel through the Rhine country buying up thousands of valuable medieval manuscripts and rare printed books from the many monastery libraries in that region for trifling sums. In most other instances, however, no attempt was even made to disguise this form of looting. In conformance with the traditions of the Thirty Years War Napoleon himself sent large numbers of books from conquered countries to Paris as war booty. They became part of the French national library. Trained agents accompanied the victorious French troops with lists of books that the library wanted and their work was done thoroughly. The Royal Library at Brussels, the Escorial Library in Madrid, the Vatican Library, the Court Library in Vienna, the Wolfenbüttel Library, and many others had parts of their collections taken away by French soldiers. In Vienna, however, the most valuable books had been sent down the Danube to Hungary, where they were kept hidden for eight years until the danger was past. After the fall of Napoleon in 1815 a considerable part of his library loot had to be returned in accordance with the terms of the Peace of Vienna, so that in the libraries mentioned we can find books bearing the stamp of Napoleon or of the Bibliothèque Imperiale (as the Bibliothèque Nationale was called in his time) as evidence of their forced excursion to Paris.

While Napoleon never managed to extend his empire to England, his wars had considerable influence on books and libraries in the island kingdom. The blockade of the continent meant that no books could be brought in from Holland or the other countries that supplied English collectors, and that resulted in a tremendous rise in the price of books already in England. Whenever the library of an English collector was put up at auction by one of the great auction firms, Leigh &

Sotheby, G. & W. Nicol, King, Evans, etc., the competition
for rare items among the great book hunters became intense.
The culmination of this trend occurred in 1812 at the auction
of the books left by the Duke of Roxburghe, where one of the
greatest English bibliophiles of the time, the Marquis of Blan-
ford, after an exciting battle with another great collector,
Lord Spencer, took home a 1471 edition of Boccaccio for
2,260 pounds sterling.   Only seven years thereafter, however
Lord Spencer was able to acquire the same book for some
900 pounds at the auction of the Marquis' estate, and in the
ensuing decades book prices dropped.

England could boast an imposing array of collectors in
the 19th century. Sir Thomas Phillips, in the course of his
travels on the continent, collected about 60,000 manuscripts
and became the greatest private manuscript collector the world
has ever known.   The position that Lord Spencer held in the
field of printed books was held by Phillips in the field of
manuscripts; later his famous collection was broken up at
prolonged auction sales.   Many such large auctions were held
in 19th century England, and here, as elsewhere in the history of bibliophilism, what is gathered by one generation is
split up by a later generation.   The largest sum realized at
any English book auction in the first part of the century was
the 50,000 pounds sterling taken in at the sale of Richard
Heber's books in 1834-36; in his insatiable mania for books
Heber had collected libraries in several cities throughout Europe.   A similar sum was realized in 1881-83 at the sale of
the famous Sunderland collection, founded by Charles, Earl of
Sunderland, toward the end of the 17th century.   At this sale
one of the largest buyers was German-born Bernard Quaritch,
who in the latter decades of the 19th century, became the
"Napoleon of the antiquarian book trade," and controlled the
European book market in this field for many years.

Many other large and valuable collections were scattered by auction.   However, Lord Spencer's collection, which
had reached 40,000 volumes, was purchased in 1892 by the
widow of the wealthy Manchester manufacturer John Rylands.
She had already made her husband's library public, and by
the purchase of Spencer's books and later the manuscripts
and fine bindings of the Earl of Crawford the John Rylands
Library was expanded to become one of England's wealthiest
book museums.

Lord Spencer's book-binder was the Roger Payne and
his librarian was a village curate by the name of Thomas
Frognall Dibdin.   Dibdin left handsomely printed accounts of
Althorp Castle where Spencer's books were housed and also

of his own travels in Spencer's service. Like Dibdin's book on bibliomania they are a hodge-podge of more or less reliable bibliographical and historical information, written in a rather affected style and interlarded with "learned" footnotes. Dibdin was probably guilty of a certain amount of foolish vanity and a rather snobbish attitude as he basked in the glory of his aristocratic surroundings, but he must be given credit for an almost religious devotion to old and rare books. He was instrumental in forming a club for this cult of the book, the Roxburghe Club. It was founded in 1812, on the occasion of the famous Roxburghe auction, and was the first of many English book clubs.

Steel Engravings. Revival
of Wood-cuts. Lithography

Several of Dibdin's works have illustrations made by steel engraving, a process that came into wide use in the first half of the 19th century alongside copper engraving. A copper engraving is quite soft and will wear rapidly when a large number of impressions must be taken. The harder steel engraving overcame this difficulty, but the general technique used was the same in both instances. Steel engravings, however, have a certain sleek and unnatural quality about them that can almost destroy their artistic effect. They were used quite extensively in England but the results attained were seldom of any great significance, and when a process was developed later for coating copper engravings with an electrolytic deposit of steel to give them a hard surface, the day of steel engravings was practically over.

At about the time when steel engravings made their appearance in English books, the poet William Blake was experimenting with a process by which copper plates were used for relief printing, and by means of this ingenious method he printed his own works in a style that closely resembled that of the illuminated manuscripts of the Middle Ages; each page, including text, headpieces and borders, was drawn by hand and then colored by hand in the manner of the old illuminators. Blake's method did not find any imitators, so that in this respect, as in his literary style, he stands alone.

More far-reaching in its effect was the work that Thomas Bewick began in Newcastle at the end of the 18th century. His work brought a revival in the use of wood-cuts for book illustration after the art had been dormant for some two hundred years. Bewick and his many pupils and followers did not build on the traditions of the past. In the old wood

94.   Vignette by Thomas Bewick in his "History of the British Birds," 1797-1804.

95.   Wood-cut by Adolf von Menzel in Franz Kugler's book on Frederick the Great, 1840.

cuts the black lines had been the most outstanding feature;
Bewick made the white line the dominant element in the picture, accentuated by a background in which the varying density
of the lines created the effect of light and shadow.   The ef-
fectiveness of these shaded wood-cuts was also due to the
fact that they were cut in very hard box-wood and the carving
was not done with a knife as formerly, but with a burin like
that used by engravers.

Bewick was an excellent draughtsman, especially when
animal subjects were involved. His major works were two
large books on mammals and birds with copious illustrations
distinguished not only by an accurate representation of each
animal's outward appearance but also by a definite feeling for
its individuality. Bewick's art reached its highest point in
the numerous small vignettes with which he decorated his
books, and in which, often with true Dickensian humor, he
depicted life in the country as lived by men as well as animals.

The wood-cut art of the Bewick school was not only
influential in England but was brought to the Continent and
also to America by English xylographers. In France J. B.
Papillon had done considerable work with wood-cuts toward
the close of the 18th century, but it was not until the advent
of English influence around 1830 that French wood-cut art
reached a high level in the work of artists like the great
satirical drawer Honoré Daumier, the brothers Alfred and
Tony Johannot and that masterful portrayer of the elegant
life of Paris, Paul Gavarni. Later in the century Gustave
Doré, whose enormous production extended from Rabelais to
the Bible, from Dante to Edgar Allen Poe, was equally great
in depicting mob scenes and individual human features. With
Doré the 19th century flowering of wood-cut art in France
came to an end.

In Germany the art of wood-cut illustration had been
kept alive more than anywhere else. Here too it was not
until along toward the end of the 18th century that the art a-
gain came into prominence, and its revival was due to the
Bewick school. Moritz von Schwind achieved great popularity
with his fairy-tale illustrations, and so did the amiable Ludwig Richter with his many charming scenes from folk-life and
fairy tales which showed kinship with the bourgeois spirit of
Chodowiecki's copper engravings. At this time Alfred Rethel
became famous for his stirring Dance of Death pictures drawn
in Dürer's style, and, later Adolf von Menzel, for his illustrations glorifying the military exploits of Frederick the
Great.

All these artists belong to the so-called Romantic period that had succeeded the neo-classical and showed its enthusiasm for the Middle Ages in various forms of expression. In Germany, Romanticism was mixed with nationalistic and religious factors, while in France the movement was of a worldly nature. French illustrative art of this period, more than that of any other country, strove for lively representation and picturesque effect.

By this time a new and very special method of reproduction had been in use in Germany for many years; it originated in 1796-98 when the actor and playwright Alois Senefelder experimented with the printing of his own works and discovered printing from stone blocks, or lithography. He used a mixture of wax, soap and lampblack to write the text on a piece of polished limestone and then poured acid and a thin gum solution over the surface; when the printing ink was then later applied to the stone it adhered only to the written lines and not to the rest of the surface. This method of printing was neither intaglio printing, as from copper engravings, nor relief printing, as from wood cuts, but plain or flat printing. The parts that were to make the impression were on the same level as the rest of the surface. Although this new method meant that the writing or drawing had to be done on stone rather than on paper and had to be done in reverse as if reflected in a mirror, the process soon came into wide use, especially for the printing of single sheets, and also for book illustrations. By using several stones it was relatively easy to print colored maps and plates for books. Since photographic methods have become available for transferring the drawing to the stone the lithographic process has been simplified, and the stone has also been superseded by modern photographic etchings in metal ("cuts" or "clichés") which are made either from line drawings or screen photographs ("half-tones"). In the half-tone engraving process the picture is photographed through a cross-ruled glass plate or screen that breaks it up into a series of dots that are dense in the dark portions and less so in the lighter portions. In this manner the shading of the picture can be reproduced with considerable accuracy. Line etchings appeared in the 1840's and the half-tone process was discovered in 1881 by the German Georg Meisenbach and is widely used today for printing illustrations.

Historical Trends in Book Collecting

When French bibliophiles were able to resume their activities after the upheavals of the Revolution and the Na-

poleonic Wars their guiding star became the "Manuel du li-
braire" of the scholar and book-seller, Jacques Charles
Brunet. This great bibliographical work appeared first in
1810 and later in several enlarged editions. It gave a detailed description of the literature that was worth collecting,
paying special attention to Latin and French and including
all particularly valuable and rare books from incunabula to
the books of 18th century. Under each entry there was historical information about the book, with the prices that had
been paid for it at auction. The influence of Brunet's handbook was very great; collectors paid more attention to early
books and became interested in the history of the various
books as they had passed from one owner to another; they
also developed an appreciation for first editions of classical
literary works, including those of the great English and German authors -- in short, the mission that Brunet performed
in France was similar to the one that Dibdin was performing
in England at about the same time. Because Brunet's work
came to be regarded as a sort of standard catalog of the
books that should be collected, it contributed to giving French
collections a rather uniform character and caused a rise in
the prices of the items that all collectors had to have.

Besides Brunet, and his work in this field, there was
also the poet Charles Nodier, who was like Dibdin in his
passion for books, albeit a more brilliant and sensitive per-
sonality. One of his best-known writings was the tale of
"Le bibliomane" told with charming irony. Like Brunet,
Nodier was one of the first to stress the historical approach
to book collecting, which became the dominant trend in France
for many years and has had permanent influence in other
countries as well. One specific manifestation of this approach
is an appreciation for the history of binding. It had been accepted practice to remove an old binding and replace it with
a new one, but collectors came to understand the value of the
original binding and to realize that even a worn and broken
binding, as long as it was contemporary with the book itself,
was more appropriate than a modern binding. Grolier bindings and other fine bindings of earlier periods were much in
demand, and the study of exlibris and super-exlibris aided in
tracing the provenance of books.

Among those working in the same spirit was Nodier
were men like Paul Lacroix (better known as "bibliophile
Jacob"), the bibliographer G. Peignot, the playwright G. de
Pixerécourt, who founded the French bibliophile society, the
book dealer Joseph Téchener, who began publishing the "Bul-
letin du bibliophile" in 1834, and Count de la Bédoyère, whose
collection of over 100,000 items on the French Revolution is

96. Red morocco binding   97. Green morocco binding in
with lace design in corners,   the cathedral style, made in the
made by the younger of the   1820's by Joseph Thouvenin, a
Bozérian brothers, who worked   pupil of the Bozérian brothers.
for Napoleon and other collec-
tors.

now in the Bibliothèque Nationale.

Some of the best hunting grounds for these bibliophiles
were the book stalls of the bouquinists, and the first half of
the 19th century became the golden age of the out-door book
trade, which included among its members even the learned
Latin scholar Achaintre. It was by no means unusual to find
books of great rarity in these dealers' stocks. Nodier came
upon a copy of "Hypnerotomachia" on one occasion and purchased this masterpiece of Renaissance wood-cut art for 30
centimes. The romantic aspects of such an experience make
it easy to understand why these daily trips along the quays of
the Seine would appeal to a poet like Nodier.

The Romantic movement, with its interest in the Middle Ages, characterized the intellectual life of this period and
provided the background for the historical interests of bibliophiles. In the Napoleonic period neo-classicism was still pre

dominant and found expression in the predilection of the Empire for the decorative features of the art of the Roman Empire. This is shown in the bindings that were produced, even though Napoleon's own binders, the two Bozérian brothers, used them only to a limited extend and often let the Emperor's coat-of-arms constitute the principle element of the decoration. With the fall of Napoleon, however, the Empire style declined and the gothic of the Middle Ages became the style to imitate; architects built "gothic" castles and villas, craftsmen made gothic furniture, and book-binders used gothic motifs for their decoration, sometimes to such a degree that the entire cover of the book was filled with adaptations of gothic pointed arches and other gothic elements from the church architecture of the Middle Ages. This style has quite properly been called "à la cathédrale." It was used a great deal by Joseph Thouvenin, a first-rate craftsman and Nodier's favorite binder. The decoration was applied by panel-stamping (French: gaufrure) in the same manner as in the 16th century, the design being engraved on a metal plate. Thouvenin's panel stamps are executed with great virtuosity, and the German-born binders Purgold and Simier also use the method with considerable skill.

Alongside the cathedral style the Empire style continued to be used, though not consistently, and the growing appreciation of earlier bindings led to imitations of the Grolier, fanfare, Gascon and other styles, often executed with considerable artistry. For a time this historical interest also involved a high regard for the rococo style; a "neo-rococo" appeared in the 1840's on many books in France as well as elsewhere. Especially in Germany and the Scandinavian countries large rococo ornaments were displayed on the covers of books and on the smooth, loose spines that had gradually become common because they were easier to decorate than the rigid spines, and because they made the books easier to open. The book-binding art of the 19th century was thus largely characterized by imitation and by mixture of styles, and only in exceptional instances was there a more or less personal contribution by the binder, as when Antoine Bauzonnet introduced a style of binding in which the entire decoration consisted of a framework of a few parallel lines stamped with great precision on leather of the most select quality prepared with the greatest possible care. Another binder who used this same style was German-born G. Trautz; he reintroduced the rigid spine, and in gilding and treatment of the leather almost surpassed his master Bauzonnet.

This concern for the styles of earlier periods led book-

binders back to mosaic and plastic work in leather; these
methods came more and more into fashion after the 1870's
and were used to produce picturesque effects on book covers.
Two French masters of plastic leather work were Marius
Michel and Léon Gruel; in Denmark there were H. C. Lerche,
D. L. Clément, and later Immanuel Petersen and J. L. Flyge.
A special variation within this style of binding was the so-
called "narrative binding" (la reliure parlante) which made its
appearance in France toward 1880; the intention -- often rather
forced in its execution -- was to have the picture on the cover
tell something about the contents of the book. This style was
imitated in other countries but quite often, especially in Germany, the results were in bad taste because of poor judgement
on the part of the artist. Its most famous representatives in
France were Cuzin, Charles Meunier and René Kieffer. England's most outstanding book-binders in the second half of the
19th century were Joseph Zaehnsdorf and his son Joseph William.

Technological Advances in Book Making

One of the most striking phenomena of the 19th century
book world is the great expansion in literary productivity. In
Germany, for instance, the annual production of printed books
around 1800 was about 3,300 titles, while at the middle of the
century this figure had already risen to 10,000 and at its close
was up near 25,000. An increase of this order presupposes a
considerable advance in the purely technical aspects of book
making and displacement of hand methods by machine operation. The beginning of this development came with the invention of the paper-making machine by Louis Robert in 1799 and
the invention of the power press by Friedrich König around
1810. The high-speed power press soon replaced the old hand
presses, and after a number of improvements made it possible
to turn out large editions in a very short time. Another significant development in printing technology was the composing
machine; the earliest experiments with mechanical typesetting
were made by a Dane, Christian Sørensen, but the machine
that became successful was the "linotype" that the German
watchmaker Ottmar Mergenthaler invented in the 1880's. Like
the various other composing machines developed later (monotype, intertype, typograph, etc.) the linotype casts the type
ready for printing; the actual composing is done by striking
keys similar to those of a typewriter. Machine composition
can be done 3 or 4 times as fast as hand composition, and the
combination of the composing machine with the high-speed press
gradually effected a revolution in the printing trade.

These technological developments were of special importance in the printing of the periodical literature that had
sprouted up so profusely since the 1820's. Newspapers as
well as the numerous popular weekly papers, magazines, etc.,
benefited by the rapid rate at which they could be produced,
especially after the rotary press with its cylindrical type-
forms came into use and paper was available in rolls. Of
equal importance was the introduction of new methods of pic-
torial reproduction, by which the tedious wood-carving and
lithographic processes were replaced by photographic etchings.
These could be made in a matter of days or even hours. Before this the illustrated press had always been the best field
for xylographers, and papers like the "Illustrated London News,"
"L'Illustration," and "Illustrierte Zeitung," all founded in the
1840's, had published many excellent wood-cuts along with
their more ephemeral illustrative material.

Reaction against Technology

These technological advances, however, had anything
but a favorable effect on the quality of the books produced.
The increased speed of the technical processes involved was
detrimental and discouraging to the esthetic aspects of book-
making. In the 1880's and 1890's a violent reaction set in
against this decadent trend, originating from a small group
of English artists of the Pre-Raphaelite brotherhood led by the
painters Burne-Jones and D. G. Rosetti. One of the most active members of this group was William Morris, whose per-
sonality was a combination of painter, architect, poet and
socialistic agitator. His versatility and unflagging energy made
him the ideal person to become the spiritual and practical
leader of the Pre-Raphaelites' counteraction against technology.
In all branches of craftsmanship their aim was to revive original methods and to recreate the purity of style that characterized the best craftsmanship of earlier periods. This was another manifestation of Romanticism, with its preference for
the art of the Middle Ages and the Renaissance.

Morris and his co-workers made furniture, wall cover-
ings, woven material, glass paintings and, in general, everything needed for the decoration of a home. In each instance
they studied the methods of the old hand-craftsmen, while
their decorative style was, like that of the French and German
romantic artists, inspired by the gothic form. Morris did not
turn his attention to bookmaking until he was well advanced in
years. He first supervised the printing of several books at
the Chiswick Press, one of the best in London, which was

owned by the publisher and antiquarian William Pickering, and
then in 1891 he established his own press, the famous Kelmscott Press, at his country estate of Kelmscott Manor on the
Thames. From then to his death in 1896 he printed about 50
books, all in small editions and now very much sought by collectors. In his printing as in his other work he went back to
the great models of the past; the types that he designed and
had cut in collaboration with Emery Walker included a roman
("Golden type") in the style of Nicolaus Jenson, and two black-
letter gothic types ("Chaucer" and "Troy") based on those of
the earliest printers. The ornamentation with which he so
lavishly decorated his pages was derived from the same
sources; the wood-cut initials and borders of vine branches
that he designed for his roman-type books were clearly inspired by Venetian wood-cut art of the Ratdolt and Aldus period. One of Morris' chief works was a large Chaucer edition with illustrations by Edward Burne-Jones. Another illus-
trator who worked with Morris was Walter Crane; he also took
Italian Renaissance wood-cuts as his models. Morris' books
produce a powerful effect with their heavy type and profuse
ornamentation; in spite of the close relationship of his work
to that of earlier periods it is not purely imitative, though it
does contain the seeds of certain mannerisms that some of
Morris' followers were not able to avoid.

Long before Morris began his printing activity there
were signs of a reaction against the spindly and insipid type
faces of the time Caslon's roman was revived by the Chiswick
Press where Charles Wittingham was the guiding spirit, and
Bishop Fell's 17th century Dutch type had been rediscovered
by C. H. O. Daniel, an instructor at Oxford University. After
Morris founded his press a considerable number of other private presses sprang up to produce books in an antique and
artistic style. However different the type used by Charles
Ricketts at his Vale Press, by John Hornby at the Ashendene
Press or by Cobden-Sanderson and Emery Walker at the Dove
Press -- to name only three of the better known types -- they
all had in common a reversion to the type forms used by the
great printers of the Renaissance, and they were all influenced
by Morris' basic principles for the artistic effect of the printed
page. Although the activity of these private presses for the
most part covered only a brief span of years, they had a definite effect on typographical art in England.

In our day, however, the United States has attained a
level of equality with the mother country in this respect. As
early as the 1630's the English brought typography to America
when Jose Glover, a pastor, and Stephen Daye, a locksmith,

98. Page from William Morris' edition of Chaucer (1893) with illustration by Burne-Jones and the characteristic Morris initials and vine-branch borders.

well-doing,'with the spirit & clear aims of a Man. He
has discovered that the Ideal Workshop he so panted
for is even this same Actual ill-furnished Workshop
he has so long been stumbling in. He can say to himself: 'Tools? Thou hast no Tools? Why, there is not
'a Man, or a Thing, now alive but has tools. The
'basest of created animalcules, the Spider itself, has a

99. Emery Walker's roman, designed from Nicolaus Jenson's
type.

founded a press at Cambridge, Massachusetts. Here in 1640
they issued the now very scarce Bay Psalm Book, which
brought $151,000 at an auction in 1947; another famous work
from the same press was John Eliot's translation of the Bible
into the language of the Indians. In the 18th century one of
the best representatives of book printing in the United States
was Benjamin Franklin, who had learned the trade in England
and then worked in Philadelphia for many years as printer,
publisher and newspaper editor. However, it is only in recent
times that American typography has attained independent importance.

Another member of Morris' circle was the former lawyer, T. J. Cobden-Sanderson, who was the founder of the
Doves Press. He was not only concerned with printing but also won special fame for the artistic bindings that he made at
the Doves Bindery in Hammersmith near London. For decorative effect he relied on the same elements used by the old
masters, and Cobden-Sanderson's importance in English book
binding was similar to that of Morris in printing. He believed
firmly that the binding should be adapted to the contents of the
book.

The movement inaugurated by Morris soon spread to
the Continent. Its influence can be traced in Belgium and
France and especially in Germany, where it was introduced
by the Belgian architect Henry van de Velde. He was one of

the most enthusiastic exponents of the Jugend style, so-called
from the periodical "Jugend." In this style of ornamentation
the effect was produced by line designs in geometrical patterns combined with animal figures and flowers. At the close
of the 19th and the beginning of the 20th century the Jugend
style had considerable influence in German and, to some extent, Scandinavian book making, but it did not attain, nor did
it deserve a position of lasting importance.

Renaissance of Scandinavian
Book Craft

The books made in Denmark in the first decades of the
19th century showed the effects of the economic crisis that the
country experienced in the years following 1807. There was
a considerable use of paper bindings, many of which were
quite attractive, and the tradition of the mirror binding period
was almost completely forgotten. The days of the great book
collectors were past, the role of the nobility had declined,
and book binders no longer found employment as before.

In Denmark as in other countries there was a revival
of the old book culture under the influence of William Morris
and his circle. Simon Bernsteen, who founded a small press
in Copenhagen in 1882 had become acquainted with Morris during a stay in England and thereafter began using a hand press
to print books designed in accordance with Morris' artistic
principles, some of them in black-letter type. Bernsteen's
work was an inspiration to the artist and wood-carver K.
Kongstad, who operated a printing business in the years 1903-
20 obtaining his types from England, Holland and Italy and
producing over 40 books printed by himself and embellished
with his own effective wood-cuts.

First and foremost, however, the guiding spirit in this
new Danish renaissance in book craftsmanship was F. Hendriksen. In the 1870's he had attained the ranking position a-
mong the many competent wood-carvers in Denmark; in his
weekly publication "Ude og Hjemme" (1877-84) he had, in collaboration with other outstanding artists, shown how high the
art of shading in wood-cuts could be carried. From 1884 on
he devoted all his energies to the task of raising the Danish
book craft out of its decadence and start it along paths like
those that Morris followed. This movement found a rallying
point in the association "Forening for Boghaandvaerk" that
Hendriksen founded in 1888 and directed for a generation;
later a school was also established for practitioners of the

art of book-making.

Book-binders also felt the new spirit. Hendriksen had strongly attacked the publishers' bindings of the period -- fancy cloth bindings often overloaded with gilded decoration -- and maintained the superiority of the plain English cloth bindings. In addition he brought about a collaboration between book-binders and artists that soon bore fruit and has continued to the present day as a characteristic feature of Scandinavian book-making.

Expansion of the Book Trade

The fight against censorship and unauthorized reprinting had been carried on by the book trade during the greater part of the 18th century; this was especially true in Germany where conditions had been disrupted and uncoordinated for a long time. Not until the end of the century did the situation begin to improve; in the beginning of the 19th century a co-operative effort was made to establish the special German conditional sale system whereby the retail book dealer could obtain a certain number of copies of any book from the publisher with the privilege of returning those remaining unsold after a certain length of time. The adoption of this system as well as the fight against censorship and the abuses of reprinting were greatly aided by the founding in 1825 of a central organization for the German book trade, the Börsenverein der deutschen buchhändler; which excluded from membership anyone engaged in reprinting. In the ensuing decades this association became increasingly influential. In 1848 censorship was abolished, and in 1870 uniform laws were established throughout the country protecting literary ownership rights for 30 years after the author's death. After a struggle of some years the Börsenverein also had effective trade agreements set up between publishers and dealers; these agreements provided a fixed retail price and established rules for the discount that the publisher should give the dealer, with a prohibition against giving discounts to retail purchasers -- it was this customer discount that had made the fixed book-store price meaningless in the past. The Börsenverein had its headquarters in Leipzig, the leading book center in the country; here was also the home of the board that controlled the relations between publishers and dealers, and here also a great book trade fair was held every spring as in earlier times. The Börsenverein published the chief organ of the book trade "Börsenblatt" with its weekly list of new books. In Leipzig were also found many of the leading German publishing houses:

100. Beowulf in combat with Grendel's mother. Drawing
by Niels Skovgaard in Thora Konstantin-Hansen's adaptation
of Beowulf for children, 1914.

Hinrichs, Brockhaus, J. A. Barth, Göschen, Reclam, Tauch-
nitz, B. G. Teubner, Velhagen & Klasing, etc., though there
were important publishers in other towns as well: Gustav
Fischer in Jena, Walter de Gruyter & Co., Julius Springer
and S. Fischer in Berlin, and Julius Perthes in Gotha. A
German publisher of recent times who has been greatly interested in Scandinavian literature is Eugen Diederichs; he came
under the influence of William Morris and has produced books
of very high quality.

One peculiarly German phenomenon is the so-called

Barsortiment, a wholesale book-store that keeps a stock of
all current German literature, usually bound, and sells it at
the regular discount to retail dealers who can thus concentrate
the major part of their purchases in one place. The largest
business of this type was Koehler & Volckmar in Leipzig,
whose complete trade catalog was a very useful tool.

While the book trade in Germany is scattered throughout the entire country, it is concentrated to a much greater
degree in the capital cities in France and England. Paris has
been the home of large publishing houses, some still in existence, like Panckoucke fils, Renouard, Otto Lorenz, known
for his "Catalogue de la librairie," Hetzel, Hachette, Le-
merre, Firmin Didot, Plon, Calman-Lévy, Larousse, which
is world-famous for its dictionaries, and Armand Colin, who
specializes in popular scientific literature; this is also a specialty of Les presses universitaires, along with university
text-books. The German conditional sale system is not used
in France, but even though publishers deliver most books only
on regular order, there is still a "système du dépot" which
has some similarity to the German system. A special French
phenomenon are the so-called "dépositaires" which have a
monopoly on the delivery of certain publisher's books to retail dealers. In France as well as in England fixed retail
prices were not established till quite recently; before that
many dealers gave their customers considerable discounts so
that the prices marked on the books became meaningless. As
a counteraction English publishers in 1901 reduced their discount to dealers (the net system). Nearly all English publishers are located in London; here we find firms like Long-
mans, Green & Co., England's oldest publishing house, John
Murray, George Allen & Unwin, William Heinemann and Mac-
millan & Co., and here we also have the Stationers' Company,
the oldest book dealers' association in the world. The conditional sales system is not used in England; English publishers work on a short range plan and deliver books only on
regular order; hence if a book does not become a success immediately after publication, only a minimum sale can usually
be reckoned with and the publisher will then put the remainder
of the edition up at auction or throw it on the market at a
greatly reduced price. Ever since James Lackington made
the beginning late in the 18th century there has been a special
type of book dealer in London, the remainder dealer, who
buys up remainders and sells them at bargain prices. An
important role has also until recently been played by the great
English circulating libraries; publishers could always count on
disposing of a certain numer of copies to them.

The situation in the United States is similar to that in England. Here book-selling is carried on in stores of quite miscellaneous character, and books have also been sold by travelling agents. There are important publishing firms in Boston, Philadelphia and other cities, but by far the greater number of the large publishing houses, as well as the largest book stores, are located in New York.

In the Scandinavian countries the book trade is organized along the same lines as in Germany, and German practice has generally been followed during the past 100 years, with fixed retail prices, prohibition against customer discount and the conditional sale system. In 1837 Boghandlerforeningen (now Den danske Forlaeggerforening) was formed on the German pattern; retail book dealers have had their own organization since the 1890's. As in Germany, so also in the Scandinavian countries it was the publishers who determined whether a retail dealer was entitled to receive a discount; this discount usually varied between 25 and 30% of the selling price, depending on the nature of the book. The practice of "prenumeration" which had originally come from England, was also taken over from Germany as early as the 18th century; this was the privilege granted to the cash customer of having his name printed in the books he purchased. The practice continued far into the 19th century but was gradually superseded by the subscription system and has now given way to installment buying.

Trade in second-hand books that have already been bought and sold once, had in the 16th century been carried on by book-binders, but in the course of the 17th century many dealers in new books also took up this business. Dealers in second-hand books alone, however, did not appear until the latter half of the 18th century, first in Germany as a consequence of the conditional sale system. The oldest German second-hand business was founded in 1785 in Frankfurt by Joseph Baer. In England at about the same time the great "Temple of the Muses" of James Lackington, with its hundreds of thousands of books, was for a long time the largest second-hand book store in the country. Half a century later Bernard Quaritch attained world renown as the greatest and best informed second-hand dealer of his time, and he and other firms like H. G. Bohn, H. Sotheran, Maggs Brothers, Francis Edwards, E. P. Goldschmidt and Robinson have made London one of the most important cities in the international second-hand trade.

Until recent times Germany has also been the home of

a large numer of flourishing second-hand enterprises, especially in Leipzig and Berlin; names like Gustav Fock, K. F.
Koehler, Otto Harrassowitz and Karl W. Hiersemann were
known everywhere in scholarly circles, for the German second-hand trade has mainly concerned itself with technical literature and not with collectors' books as much as other European dealers. Exceptions, however, were Martin Breslau
and Jacques Rosenthal (now moved to London and New York)
who like many English, French, Dutch, Swiss and Italian
second-hand dealers dealt mostly in manuscripts, old and
rare printed books, wood-cut books and fine bindings, both
historical and modern. To this category of second-hand
dealers belongs Martinus Nijhoff of the Hague, who also operates one of Holland's largest publishing firms and retail book
stores; also Menno Hertzberger in Amsterdam, L'art ancien
in Zurich, Nic. Rauch in Geneva, Ulrico Hoepli in Milan,
Leo S. Olschki in Florence and C. E. Rappaport in Rome.
In America the second-hand trade in fine and rare books has
prospered because of the many wealthy collectors of the last
hundred years; of particular fame is A. S. W. Rosenbach, who
like another great second-hand dealer in the same city, H. P.
Kraus, was born in Germany. Other important firms are
Lathrop C. Harper and James F. Drake in New York and
Goodspeed's in Boston.

In France, where the second-hand book trade had its
golden age in the period following the Revolution, and where
G. F. Debure in the middle of the 18th century published some
of the earliest catalogs designed for bibliophiles, Paris was
the home of many great second-hand dealers all throughout
the 19th century and down to our time. Among the best known
of the older ones are A. A. Renouard and J. Téchener, and
of the more recent, E. Rahir, Maisonneuve & Cie. and De
Nobele. Many of the European and American second-hand
dealers have issued catalogs that contain detailed descriptions,
historical information and facsimiles of the books offered for
sale. Like the great auction catalogs they have been valuable
for bibliographical and historical purposes. Several of these
dealers have been well versed in literary history and bibliography, and some have passed this knowledge on in works of
a high scholarly standard.

The Scandinavian countries have not been large enough
to offer second-hand dealers the same opportunities as other
countries; with a few exceptions these dealers have concentrated on the national literature, and neither their catalogs
nor their prices have reached the level of the great foreign
second-hand dealers. Among those dealing exclusively in sec-

ond-hand books in Denmark the most important in the 19th
and the beginning of the 20th century have been Herm. H. J.
Lynge & Søn (established 1853, now directed by Arne Stuhr),
J. Grubb, Magnus Hansen and Jeppe Poulsen Skadhauge (the
last two now combined under the direction of E. Grønholt
Pedersen); in Norway, N. W. Damm; in Sweden, O. H. Klem-
ming, Robert Sandberg, and Björck & Börjesson, who now
probably hold the leading position in the Scandinavian countries. In more recent times, however, a large number of
publishing firms and regular book-dealers have taken up the
sale of used books.

Growth of Libraries

The reason for the enormous increase in literary production during the last 150 years is in part the growth of scientific research with its increasing specialization, which has
given rise among other things to innumerable scientific and
technical journals, and in part the increased interest in reading and desire for information by the public at large as a
consequence of the spread of democracy, a situation that is
particularly characteristic of the Anglo-Saxon, Germanic and
Scandinavian countries. These are then the factors that have
been the basis for the tremendous growth of libraries in the
same period.

This growth, however, has not manifested itself so
much in increased size of book stocks, although it was an impressive increase that the libraries of Paris received after
the Revolution or that the secularization of monastery book
collections gave south German libraries in the early years of
the 19th century -- about 150 such old book collections were
incorporated in the Court library in Munich alone. Instead,
the growth appears much more in the new spirit that began to
permeate the activities of libraries, outwardly as well as in-
wardly, along toward the middle of the last century. An entirely new conception gradually evolved of the library's obligations as a public institution. One of the pioneers in this
respect was the illustrious Italian-born director of the British
Museum, Antonio Panizzi, who drew up a program for this
library in which he emphasized that the aim should not be to
collect books for museum purposes but to create a center for
the spread of knowledge and culture. In the present-day con-
cept of library service, the primary concern is for the useful-
ness of the library, whether the books are used for strictly
scientific purposes or for more popular ends. This principle
governs all aspects of the library's organization and work:

the design of the building, arrangement of the catalog, book purchases, etc. One of Panizzi's greatest projects was the printing of the catalog of the British Museum library in collaboration with Richard Garnett; this gigantic bibliographical task resulted in a work of over a hundred folio volumes. Another of Panizzi's memorable accomplishments was the initiative he took in the construction of a new reading room, circular in shape and covered by a large glass dome, with several hundred seats and an impressive reference collection. Around the outside of the reading room were the book stacks, so arranged as to make best possible use of the space and provide convenient access to the books. The stacks had adjustable shelves and their height from floor to ceiling was so low that the top shelf could be reached without a ladder. These stacks, which were built in 1854-57, represented a break with the earlier tradition of a large library hall, and they were soon adopted in other new library buildings throughout the world. Unfortunately the stack system had not yet reached Denmark when the new University Library building was erected in 1857-61 at the University of Copenhagen, after the old library quarters in the loft of Trinity Church had long been overcrowded. On the other hand, the system was adopted in the new building for the Royal Library in Copenhagen, which was opened in 1906, and in the Statsbibliotek at Aarhus, built in 1898-1902, the University Library of Oslo, 1907-13, Lund University Library, 1907, and in several other Scandinavian library buildings.

France had a first-rate library architect in Henri Labrouste. In the middle of the 19th century he designed a new building for the Bibliothèque Sainte-Geneviève that was fully adapted to its purpose. With a reading room containing 700 seats and a reference collection of over 100,000 volumes this library is the most used of any in Paris, the average number of visitors per day reaching some 4,000. In 1864-68 Labrouste introduced modern stacks in France when remodelling the Bibliothèque Nationale, and on that occasion the library also acquired its monumental reading room, lighted through 9 domes. In the French national library there were still hundreds of thousands of books and magazines from the period of the Revolution that had not been organized or cataloged -- until in 1874 Leopold Delisle, a man of wide knowledge and great administrative ability, became director of the library; in the course of the next twenty years Delisle accomplished the extraordinary feat of cataloging this enormous collection. In 1897 he was able to begin the printing of an author catalog of the library. In spite of the difficulties caused by two world wars this project is still being continued and has now reached the letter T.

In Germany the library at Göttingen had long been a model. Here and there throughout the country some steps were being taken toward reorganization, but the majority of German libraries were still marked by neglect. There was no appreciation of the special qualifications required for library work and the management of a library was not even considered a full-time task; usually it was entrusted to a member of the university faculty as a secondary assignment; and while it is true that a number of these professor-librarians, like Robert von Mohl in Tübingen, did outstanding work the arrangement was a hindrance to library development. Not till the 1870's was there a change in this situation, when the state governments, especially that of Prussia under the leadership of Fr. Althoff, began to recognize their obligations toward libraries and demonstrated this recognition in the form of increased appropriations and in the development of a separate library profession and the provision of special education for library work.

Panizzi's stack system was first used in Germany when a new building was erected for the University library at Halle in 1878-80 and throughout Germany the various state and university libraries now began to be reorganized.

In 1914, just before the outbreak of the first World War the country's largest library, the Royal Library in Berlin, finally acquired a new building; one that was distinguished rather by its extraordinary size than by its practical design. From this point of view a much better result was attained shortly thereafter when a building was erected for the Deutsche Bücherei in Leipzig, a library that had been founded in 1912 by the German book dealers' trade association in an effort through voluntary deposit of books by publishers to build up a national library where all the current literature of the country could be gathered, and thus also constitute a center for German national bibliography. Among other cooperative library projects in Germany during this period there were a number of centralized or union catalogs and especially the preparations for the great "Gesamtkatalog," which began to appear in 1929 but soon proved impractical to complete. Of great importance for the growing inter-city library loan program was the information office at the Royal Library in Berlin (Auskunftbüro) which also facilitated loans between German and foreign libraries.

In Germany, however, it was impossible to achieve

centralization to the same extent as in France following the
Revolution or as had been effected among Italian libraries;
each separate German state pursued its own course even
though there were certain common features in the methods and
procedures of German scholarly libraries. German library
practice, as reflected in the distinguished journal "Zentral-
blatt für Bibliothekswesen" that began publication in 1881, has
been of great importance for the development of scholarly librarianship in the Scandinavian countries; in the 20th century,
however, there has also been an influence from the Anglo-
Saxon library world, which came to Denmark in particular
under the inspiring leadership of H. O. Lange.

English, American and Scandinavian
Public Libraries

There is one field in which the influence of the English-
speaking countries has been predominant. The development
of free public libraries in those countries has surpassed that
in all others and must be counted as one of the greatest cultural contributions made by the Anglo-Saxon world.

In England and the United States the development began
around the middle of the 19th century when laws were adopted
giving governmental units the right to assess a special tax for
the establishment of public libraries, not to serve scientific
research but to meet the literary needs of the general public.
In England the beginning was made at Manchester, and the
free public library of this great manufacturing town is still
one of the largest and most active in England, having an annual circulation of 5-1/2 million volumes. In the United States
the first significant steps were taken in Boston, and American
free public libraries have become a cultural factor of even
greater importance than those of the old world.

Enormous sums have been and are being spent on libraries in the United States, not only by the states and cities
but also by individuals. Such library "patrons" represent a
type that is just as common in the new world as it is uncommon in the old. At the head of them all stands Andrew Carnegie who provided funds for the erection of almost two thousand library buildings.

American appreciation of the importance of public libraries has also found expression in the formation of organizations (Friends of the Library) to provide financial support
for libraries, and in the fact that many of the country's large

book collectors have made their own libraries accessible to the public or have donated them to public libraries. We can say without exaggeration that America could not have brought so many and such valuable book treasures away from Europe if her private collectors had not been so numerous and so active and had such extensive financial resources.

In the front rank of these collectors stands the financier John Pierpont Morgan, who, with some justification, has been compared to the Medici in Florence; at his death in 1913 his private library was valued at around 10 million dollars. Among his 20,000 printed books there were many with bindings of historical interest; of the 1,300 manuscripts a large number were illuminated manuscripts from the Middle Ages, but Morgan had also bought most of the Coptic manuscripts from the 9-10th century that the Arabs found buried in a monastery ruin near Faijum in 1910. Morgan's library is now public property and is housed in a marble building in New York where additions are still being made to it. Still greater in size and value is the collection that the railroad magnate Henry E. Huntington, brought together in a palatial library building on his estate in San Marino, near Los Angeles, and which is now owned by the State of California. Huntington did not begin his collecting activities until he was along in years, but he had a good knowledge of books and often bought entire private libraries in order to pick out the best items; his fantastic purchases contributed in a considerable degree to raising the prices of rare books. The Huntington Library is, like the Morgan Library, still being added to; some 20 years ago it was already up to a quarter million volumes, including 5,000 incunabula, besides thousands of maps and also manuscripts and letters of famous authors.

Among the auctions at which Huntington made extensive purchases were those held in 1911-12 in London to dispose of the library left by the English banker Henry Huth, whom we have already mentioned, and also the New York auction of the library of the American bibliophile Robert Hoe, who owned the world's leading factory for the manufacture of rotary presses. Hoe had brought together a library in the true collector's tradition; he was also the founder of the famous association of bibliophiles, the Grolier Club, in New York, and like Morgan he was especially interested in historical bindings. The auction of his books brought in almost 3 million dollars for about 15,000 items. At the Huth and Hoe auctions many other American collectors appeared as buyers, among them the young and wealthy Harry Elkins Widener, but on his way home from London with his purchases from the Huth auction

101.   The palatial Henry E. Huntington Library in San Marino, California.

Widener drowned in the shipwreck of the Titanic, and the books
were lost. His own library, which was distinguished among
other things by its many Stevenson and Dickens items, was
donated to Harvard University. Like Widener, other American bibliophiles have given special attention to particular authors or certain fields of literature. Prof. D. W. Fiske, for
instance, was especially interested in Icelandic literature and
in Dante and Petrarch; he presented his books to Cornell University, except for a section of chess literature that went to
the library at Reykjavik. We have already mentioned Henry
Clay Folger's unique library of Shakespeare editions and material from the shakespearean period; it was presented to Am-
herst College and now contains about 200,000 volumes housed
in a monumental building in Washington, D. C., alongside the
Library of Congress.

As was natural, early American printed books as well

102. Interior of the circular domed reading room of the
Library of Congress.

as books about the colonization of America, the Indians, and
the later history of the country were given preference by a
large number of collectors in the United States, so that the
prices of rare Americana have gradually risen to fantastic
heights. Many private collections of great national importance
have been brought together in this field, containing both manuscript and printed material for the study of the history of the
country. Among the older collectors of Americana were
James Lenox, whose collection is now in the New York Public
Library, and John Carter Brown, who presented his books to
Brown University in Rhode Island. The Newberry Library in
Chicago contains a large portion of the books collected by
Edward E. Ayer; besides ornithology his field was literature
on the Indians and about Mexico and Central America. The
University of Michigan Library acquired by gift the collection
made by William Lawrence Clements, which provides an ex-
ceptional fund of material for the study of the Revolutionary
War and the wars with the Indians.

Some of the university libraries of the United States
have been mentioned along with other large libraries, but the
greatest of them all, the Library of Congress in Washington,

D. C., with its nine million printed volumes and enormous
special collections of manuscripts, maps and music is one of
the largest libraries in the world.   It was founded in the year
1800 as a reference library for the members of Congress,
but in the second half of the 19th century, mainly under the
direction of A. R. Spofford and later Herbert Putnam, it developed into the national library of the United States.   The
building of the Library of Congress was dedicated in 1897, and
is one of Washington's most striking government buildings;
like the British Museum it has a large domed reading room.

The next largest library in the United States is the New
York Public Library, which came into being in 1848 when the
German-born merchant, John Jacob Astor, presented the city
with a book collection to form the nation's first public library;
it has since benefited greatly from Carnegie's generosity.   The
main library structure on Fifth Avenue is a huge cultural center that is visited annually by some 3 to 4 million persons.
It offers exhibits, lectures, concerts, film showings, and en-
tertainment for children, and its many reading rooms provide
material for research as well as general information.   The
New York Public Library is both a scholarly and a popular library, and its finances are based mainly on private funds.
In both these respects it is typical of many similar cultural
institutions that are found in the larger American cities, while
other libraries in the smaller towns are provided for by special legislation.   In this variegated American library picture
an important place is held by the technical and research libraries of universities and other institutions of learning.   A-
mong the largest university libraries are those of Harvard,
Chicago, Columbia, Princeton, Illinois, Yale and California.

One requirement for an enterprise of the proportions
represented by American library service is highly developed
library technique.   In the arrangement and the equipment of
library buildings, the cataloging and classification process,
the recording of loans and in the expansion of the libraries'
effective range to out-of-the way localities modern technology
has been extensively applied, resulting in the development of
practical procedures that are used throughout the country and
have helped give the many thousands of separate institutions
a generally uniform character in spite of their individual differences.

These shadows in the picture cannot, however, detract
from the glory that belongs to the American library world.
It was, in fact, from the United States that several European
countries, especially the Scandinavian, derived the impulses

for the growth that their public libraries have experienced in the last generation. Most of the small reading circles and parish libraries that, like the diocesan libraries, had been established throughout Denmark during the time of the Enlightenment had died out. The Danish government did begin in the 1880's to grant small sums for popular libraries but these did not attain any real significance until a new movement with English and American public libraries as models laid the foundation for the modern development of Danish libraries; the chief person in this movement at the turn of the century was Andreas Schack Steenberg. In Norway the country's largest public library, the Deichmanske Bibliotek in Oslo, was thoroughly reorganized about 1898 on the American pattern with Hakon Nyhuus as the motivating force, and in Sweden American influence became effective through the proposal by Valfrid Palmgren in 1911, which resulted in a complete reorganization of the Swedish public library system.

The Period Since 1914

The period since 1914 is still so close to us that it cannot be treated historically in the same manner as earlier periods. But with this reservation an attempt will be made to present a picture of the developments in our field during this unsettled and confused era, however hazy and uncertain this picture may be. To some extent it will be necessary to discuss persons and events belonging to the very beginning of the century in order to illustrate, among other things, the continuity which has not been entirely severed by the destruction and upheavals brought on by two world wars. On the other hand, names and events of the most recent years will only be mentioned to a very limited extent.

Book Production and Book Arts

The triumphs of technology has been just as remarkable in this field as in other fields; the book-making craft has become the graphic arts industry, but the earlier methods have not been entirely superseded. Even though by far the greater part of modern book printing is done by the use of composing machines and power presses, there is still some work that requires hand setting, and while binderies also make extensive use of machinery, there is still a demand for the type of fine binding that can be done only by hand. But new technical methods will nevertheless continue to be adopted. For printing very large editions, especially of illustrated magazines, an intaglio (photogravure) process is now used, the text and illustrations being etched into a copper plate from which the impressions are taken; a modern rotogravure press can make 20,000 or more impressions per hour. Another method of printing large editions, offset printing, has come more and more into use for advertising matter, etc., as well as for books; in this process the impression is transferred from a zinc plate to a rubber blanket from which a good impression can then be obtained.

Both the gravure and the offset method can be used for color printing, but pictures in color are also produced by the

three- or four color process in which the original is broken
up into 3 or 4 colors which are then printed one on top of the
other from separate plates. A very high quality of color reproduction is obtained with the collotype process, in which the
printing surface is a specially treated glass plate, but this
method is best suited to small editions and is used mainly for
facsimiles; the accuracy of reproduction is so great that it is
almost impossible to tell the original from the printed copy.
These various mechanical processes, which are due to the
advances made in photo-chemistry, have outdistanced the older
methods of printing illustrations from wood-cuts and copper-
plate engravings, and the latter are no longer of importance
in ordinary printing work. Recently, however, wood-cuts
have again come into use in special fields. In various countries there are a number of modern artists making wood-cuts
for book illustrations. They work in the style of the illustrations in the earliest printed books rather than in the manner
introduced by Bewick, but with a much greater personal quality. Some of these artists also work with etching and lithography although these processes are so fundamentally different
from book printing that fully homogeneous results are difficult to obtain.

For the textual matter machine composition is now in
general use, and beautiful books can, in fact, be composed
by machine. The determining factor is the type face itself
and the way it is used to produce harmonious and readable
text pages, as well as the care that is used in the inking and
press operation -- and here again too great haste is a bad
thing. There are many modern types designed for machine
composition, several of which are based on the models of the
great type designers of earlier periods -- Jenson, Garamond,
Caslon, Bodoni, Baskerville and several others are represented in the machine composing rooms of the present day.
But alongside these an entirely new series of types has been
created, including some that are close to the historical forms,
others of a calligraphic character and still others in which
the striving for originality has produced a result that is often
more outré than pleasing and which have consequently been
short-lived.

Increasing emphasis is being placed on the importance
of adapting the typography and the other outer features to the
nature of the book itself. This has given rise to a new category of personnel in the graphic arts field, namely book con-
sultants who design and supervise the various steps in the
production of a book. Their work involves the proper choice
of format and selection of paper and the most suitable type

face in the best size and with the correct amount of leading, as well as decisions regarding the placing of illustrations in the text and particularly the design of the title page. The principles on which these decisions are based have gradually been evolved in the many books about paper, printing and illustration that have appeared in recent years, representing historical, esthetic and technical points of view. These same topics are also discussed in numerous trade journals and are taught in the schools of graphic art that can now be found in most countries. One current practice that helps to maintain interest in the quality of book production is the annual selection of well-made books by groups in several countries including the Scandinavian -- an idea that originated in the United States.

As in earlier periods we also find it true today that changing styles and fashions in art have their influence on book arts. A clear example of this occurred in the years between the two world wars when functionalism appeared in Russia and Germany and its principle that whatever is practical is also esthetically correct was transferred to book-making with the creation of functional or elemental typography. The basic functional type became the so-called grotesque, or gothic (Fig. 106), originally an English type from about 1815 in which all the lines are the same thickness. Another characteristic of functionalism was the division of the text into irregular sections and an unsymmetrical arrangement of the title page; the purpose of this was to emphasize the important matter and to attain the greatest effect through extreme simplicity. One of the most enthusiastic proponents of the movement was Jan Tschichold, who was born in Germany but lived in Switzerland; his influence was also felt on book-making in the Scandinavian countries. Later, however, he came to realize that this elemental typography was better suited to commercial printing than to books; in 1946 when he undertood to redesign the inexpensive English Penguin Books he had gone back to traditional typography. Although elemental typography is thus no longer used to any extent for books, it has performed a useful service in freeing book printing from the earlier dependence on traditional type faces and on the heavy ornamentation that William Morris made fashionable in the first decade of this century.

In general, England and the United States lead in typography today. English private presses continue their role of keeping up interest in high quality, and England also has firstrate type and book designers who, in contrast to Morris, have fully accepted modern technology. Names like Eric Gill, Stan-

THE PERPETUA TYPE

CUT FROM THE DESIGNS MADE BY

ERIC GILL

FOR THE LANSTON MONOTYPE CORPORATION

LONDON

The following founts only have been made to date; it is projected
to cut the usual sizes for book and display work

103.   Eric Gill's Perpetua type.

ley Morison, Oliver Simon and Francis Meynell have become
known throughout the world. Another great name has been
that of Edward Johnston, whose book "Writing, Illumination
and Lettering" issued in 1906 attained great influence both in
England and in Germany; his pupil Anna Simons has inspired
many German type designers. The periodical "The Fleuron"
issued by Stanley Morison and Oliver Simon from 1923 to
1930 was devoted to serious discussions of the esthetic problems of book printing. Several new type faces have made
their appearance, among them the Perpetua designed by Eric
Gill, which is one of the best book types of our day. As consultant to the Monotype Corporation Morison brought out Garamond, Baskerville and especially Caslon type in forms suitable
for machine composition, and for the London Times he also
created the first really good newspaper type, the very readable "Times roman" which has also been adapted for use in
book printing. Among the best English printed books of the
present day are those issued by the two university presses,
Oxford and Cambridge, which date back to the 16th century;
the clear, quiet effect of their books is typically English.

Since the close of the last century several organizations
have been established in the United States for producing fine

printed books in limited editions, and a number of private
and university presses have been set up on the English pattern.   The outstanding typographer, Daniel Berkeley Updike,
was active at one of these private presses, "The Riverside
Press," in the 1880's, and in 1893 he set up his own press,
"The Merrymount Press;" he was also well versed in the history of the craft, and his book "Printing Types" is one of the
chief works in the history of this subject.   While Updike was
a printer, two of the other great men in modern American
typography, Bruce Rogers and Frederic W. Goudy, were primarily type designers.   Rogers, like William Morris, started
with Nicolaus Jenson's roman type and from it he designed a
series of types that gradually took on more and more of his
"Centaur" he created a completely original modern type face;
one of the best works printed with it is the monumental "Oxford Lectern Bible," clear and simple in its typography without any decoration whatever.   Goudy, who owned "The Village
Press" designed some 100 type faces, inspired by historical
forms all the way from old Roman inscriptions to black-letter
missal types of the 15th century; his Kennerly roman has been
of great importance in modern printing in the United States.

In Germany there was a time in the 1880's when printers
had recourse to the models of the 15th century, and attempted
to give their books an "old-German" appearance such as by
extensive use of Schwabacher type.   The Jugend style came
later but when it died out shortly after the turn of the century
the influences from England and America began to be felt.
Count Harry Kessler of the Insel-Verlag, founded in 1899, had
established contact with Emery Walker, Eric Gill and other
leading English type designers, and when Carl Ernst Poeschel,
who had studied his craft in the United States, returned to
Leipzig he and type-founder Karl Klingspor became pioneers
in modern German typography, working closely with a number
of outstanding type designers.   Poeschel founded a private
press (Janus Presse) in company with the type designer Walter
Tiemann.   Most of the new types that Germany experimented
with in the 1920's were roman types, but many "fraktur"
types were also designed, such as Koch's Deutsche Schrift.
During the first World War fraktur type came into vogue, and
in the 1930's the Nazis enforced its use as the "national" German type.   Not until after 1945 did roman type again become
prevalent in Germany as in other countries.

Modern German book illustrators include three artists
who deserve special mention, Max Slevogt, Hans Meid and
Alfred Kubin; Slevogt's impressionistic pictures are particularly effective and include more than 500 illustrations that he

THE

HOLY BIBLE

Containing the Old and New
Testaments : Translated out
of the Original Tongues and
with the former Translations
diligently compared and revised by His Majesty's special
Command

Appointed to be read in Churches

OXFORD
Printed at the University Press
1935

104.   Title-page of the Oxford Lectern Bible, printed by Bruce
Rogers with his Centaur type in 1935.

Angſt iſt nahe + denn es iſt hie kein Helfer. + Große Farren haben mich umgeben + gewaltige Stiere haben mich um= ringet + ihren Rachen ſperren ſie auf wider mich + wie ein brüllender und reißender Löwe. + Ich bin ausgeſchüttet wie Waſſer + alle meine Gebeine haben ſich zertrennet; mein Herz iſt in meinem Leibe wie zerſchmolzen Wachs. + Meine Kräfte ſind vertrocknet wie eine Scherbe + und meine Zunge klebt an meinem Gaumen, und du legeſt mich in des Todes Staub. + Denn Hunde haben mich umgeben + und der Böſen Rotte hat mich umringt + ſie haben meine Hände und Füße durchgraben. + Ich kann alle meine Gebeine zählen. + Sie

105.   Rudolf Koch's Deutsche Schrift.

Es hat wenig Sinn, über die Zukunft der Schriftentwicklung nachzudenken. Mag die Schrift der kommenden Zeit den Charakter der Groteskschriften behalten oder zu den Schriften der älteren Antiqua zurückkehren: jedenfalls haben wir heute den historischen Vorbildern gegenüber eine innere Freiheit wiederge- wonnen, mit der wir auf diesem neuen Anfang weiterbauen können.

106.   "Grotesque" type designed by Rudolf Koch.

drew for "Faust."

In France the printing types of the Empire period con- tinued to be the dominant forms for a long time, but in the present period types have also been designed from earlier models, such as the rococo-like Cochin (Fig. 110) that was very popular for a number of years, and several types in the style of Garamond, in addition to types of original modern design.   It is not so much in the field of typography that present-day France lives up to her earlier traditions, but rather in the field of book illustration, where she still holds the lead.   There was, it is true, a period of decline in the latter part of the last century, but with the 70 or so books that the Edouard Pelletan issued between 1896 and 1912 French illustrative art again came into its own.   First-rank artists working with competent wood-carvers created pictures that harmonized with the text of the books, and Pelletan saw to it that the typography in each book was suited to its contents. One of his contemporaries, Ambroise Vollard, published a number of fine books in small editions, illustrated with orig- inal drawings by such outstanding artists and sculptors as Pierre Bonnard, Aristide Maillol, Henri Matisse, Pablo Pi- casso, Auguste Rodin, Georges Rouault and André Dunoyer de Segonzac.   Other publishers have also made a point of issuing books with original drawings in the form of wood-cuts, litho-

107.   Wood-cut by Aristide Maillol for Longus' Les Pastor-
ales, ou Daphnis et Chloe, 1937.

graphs and etchings, and have given a large number of
"peintres-illustrateurs" an opportunity to put their own personal stamp on modern French book art. Many of these luxury books -- most of them editions of contemporary writers
-- are of high artistic quality and represent the work of great
artists, too numerous for their names to be mentioned here.
Taken together they constitute just as strong a manifestation
of the French spirit as did the work of the great illustrators
of the rococo period. Unfortunately, as was the case then
there have also been produced "bibliophile" books with a handsome exterior that cannot hide the fact that they represent
primarily a speculative appeal to the dubious taste of a wealthy
parvenu clientele.

Wood-cuts received special attention in Bewick's homeland, England. In the periodical "The Dial" artists like
Charles Ricketts, Charles Shannon and Lucien Pissarro had
a chance to express themselves. Pissarro's private press,
the "Eragny Press" issued a series of books with colored illustrations made from wood-cuts that had been transferred to
lithographic stones. William Nicholson and Gordon Craig also
used colored wood cuts. Other modern English book artists,
besides Eric Gill are Paul Nash, Hughes-Stanton and Clifford
Webb.

Wood-cuts have had considerable use in Belgium in
recent times; the vigorous and dramatic pictures of the versa-
tile Frans Masereel are reckoned among the best in this field,
being on a level with the work of the great French artists.
In Poland, Czechoslovakia, Hungary and Russia wood-cut illustration is also important; Russian childrens' books with
illustrations by Wladimir Lebedew and Konstantin W. Kusne-
zow have attracted particular attention in a period when the
Soviet government's demand for a realistic and directly intel-
ligible art has limited artistic freedom of expression in the
field of book illustration.

The Scandinavian countries, especially Sweden and Denmark, have kept abreast of foreign developments in typography in the period since 1914. After the introduction of sturdy
types and close-set text pages by F. Hendriksen, Denmark
had gradually adopted a more varied typography. Architects
like Knud V. Engelhardt and Gunnar Billmann Petersen have
had considerable influence as type experts and have designed
books of great esthetic appeal, as have also Steen Eiler Ras-
mussen and other architects, as well as the art historian Vil-
helm Wanscher and the author Kai Friis Møller. Some have
received their inspiration from English sources, and a few

Betragtninger over anbringelse

af illustrationer i bøger

Af Ejnar Philip

BEMÆRKNINGER OM DANSK BIBLIOPHILIS OPGAVER

Af H.O.LANGE

Aaret 1891 udkom i Forening for Bog-
haandværks Aarsskrift Emil Hannovers
Afhandling: Om at samle paa Bøger. Det
var vel nok den førsteVejledning for danske Bibliophiler, og ved sine kløge og kyn-
dige Anvisninger til Indkjøb, Indbinding og Ordning
af Bøger har denne Afhandling sikkert havt en ikke
ringe Betydning for begyndende Bogsamlere, sparet
dem Penge og Ærgrelser og særlig de Græmmelser,
som principielle og methodiske Fejltagelser og Mis-
greb i Begyndelsen forvolde den Bogven, der først
efterhaanden bliver klar over sine Maal og erhværver
dybere Indsigt og videre Kundskaber.

Siden den Tid er Samlerlysten og Interessen for
den gode, den smukke, den sjældne Bog mangedoblet
i vort Folk. Bibliophili er ikke, som det synes for
mange, en overflødig Luxus, en Udvæxt paa Kultu-
ren, en Udvendiggjørelse af indre, aandelige Værdier;
Bibliophilien er i Virkeligheden et selvfølgeligt Ud-
slag af Aandskulturen, en af de ædle Passioner, der
kun slaa Rod i Kultursamfund, som have naaet en vis
Grad af Modenhed, et nødvendigt og naturligt Ud-
slag af historisk Sans og Følelse for Sammenhængen

Der findes naturligvis elementære regler, som enhver sætterlærling
faar banket ind i hovedet i løbet af sin uddannelse, og som gør det
muligt for ham at gaa i lag med alle almindelige opgaver, der i sig
selv ikke rummer særlige problemer. De findes aftrykt i de fleste
lærebøger om typografi, f. eks. i „Selmars Typografi", og bl. a.
Jan Tschichold har behandlet de lidt mere komplicerede proble-
mer, som anbringelse af billeder i plancheværker frembyder; de er gengivet i Grafisk Teknik nr. 2, juni 1946.

I snart adskillige aar har vi arbejdet med friere titelopbygninger,
som, selvom langt fra alle de eksempler, vi har set, har virket
overbevisende, dog har været en gevinst for typografien, fordi de
har frigjort os for vaneforestillinger, og navnlig fordi de har
bidraget til, at hele bogens typografi blev genstand for større
interesse. Paa samme maade kan det være nyttigt at anskue
problemet billedanbringelse fra andre end tilvante synsvinkler.
Det maa heller ikke glemmes, at de faste regler ofte forflygtiges
i omgangen med reklametypografien, som i kataloger, brochurer,
annoncer og ugeblade arbejder med andre og mere direkte virke-
midler, der ikke ubetinget kan bringes i overensstemmelse med
bogens typografi, selvom de ofte kan virke forfriskende og
inspirerende.

For den læge læser kan det forekomme pedantisk at ville hævde,
at det ikke er ligegyldigt, hvordan man anbringer billederne i en
bog, men den, der har beskæftiget sig med tingene, vil vide, at

7*

108. Page from first issue of Aarbog for Bogvenner (Year-book for Bibliophiles) printed in 1917 by C. Christensen with Scandinavian roman type. Greatly reduced.

109. Page from "Bogvennen," 1955, set in Garamond by F. E. Bording.

can be said to have been fore-runners of the functional trend
that was somewhat in vogue in Denmark for a number of years
at the beginning of the 1930's. Among the most active professional book designers are Viggo Naae and Erik Ellegaard
Frederiksen.

Besides the older Danish presses, some of which have
been mentioned, and which also include the firms of Fr.
Bagge, Nielsen & Lydiche, A. W. Henningsen, Egmont H.
Petersen, J. Jørgensen & Co., Langkjaer, Bording, and others,
there are now several new ones that maintain a high standard,
such as Det Berlingske Bogtrykkeri (Axel Danielsen), Valdemar Pedersen and C. Volmer Nordlunde. The last of these

has also made important contributions to the literature of the history of printing and has been one of the most enthusiastic spokesmen for the modern typographic style of England and America and for their better type faces, which are now seen more and more in Danish books. By far the majority of these presses are found in Copenhagen, but there is also the cooperative press in Odense, as well as the diocesan presses in Aarhus and Aalborg, and three West-Jutland presses, which have all contributed to the progress of Danish typography.

In this period pen-and-ink artists have been active in book illustration. In many instances they had previously made drawings for newspapers where the intimate combination of illustration and text gave them an understanding of modern printing methods and a feeling for the harmony of text and picture. The pioneers in this group were Valdemar Andersen and Axel Nygaard, both naturally gifted artists, and they were followed by many others. Besides these newspaper and periodical artists a number of highly individualistic painters have devoted themselves to book illustration. Of particular interest has been the work of the painter Aksel Jørgensen, as seen in his wood-cut illustrations for the monumental edition of the first part of Oehlenschläger's "Gods of the North;" he also founded a school of graphic art at the Danish Art Academy in 1920, where a number of important wood-cut artists have been trained. Jørgensen's most gifted pupil in this field was Povl Christensen, who made a number of illustrations for Blicher's and H. C. Andersen's works that show his great imaginative powers and his craftsmanship as a wood-carver. This younger group also includes other types of graphic artists.

In Norway and Finland the development in typography has proceeded somewhat more slowly than in the other Scandinavian countries, but in Sweden it has been quite rapid. A notable advance was made there when Akke Kumlien in 1916 became artistic advisor to the Norstedt publishing firm and in the course of a few years completely changed the character of its books. He reacted against the heavy tone of the previous period and through his fondness for Gustavian classicism gave the books a less formal appearance, especially when in the 1920's he introduced the French rococo type, Cochin roman. He was aided by artists like Yngve Berg, whose illustrations for Bellman's works represent a fine adaptation of the Gustavian style, and by Bertil Lybeck whose work still has a tendency toward the grandiose. At this time type faces like Garamond and Bodoni began to take their place in Swedish printing, and in the 1930's the consultant to the great Nordisk Rotogravyr press, Anders Billow, became a spokesman for

UR SVENSKA AKADEMIENS
ARKIV

*

SVENSKA AKADEMIENS

DAGBOK

1 7 8 6 · 1 7 8 9

UTGIFVEN

AF

HENRIK SCHÜCK

STOCKHOLM

P. A. NORSTEDT & SÖNERS FÖRLAG

110.   Title-page designed by Akke Kumlien in the Cochin
style, a modern imitation of the work of the 18th century French
book-artist Cochin.   The type used here was produced at the end
of the 19th century under the name of Cochin roman by the Peignot type foundry in France; it was designed from one of
Pierre Simon Fournier's 18th century types.

elemental typography, which was also accepted even by Hugo
Lagerström.   In our day Swedish printing has been influenced
by modern British typography through the instrumentality of
such men as Carl Z. Häggström, who directs the great press
of Almqvist & Wiksell in Uppsala, and English and American
type faces are now as much used in Sweden as they are in
Denmark.   One modern type designer of considerable significance is Karl-Erik Forsberg, known among other things for
his Berling roman.

In the field of illustrative art newspaper artists have
not played the same role in Sweden as in Denmark, but there
are two that have attained fame as book illustrators: Adolf
Hallman, a master of the French style, and Birger Lundquist,
who achieves his effect with a few quick, bold strokes.   A
number of modern illustrators have also gone back to the 19th

century romantic period for their models, such as Bertil
Bull Hedlund, who also shows evidence of influence from sur-
realistic mysticism. In the 1940's Sweden reissued her illustrated children's books, undoubtedly under the influence of
the revival that Danish children's books experienced in the
previous decade. The fact that modern Swedish book art is
on such a high level is due to the contributions of many individuals as well as of three technical schools: the School for
Book and Advertising Art, the Trade School for Bookmaking
and the Graphical Institute, the latter of which is similar to
the Danish School of Graphic Arts.

In the field of book-binding there was a period toward
the close of the last century when, as in typography, old
models and styles were imitated and with inferior results.
Even though the craftsmanship was of a high order and the
stamps were accurate copies of the old models, these imitations usually lacked the artistic touch and faultless taste of
the old masters. Later, the decoration on many books was
influenced by the plant and animal figures of Japanese art, executed in gold or multicolored leather appliqués, while others
belong rather to the Jugend style, called "Skønvirke" in Denmark.

Thus, as in typography, various modern fashions have
also set their mark on the decoration of book bindings, without however entirely excluding imitations of earlier models.
A very special development in recent English binding is represented by T. J. Cobden-Sanderson and his pupil Douglas
Cockerell. At Cobden-Sanderson's "Doves Bindery" which he
operated from 1900 to 1916, he himself bound the books and
decorated the covers with his own designs, consisting of small
conventional flowers and leaves arranged in groups framed by
straight lines. The title was combined with the decoration of
the binding to form an artistic unit. Of special importance
are also the Danish bindings that Anker Kyster and others
made from designs by the architect Thorvald Bindesbøll.

Bindesbøll might be considered a precursor of cubism,
which played such a great role in art during the years that
preceded the first World War, and which was also frequently
evident in book bindings.   Functionalism, which flourished
between the two World Wars likewise had an influence on the
art of book-binding; it encouraged the greatest possible simplicity in decoration. This influence has continued, and many
of the best bindings of today produce their effect by the high
quality and the treatment of the leather and the other materials
and by the proper combination of colors.

111. Binding in dark green morocco by Anker Kyster with decoration by Thorvald Bindesbøll.

112. Binding in reddish-brown morocco designed and executed by August Sandgren.

Along with the trend toward simplification in the form of this refined functionalism, there are still bindings that make use of excessive gilding or elaborate symbolism. Many modern French bindings are characterized by an overdevelopment of the "reliure parlante" idea. Like the original "narrative bindings" these attempt to indicate the contents of the book, and in many instances the decoration continues as a unit over both the back and the sides. However, instead of direct representation of the contents of the book the attempt is rather to produce an idealized expression of its essence through abstract designs and the use of color. Surrealist tendencies have also appeared in book decoration in France and other countries. One of the most important French binders of our day, along with René Kieffer and Léon Gruel, is Pierre Legrain, who has made extensive use of geometric designs as decorative elements. Others that deserve to be mentioned are Georges Cretté, Paul Bonet, Pierre Martin and women like Jeanne Langrand and Rose Adler; a number of these draw their own designs while others use designs made by other artists.

113. Binding by Paul Bonet in black morocco with white
leather mosaic work and gold-tooled lines.

In Germany, both the Jugend style and cubism have
been much in vogue. The leading German book-binders of the
recent period include Paul Adam and Paul Kersten, later also
Ignaz Wiemeler and Otto Dorfner. The work of the last two
exhibits extreme simplicity in decoration; on many of Dorfner's
bindings the title is also used very effectively as a decorative
feature of the front cover.

The dominant figures in Swedish book-binding have
been Gustav Hedberg, who died in 1920, and his brother Ar-
vid. Their work is in many styles, and they show the influence of Cobden-Sanderson. At the present time the Swedes
have Nils Linde in Gothenburg, a book binder of European
standing; with his faultless taste and daring imagination he and
his collaborators have actually effected a revival in modern
Swedish binding. In other countries there are also binders of
the same stature as those already mentioned but their names

alone would mean little. Anyone desirous of studying modern
fine binding should follow the reports in bibliophile journals
of the exhibitions at Le salon international du livre d'art in
Paris, where most countries, at least those of the western
world, periodically exhibit their finest work, not only in binding but in book arts in general.

Even though artistic bindings are usually done entirely
in leather there are still the far more numerous half-leather
bindings, in which only the spine and the corners are of
leather, the rest being covered with paper, cloth or other material. In these bindings the combination of colors has a significant effect. There are many kinds of paper available to
bookbinders and very attractive bindings can even be made entirely of paper. This is done to some extent in current publishers' bindings, but aside from these and the sturdy English
cloth bindings that usually have no decoration other than the
title on the spine, publishers' bindings are usually in half-
leather. In recent years many so-called "fine" bindings have
been put on the market; bindings with elaborate gilded decoration, but made of poor materials by mass production machine
methods. Still more recently, however, there has been a
clearly detectable improvement in this field; nearly all countries, including Denmark, now produce each year a number of
publishers' bindings that are simply and artistically decorated,
are made of good materials with pleasing color combinations,
and of greater durability than in the past.

No one country can be singled out as the recognized
leader in bookbinding today, nor can we speak of a definite
national style in each country. In general, however, we can
probably say that the reform movement instigated by William
Morris -- including the Jugend offshoot -- has had its greatest
influence on English, American, German, Dutch and Scandinavian book binding. The fine bindings produced in France
present the same variegated appearance that we see in modern French illustrative art; it is generally inclined toward the
picturesque, while that of the southern European countries
follows the historical tradition more closely. In the present
period there is no common or uniform style for all countries
and for all aspects of book art as there was in the baroque
and the rococo periods, and even during the Empire. In fact,
it is questionable whether any such uniformity, in spite of
the greater intercommunication among nations, would be able
to develop today when artistic considerations must often give
way to demands for speed, and life itself is seldom distinguished by any balance or harmony.

The Book Trade

During the first World War the book trade and the publishing business had a prosperous period in the neutral countries, while in the countries at war they were beset by great difficulties, although they did issue a steady stream of small propaganda items in large editions. The German book trade was particularly hard hit, and its fixed retail price and conditional sale system was disrupted for a long time. Its extensive export business also dropped to a minimum. After the Nazis came to power the Börsenverein was incorporated into the so-called Reichskultur office in 1933, and thus the book and publishing trade was brought completely under state control. In May of 1935 a large number of "undesirable" books were confiscated and burned; many authors, publishers, and new and second-hand book dealers to whom the government objected for racial or political reasons left the country and some of them started business anew in other countries, several in the United States.

With the outbreak of the second World War the fateful hour struck for the German book trade. Millions of books in publishers' and book-dealers' stocks were destroyed by aerial bombardment, and when Germany collapsed in 1945 its greatly diminished literary production dropped to almost nothing for a time. The book trade was split up between East and West Germany; the Börsenverein was divided into separate organizations in Frankfurt and in Leipzig, and the large Barsortiment of Koehler & Volckmar was similarly divided. Within West Germany the division into zones created further difficulties, while dealers and publishers in East Germany became subject to the rigid control of the new state. Under these conditions a number of large scientific works that had previously been published in Germany were now issued in America or England, and many German authors had their works published in Holland and Switzerland (several by the leading Swiss publisher, Orell Fussli in Zürich). For a time it appeared that Switzerland might become the center of publishing on the continent, but in very recent years the German book business has again revived and has shown that it is capable of handling projects of considerable size. German second-hand dealers, however, have not as yet recovered their former position, except to a limited extent, and several of the most outstanding of the former second-hand dealers are now carrying on their business in other countries.

In France and England, in spite of the disruption and destruction caused by the two wars the book trade suffered less, even though the aerial bombardment of the second World War caused great losses to London book stocks, and the head-quarters of the English book dealers' association, Stationer's Hall, was destroyed. In England the fight for the adoption of a fixed retail price continued down into the 1920's, but it has now been won to the extent that no books marked "net" may be sold at a price below that printed on them. The disposal of remainder stocks is still a characteristic feature of the English book trade, although there are signs in very recent years that publishers will instead adopt the practice of making annual price reductions as is commonly done in the Scandi-navian countries.

As mentioned earlier, most of the larger American publishing firms are located in New York, where the larger book dealers are also found. One of the most important of modern publishers is Doubleday & Co., which also operates a score of book stores in various cities and several book clubs with a total of over 2 million members. These clubs bear witness to the wide-spread interest in reading as do al-so the inexpensive Pocket Books editions, which, like the Penguin Books issued in England since 1935 make popular sci-entific works and classical literature available to large sec-tions of the population. An important part is played by the presses that are operated by the larger American universities on the pattern of those at Oxford and Cambridge, and a num-ber of book clubs also engage in the publication of limited ed-itions of fine books. On the other hand American publishers every year print enormous editions of "best-sellers," which are distributed in large quantities in other English-speaking countries. Along with retail bookselling, direct canvassing by agents is carried on to a greater extent in the United States than in Europe, where it is still an important factor in the book business and is an economic necessity for some pub-lishing firms; many encyclopedias, reference books, and col-lected works of literary writers would be difficult to publish without this method of distribution.

The United States has not subscribed to the Berne Convention, which was adopted in 1886 by the majority of European countries for the mutual protection of literary and artistic property rights; since 1948 this right is effective for 50 years after the death of the author. The United States, however, has its own Copyright Act, adopted in 1909, which in general protects an author's rights for 28 years after pub-lication when the book carries a notice of copyright. Each book is entered on a list issued by the Library of Congress; it is al-so required that two copies of the book be deposited in the

Library. In 1952 a World Copyright Union was established
in Geneva but it did not go as far as the Berne Convention,
which is still in force.

Along with the United States the Soviet Union is also
outside the Berne Convention, and hence foreign books can be
published there without remuneration to the author. However,
many works of foreign authors are not acceptable for publication in Soviet countries or the countries under Soviet domina-
tion, since all publishing is under the control of the State and
books that do not agree with its ideology are rejected. Nevertheless, there is a great need for books in Russia today, and
even though book production figures have been up in the millions in recent years it is still far from adequate. Besides
the great Russian and foreign classics, literature on questions
of national economy and on technical subjects is very much in
demand, and there is also an unusually good market for children's books.

In the book trade in the Scandinavian countries the influence from Germany has continued, but in recent years
there have also been influences from the Anglo-Saxon world.
Book production figures for the Scandinavian countries are
very high in relation to the population figures; the ratio is
highest in Iceland where the capital city has about 20 book
stores for some 60,000 inhabitants. In 1949 slightly over
4,000 book titles were published in Denmark, but since then
the annual production has been going down as the price of
books has risen; in 1955 it was down to about 2,600 titles in
an average edition of 6,000 copies.

In addition to the Danish publishing firms mentioned
earlier there are now many new firms. The firm of Ejnar
Munksgaard is somewhat in a class by itself and since the
1920's has become internationally known for its large facsimile editions of Icelandic, Swedish, Old Persian and Mexican
manuscripts and for the many scientific journals that it pub-
lishes; facsimiles are also issued by Rosenkilde og Bagger.
During the years between the two wars the librarian Aage
Marcus was engaged in publishing important humanistic literature in books of high technical quality. Finally, a publishing
business was started by the Danish cooperative movement in
1941 on the Swedish pattern; Det Danske Forlag it is called,
and its books are sold through cooperative retail outlets and
also through regular book stores.

One of the new book stores that have been opened in
Copenhagen in recent years is Boghallen; the large department

stores like Illum and Magasin du Nord have also set up book
departments as in the United States.   In addition, several of
the new publishers, like the older ones, also operate sizable
book stores, usually with second-hand departments.   This is
true, for example, of Munksgaard and Rosenkilde og Bagger.
With Branners Antikvariat and Boghallen these firms are among
the best known of Danish second-hand dealers.

New publishing firms have similarly been established
in Norway and Sweden in the recent period; as in Denmark
they often operate retail book stores with second-hand departments as well.

Libraries

The period from 1914 to the present has been one of
the strangest in the history of libraries.   While public libraries have achieved a stronger position than every before and
have experienced an extraordinary growth in both their internal
and external functions, this period has also witnessed the
greatest destruction of books and libraries that the world has
probably known since the days of the barbarian invasions.

In the first World War the losses were relatively small
and the only library that was completely destroyed was that of
the University of Louvain, which was burned when German
troops captured the town.   In return German libraries felt the
effects of the war and the subsequent period of inflation by
being cut off from foreign book markets and having their financial support undermined.   Between 1920 and 1930, however, the "Notgemeinschaft der deutschen Wissenchaft," which
had been organized after the war, provided considerable financial aid, but when this came to an end, the situation a-
gain deteriorated.   In 1933 the Göttingen library, for example,
had to discontinue all its periodical subscriptions.   Other difficulties also arose at that time when the new Nazi government came to power.   The Nazis' plan of bringing the entire
German library system together in a single unit may have
been good, but the unfortunate aspect of it was that libraries were made a political instrument subject to the ideology
of the party, with all book purchases controlled by a central
purchasing office in Cologne.   Long lists were compiled of
prohibited books that were to be removed from libraries,
Jews were denied the use of public libraries, and at the same
time a special library was established in Frankfort for the
study of international Jewry.

Some of the books added to this library had been
seized by the Germans in the countries that they occupied
during the first period of the second World War. Like Napoleon's armies of an earlier day, the German troops were
also accompanied by experts who picked out the most valuable
parts of the libraries that were taken over. This was done
extensively in the Balkans and even more so in Poland; here
the books that were not taken back to Germany were in large
part collected at the Krasinski Library in Warsaw, and shortly before the German troops had to leave the city in 1944
they set fire to this library as well as to the municipal library. Many Polish public libraries were also burned, at least
the Polish parts of their collection. Similar action was taken
in the case of book dealers' and publishers' stocks and numerous private collections, all for the purpose of destroying
Poland's national culture. Fortunately the old Jagellon Library in Krakow was saved; its book treasures as well as the
magnificent new building that had been provided for it just before the war.

Other countries also had their libraries plundered and
destroyed by the Nazis, but a frightful nemesis was to visit
German libraries when aerial warfare began in earnest. It
has been calculated that German libraries lost about a third
of the more than 75 million volumes that they contained before the war. At the outbreak of the war the most valuable
portions of the collections had been moved to the library cel-
lars, and it was not till very late in the war that they were
evacuated to castles, churches, monasteries and mines, where
some of the material was destroyed by dampness or fire.
Before this evacuation took place bombs had already partly or
wholly destroyed a large number of library buildings. The
two most magnificent of German libraries, the Preussische
Staatsbibliothek in Berlin and the Bayerische Staatsbibliothek
in Munich, were largely in ruins at the end of the war, and
the buildings of the following libraries were totally or almost
totally destroyed; the university libraries of Bonn, Breslau,
Frankfort, Giessen, Hemburg, Münster and Würzburg, and
the regional libraries in Dresden, Darmstadt, Karlsruhe,
Kassel and Stuttgart; several of the old city libraries and a
number of technical and special libraries were also destroyed.
Many other libraries were heavily damaged, and several lost
their entire catalog or parts of it.

It was unavoidable that this catastrophe should have
serious effects in the years immediately following the war;
German culture and science had suffered an irreplaceable and
almost inconceivable loss. The Preussische Staatsbibliothek

alone had lost a million and a half printed books, almost
6,000 incunabula and about 6,700 manuscripts, or more than
the entire contents of the Royal Library in Copenhagen.
Most of what remained was taken to Marburg where it was
to form the basis for a new West German central library.
Many of the ruined libraries found temporary, though often
very unsuitable quarters, but to build up their book collections
again was another problem; only slight assistance was provided by the "Deutsche Forschungsgemeinschaft," a revival of
the earlier "Notgemeinschaft," or by the gifts from abroad.
But the ability of the German people to rally in an apparently
hopeless situation and under harsh living conditions, as well
as their organizational ability has asserted itself also in the
field of library activity. At various places throughout the
country regional union catalogs are being compiled, and liberal loan arrangements have been instituted between the individual libraries. To replace the Deutsche Bücherei, which
now operates only in East Germany, a new library was established in Frankfort in 1946 where all new German books are
collected and a current German bibliography is compiled. In
spite of all these efforts, however, the great libraries of Germany will always carry the marks of the catastrophe of the
second World War, and will always be limited in their ability
to maintain the cultural contacts with the past that are of special importance today with our rapid advances in technology.
One ray of hope for German popular libraries appeared in
1954 when the Americans gave West Berlin a great "Berliner
Zentralbibliothek," built and arranged on the pattern of an
American public library. In it Germany has for the first time
a completely modern public library which will certainly in
time be imitated in other cities of West Germany. An en-
couraging event for the scholarly library system is the reap-
pearance of Milkau's great "Handbuch der Bibliothekswissenschaft," originally published in 1931-42. Publication of the
new and greatly expanded edition began in 1952 under the direction of the former head of the University Library in Tübingen, Georg Leyh.

Germany was not the only country that was damaged
by aerial bombardment, although nowhere else was the damage
nearly so great. In Bulgaria the National Library in Sofia
was completely destroyed, and in Yugoslavia the Germans destroyed or carried off great quantities of books and the national library in Belgrade was extensively damaged. Libraries in Czechoslovakia lost over 3 million volumes, mainly
in the Sudeten area. In Austria and Hungary, and presumably
also in Russia, the damage was less serious; the same is true
of Holland and Belgium, but the Louvain University Library

was destroyed a second time. In France the university libraries of Caen and Strasbourg were destroyed and also the
municipal libraries of Caen, Douai, Cambrai and Tours, and
in the towns of Beauvais, Brest, Chartres, Dunkerque, Lori-
ent, St. Malo, Vitry-le-françois, Metz and others the libraries were partially destroyed. In all, French libraries lost
over 2 million volumes, but none of the large collections in
Paris were affected. Neither did Italy fare as badly as might
have been expected, although part of the Monte Cassino monastery was hit and the libraries in Bologna, Messina, Milan,
Naples, Parma, Pisa and Turin suffered considerable losses.
The most important library treasures from Monte Cassino and
other monasteries and churches as well as from the various
state libraries had already been taken to the Vatican Library,
which like the other libraries of Rome escaped damage. In
England libraries in Liverpool, Bristol, Plymouth, Portsmouth
and other towns were hit, but in general the bombardment was
as we know, concentrated mainly on the capital and its surroundings. The University College Library in London was destroyed, and at the British Museum Annex outside the city a
bomb did away with a great part of the collection of English
provincial newspapers. At the National Central Library more
than 100,000 volumes were lost.

This last chapter in the history of libraries is not,
however, merely an account of war disasters and the destruction of books. There are also many brighter developments
to be noted. Among these we naturally think first of the many
new modern library buildings that have already been erected
to take the place of those that were destroyed, such as the
new National Library in Sofia and the University College Library in London, and also those that have been built to replace existing but antiquated and overcrowded structures, and
the additions that have been made to other libraries, the most
impressive of the latter being perhaps the new Annex to the
Library of Congress providing stack space for an additional
10 million volumes. To list the new library buildings of recent years in the various countries would require too much
space, and however impressive and significant an advance they
represent, it is equally important to point out the new attitude that libraries have adopted in recent years in their relations with their patrons and the intensive work that many of
them are doing to make their contents as easily accessible as
possible. In this respect technical libraries have made the
greatest advance through their work in documentation, which
covers not only books and periodicals but also includes pamphlet material, patents, standards and other literature; new
technical features and new principles for subject cataloging

114. Left, library interior with alcoves in the old section of the Bodleian Library at Oxford; reading desks in each alcove. Right, steel book-stacks with adjustable shelves in the new section of the same library.

are constantly being adopted.

No less important is the increasingly difficult fight that libraries are waging to master the enormous book production of the present. During the war years this production decreased temporarily, but now new countries have come into the field. Libraries are faced with an eternal space problem; although the capacity of book stacks is being fully utilized, the problem of additional space continues to increase and will require new solutions; one of the latest of these is the solid stack with its double sections of shelves enclosed in dust-tight cases and running on rails so they can be pushed tightly together or rolled apart by electrical power. This type of stack can hold twice as many books as the standard type, and its use has spread from Switzerland, where it was invented, to German, French and Scandinavian libraries; it is used especially for collections of manuscripts, rare and little-used books and periodical files.

With the great increase in the world's literary productivity it has become more important than ever before that
libraries be assured of adequate financial support, and on the
other hand that careful decisions be made regarding book purchases and periodical subscriptions. The selection of books
has always been the most difficult of the librarian's tasks,
and in the present age of intensive specialization the difficulty
as well as the importance of making the proper choice from
the large number of possibilities is even greater. Here as
in the case of so many other library problems the proper
course is to establish cooperative arrangements among the libraries of any one country; with respect to book acquisition
this means that the purchase of unnecessary duplicates can be
avoided and instead a greater number of different titles and
periodicals can be acquired by the cooperating libraries. As
an example is the division of subjects that was adopted in
1927 by Danish research libraries, or the commission that was
appointed some years ago to coordinate the book purchasing
of the larger libraries of Paris, or finally the so-called
"Farmington plan" by which the various fields of literature
have been distributed among a number of the leading American libraries under a large-scale cooperative purchasing program that would insure the acquisition of a copy of every
foreign book that could conceivably be of interest to Americans
by at least one American library. West German libraries
have had to adopt a similar distribution of fields because of
their limited funds. The international exchange of the publications of scientific societies and institutions and of official
government documents has also been important to libraries.

Another feature of library cooperation has been the establishment of union catalogs for certain groups of libraries,
such as the one that was set up in the Royal Library at The
Hague for about 50 Dutch libraries, or the one that is being
compiled at the Bibliothèque Nationale to cover the foreign
book holdings of some 400 French libraries. German union
catalogs have already been mentioned, and in Great Britain
the National Central Library is performing a similar function
to that of the Library of Congress in the United States. The
Library of Congress also issues printed catalog cards of its
accessions and distributes them to other libraries. However,
with the growing complexity of cataloging it has become more
and more difficult to keep library catalogs up-to-date; even
the cataloging divisions of many large American libraries,
where hundreds of people are employed, are plagued with
backlogs.

When speaking of union catalogs it is natural to men-

tion the cooperation that is being practiced in the loan of
books among libraries within the same country and also between the libraries of different countries. Photostating and
microfilming are, however, coming more and more into use
so that instead of sending out the book or periodical, the library sends a photostat or a micro-film of the portion that
the borrower needs. In the case of periodical articles, manuscripts and rare books in particular this method has become
an important feature of library loan work, and in time even
more practical and less expensive methods will undoubtedly be
found. Microfilming is also one of the devices that is being
used to meet the problem of space, especially for large collections of newspapers and it also protects these from damage
by frequent handling. Similarly, microfilming can be used
to preserve copies of manuscripts and rare or irreplaceable
books should the originals be destroyed, and also for acquir-
ing copies of books and manuscripts from other libraries.
For example, American libraries are now in the process of
filming everything in the way of source material for American
history that is to be found in European libraries and is not already in the United States.

The many problems that the intensive library activity
of the present day gives rise to, and of which only a part have
been mentioned here, are continually being discussed in library periodicals and at library meetings, such as those held by
UNESCO and the international library and documentation organizations. There is also great interest in the training of librarians; in some cases this is done at special schools while
in other cases library training is offered by universities and
in still others it is provided by courses at the libraries themselves. Great progress has been made in teaching the technical skills involved; the weak point, especially from the standpoint of scholarly libraries, is knowledge of books and of their
history, and in this respect the librarians of today cannot
measure up to the scholarly librarians of earlier times.

This situation has caused considerable difficulty particularly in the United States as large quantities of manuscripts
and rare old books have found their way to American libraries.
In most other respects, however, it is the Americans that are
the leaders in the library world today, partly because they usually have financial means at their disposal far beyond what
European libraries can hope for. Throughout the United States
and Canada libraries of all types and sizes have either recently built or are planning new buildings. The American Library
Association has appointed a permanent committee where librarians discuss their experiences and problems with architects

115. Iowa State University Library building, erected in 1951.

in an attempt to arrive at the most practical building design
to meet the actual needs of everyday library service. The
catalog now occupies a dominant location, reading desks have
been provided even in the stacks, and the building is designed
on the principle of flexibility so that its interior can be arranged whenever a new distribution of the space is required.
The first library depots or warehouses have been built near
Boston and in Chicago; in these, libraries within the area can
store their little-used books and thus save their own valuable
space.

Turning to the other great world power of today, the
Soviet Union, we find that the library movement has had a
much later development than in the United States and did not
become effective until after the Russian Revolution. The largest library in the Soviet Union, the Lenin Library in Moscow,
is now said to contain 15 million volumes besides large collections of manuscripts, incunabula and oriental material; it is also a great cultural center like the New York Public Library,

being a combination of research library and popular library.
In the capitals of the various Soviet republics there are also
state libraries, many of them rich in manuscript and printed
material for the study of the history of the county. These
function as centers for the network of popular libraries that
now covers the entire Union. They also send travelling book
collections to out-of-the-way places by bus, sleigh, motor-
boat and airplane -- a rural service similar to that provided
by English regional libraries or the Scandinavian central libraries.

  The uniformity that characterizes library service within both the United States and the Soviet Union is not found to
the same degree in Western Europe. Here there is considerable variation from one country to another, partly because of
different historical backgrounds and strong national traditions.
In countries like Italy and France centralization had gradually
been achieved and in the case of France became still more
effective when a unified administration was established in 1951
for all the libraries of the country. In England the situation
has been exactly the opposite; here the individual libraries are
largely independent and the initiative for cooperative projects
comes from the British Library Association rather than from
the government. In Switzerland the division into cantons has
hindered any uniform development, though the founding of the
Landesbibliothek in Berne in 1895 did provide a national library for the entire country, and the Schweizerische Volks-
bibliothek, founded in 1920, functions as a central agency for
popular libraries. In countries like Italy and Spain popular
libraries are still lagging and the same can in general be said
of Holland and Belgium where strong religious oppositions
have hindered their growth; Antwerp is the only city of the
Netherlands with a modern system of public libraries. These
countries have not yet accepted the impulses from England
and the United States; on the other hand the influence from
these two sources has been very effective in the Scandinavian
countries. In 1920 Denmark became the first of them to
adopt public library legislation, with state support based on
local contribution; since then Danish popular libraries have
had a rapid development, those of the other Scandinavian countries following somewhat more slowly.

  Research libraries in both America and Europe have
not profited so much from the work of private collectors in
recent years as they did in earlier times; nevertheless, the
collections of David Simonsen and Lazarus Goldschmidt have
made the Royal Library in Copenhagen a center for Jewish
studies, and the University Library in Uppsala has received

from the physician Erik Waller the gift of his internationally
famous collection for the study of the history of medicine.
Other Scandinavian library "patrons" of the present time are
the Danes V. R. Christiansen and A. Jurisch and the Swedes
Gustaf Bernström and Thore Virgin.

The stream of books going to the United States from
Europe is not so great now as formerly; in Switzerland, for
example Martin Bodmer in Coligny near Geneva has in the
course of the last three decades built up a collection of manuscripts, incunabula and first editions that can compete in
monetary value with the Huntington Library in California.

In Asiatic as well as in eastern European countries,
where illiteracy still creates enormous difficulties, modern
public library systems are beginning to develop. This is
true, for instance, in India, Indonesia, the Chinese People's
Republic and Japan. There is no doubt, either, that other
countries that are gradually freeing themselves from European
control and developing their own national culture will recognize the importance of public libraries as a cultural factor.

Pessimistic voices are heard from time to time pre-
dicting that the day of the book will be displaced by newspapers and magazines, motion pictures, radio and television.
It cannot, of course, be denied that many persons' reading
does not go beyond the daily newspapers, picture magazines,
and comic books, or that motion pictures, radio and television take up much of their free time. The amount of this
free time will increase as the standard of living rises, but
no one can say whether this will mean greater possibilities
for the use of books. New technical discoveries in the field
of what is called "mass communication" will be competing
with books to an even greater degree than at present, and
hence no comforting parallels can be drawn from earlier periods.

In spite of all this there is still reason to believe that
the history of the book will not end with the end of the 20th
century. It is no accident, for example, that illiteracy is
being combatted so vigorously where it still exists, and that
books play an important role in the program of UNESCO.
There will continue to be a place for the book as a practical
means of communication, since it has a very significant advantage over the other transitory and ephemeral means -- the
book is an enduring repository for the thoughts, knowledge, emo-
tions and imagination of mankind, every ready to open itself anew.

Bibliography

Books and the History of Books in General

Das alte Buch und seine Ausstattung vom 15.-19. Jahrhundert. Hrsg. von M. Gerlach. Wien [1915]. (Die Quelle. Mappe XIII).

Otto Andersen: Boghaandvaerket. 3. udg. Kbh. 1954.

J. Christian Bay: The Fortune of Books. Essays, Memories and Prophecies of a Librarian. Chic. 1941.

André Blum: Les origines du papier, de l'imprimerie et de la gravure. Paris 1935.

En Bog om Bogen. Under Redaktion af Aage Marcus. Kbh. 1950.

Bogen. En Haandbog for Boghandlere og Bogvenner. Udg. af Otto Andersen og Aleks. Frøland. Kbh. 1925.

Hans Bohatta: Einführung in die Buchkunde. Wien 1928.

Bokvandringar. Uppstatser om böcker och samlare under red. av J. Viktor Johansson. Sthlm. 1945.

F. Calot, L. M. Michon et P. Angoulvent: L'art du livre en France des origines à nos jours. Paris 1931.

Albert Cim: Le livre. Historique, fabrication, achat, classement, usage et entretien. Tome 1-5. Paris 1905-08.

D. W. Davies: The World of the Elzeviers, 1580-1712. Haag 1954.

K. Fleischhack: Wege zum Wissen. Buch, Buchhandel, Bibliotheken. 2. erweit. Aufl. Würzburg 1940.

Eric de Grolier: Histoire du livre. Paris 1954.

Haandbog i Bibliotekskundskab. Udg. af Svend Dahl. 3. forøgede udgave. Bd. 1-2. Kbh. 1924-27. -- Svensk udgave ved Samuel E. Bring. Bd. 1-2. Sthlm. 1924-31.

Handbuch der Bibliothekswissenschaft. 2. Aufl. hrsg. von Georg Leyh. Bd I: Buch und Schrift. Wiesbaden 1952. -- Bd. 3: Geschichte der Bibliotheken. Sst. 1955 ff. (endnu ikke afsluttet).

J. Viktor Johannson: Från Gutenbergbiblen till Gösta Berlings Saga. Vandringar i Bibliotheca Quarnforsiana. Sthlm. 1952.

Wilhelm H. Lange: Das Buch im Wandel der Zeiten. 6. Aufl. Wiesbaden 1951.

Hellmut Lehmann-Haupt: A History of the Making and Selling

of Books in the United States. 2. ed. New York 1951.
Lexikon des Buchwesens. Hrsg. von Joachim Kirchner. Bd. 1-4. Stuttg. 1952-56.
F. C. Lonchamp: Manuel du bibliophile français (1470-1920). Tome 1-2. Paris 1927.
Wilhelm Munthe: Boknåm. Essays for bokvenner. Oslo 1943.
Bert Möller: Svensk bokhistoria. Sthlm. 1931.
Lauritz Nielsen: Den danske Bog. Forsøg til en dansk Bog-historie fra de aeldste Tider til Nutiden. Kbh. 1941.
Nordisk Leksikon for Bogvaesen. Red. af Esli Dansten, Lauritz Nielsen og Palle Birkelund. Bd. 1 ff. Kbh. 1949 ff. (endnu ikke afsluttet).
Leo S. Olschki: Le livre italien à travers les âges. Florence 1914.
W. Dana Orcutt: The Book in Italy during the 15th and 16th century. London 1928.
Johs. Pedersen: Den arabiske Bog. Kbh. 1946.
K. F. Plesner: Bøger. Kbh. 1942.
K. F. Plesner: Mellem reoler. Kbh. 1947.
G. J. Poršnev: Das Buchwesen in der U.S.S.R. Ein kurzer Abriss. Berlin 1927.
Karl Schottenloher: Bücher bewegen die Welt. Eine Kultur-geschichte des Buches. Bd. 1-2. Stuttg. 1951-52.
Karl Schottenloher: Das alte Buch. 3. Aufl. Braunschweig 1956.
Albert Schramm: Das Schreib- und Buchwesen einst und jetzt. Lpz. 1928.
Henrik Schück: Bidrag till svensk bokhistoria. Sthlm. 1900.
O. Weise: Schrift- und Buchwesen in alter und neuer Zeit. 3. Aufl. Lpz. 1910.

Papyrus and Paper

En bok om papper tillägnad Carl Joh. Malmros. Upps. 1944.
Ch. M. Briquet: Les filigranes. Dictionnaire historique des marques du papier 1282-1600. Tome 1-4. Genève 1907. (Nytryk Lpz. 1925).
W. A. Churchill: Watermarks in Paper in Holland, England, France etc. in the XVII and XVIII Centuries. Amst. 1935.
Dard Hunter: Papermaking. The History and Technique of an ancient Craft. 2. ed. New York 1947.
Karl Preisendanz: Papyrusfunde und Papyrusforschung. Lpz. 1935.
Armin Renker: Das Buch vom Papier. 4. Ausg. Lpz. 1951.
Wilhelm Schubart: Einführung in die Papyruskunde. Berlin 1918.

Writing, Manuscripts and Illumination

P. d'Ancona: Le miniature italienne du 10e au 16e siecle. Paris et Brux. 1925.

P. d'Ancona et E. Aeschlimann: Dictionnaire des miniaturistes. 2. éd. Milano 1949.

Erich Bethe: Buch und Schrift im Altertum. Lpz. u. Wien 1945.

Erich Bethe: Buch und Bild im Altertum. Lpz. u. Wien 1945.

Theodor Birt: Das antike Buchwesen. Berlin 1882.

P. Blanchon-Lasserve: Écriture et enluminure des manuscrits du 9e au 12e siècle. Paris 1926-31.

A. Blum et Ph. Lauer: La miniature française aux 15e et 16e siècles. Paris et Brux. 1930.

A. W. Byvanck: La miniature dans les Pays-Bas septentrionaux. Paris 1937.

Albert Boeckler: Abendländische Miniaturen bis zum Ausgang der romanischen Zeit. Berlin u. Lpz. 1930.

L. Coellen: Die Stilentwicklung der Schrift im christlichen Abendlande. U. st. 1922.

E. Crous und J. Kirchner: Die gotischen Schriftarten. Berlin 1928.

H. Delitsch: Geschichte der abendländischen Schreibschriftformen. Lpz. 1928.

Karl Dziatzko: Untersuchungen über ausgewählte Kapitel des antiken Buchwesens. Lpz. 1900.

J. G. Fevrier: Histoire de l'écriture. Paris 1948.

A. Goldschmidt: Die deutsche Buchmalerei. Bd. 1-2. Firenze u. München 1928.

Greek and Latin Illuminated Manuscripts in Danish Collections. Kbh. 1921.

Gyldne bøger. Illuminerede middelalderlige håndskrifter i Danmark og Sverige (Nationalmuseet). (Katalog of Kåre Olsen og Carl Nordenfalk. Indledn. af Carl Nordenfalk). Kbh. 1952. -- Svensk udg. Sthlm. 1952.

J. A. Herbert: Illuminated Manuscripts. 2. ed. London 1912.

H. Hermannsson: Icelandic Illuminated Manuscripts of the Middle Ages. Copenh. 1935.

Hermann Hieber: Die Miniaturen des frühen Mittelalters. München 1912.

Carsten Høeg: Skrift og Bog i den klassiske Oldtid. Kbh. 1942.

M. Rh. James: The Wanderings and Homes of Manuscripts. Cambr. 1928.

H. Jensen: Die Schrift in Vergangenheit und Gegenwart. Glückstadt u. Hamburg 1935.

F. G. Kenyon: Ancient Books and modern Discoveries. Oxford 1927.

F. G. Kenyon: Books and Readers in ancient Greece and Rome. 2. ed. Oxford 1951.

Karl Löffler: Einführung in die Handschriftenkunde. Lpz. 1929.

F. Madan: Books in Manuscript. London 1893.

H. Martin: Les miniaturistes français. Paris 1906.

H. Martin: La miniature française du 13e au 15e siècle. 2. éd. Paris et Brux. 1924.

W. A. Mason: A History of the Art of Writing. New York 1920.

E. G. Millar: La miniature anglaise. Paris et Brux. 1926-28.

Lauritz Nielsen: Danmarks middelalderlige Haandskrifter. En sammenfattende boghistorisk Oversigt. Kbh. 1937.

H. L. Pinner: The World of Books in Classical Antiquity. Leiden 1948.

M. Salmi: Italian Miniatures. New York 1956.

O. Elfrida Saunders: English Illumination. Vol. 1-2. Firenze and Paris 1928.

Wilhelm Schubart: Das Buch bei den Griechen und Römern. Berl. u. Lpz. 1921.

Franz Steffens: Lateinische Paläographie. 125 Tafeln in Lichtdruck mit einer systematischen Darstellung der Entwicklung der lateinischen Schrift. Trier 1909.

E. M. Thompson: An Introduction in Greek and Latin Palaeography. Oxford 1912.

W. Wattenbach: Das Schriftwesen im Mittelalter. 3. verm. Aufl. Lpz. 1896. F. Winkler: Die flämische Buchmalerei des 15. u. 16. Jahrhunderts. Lpz. 1925.

The Art of Printing and Book-Making

Harry G. Aldis: The Printed Book. Cambr. 1916.

H. Barge: Geschichte der Buchdruckerkunst von ihrn Anfängen bis zur Gegenwart. Lpz. 1940.

Konrad F. Bauer: Aventur und Kunst. Eine Chronik des Buchdruckgewerbes. Frankf. a. M. 1940.

Carl Björkbom: Gutenberg. Upps. 1951.

G. A. E. Bogeng: Geschichte der Buchdruckerkunst. Bd. 1-2. Lpz. u. Berlin 1930-41.

Bogtrykkerbogen. Laerebog ved Mesterprøven. Red. af O. Hassing og C. Volmer Nordlunde. Kbh. 1946. (Ny udg. under udgivelse).

Der Buchdruck des 15. Jehrhunderts. Eine bibliographische Übersicht hrsg. von der Wiegendruckgesellschaft. Berlin

1929-36.

Isak Collijn: Svensk boktryckerehistoria under 14- och 1500-talen. Sthlm. 1947.

Isak Collijn: Svensk typografisk atlas. 1400- och 1500-talen. Sthlm. 1952.

Svend Dahl og Thomas Døssing: Bogtrykkerkunsten. Kbh. 1940.

Dansk Boghaandvaerk gennem Tiderne. 1482-1948. Kbh. 1949.

Deutscher Buchdruck im Jahrhundert Gutenbergs. Hrsg. von der Preussischen Staatsbibliothek und der Gesellschaft für Typenkunde des 15. Jahrhunderts. Berlin 1940.

E. Gordon Duff: Early Printed Books. London 1893.

E. Gordon Duff: Fifteenth Century English Books. Oxford 1917.

F. H. Ehmcke: Die historische Entwicklung der abendländischen Schriftformen. Ravensburg 1927.

E. P. Goldschmidt: The Printed Book of the Renaissance. Cambridge 1950.

Grafiska yrken. Red. av Bror Zachrisson. Bd. 1-2. Sthlm. 1956.

Henry Guppy: Stepping Stones to the Art of Typography. London 1928.

A History of the Printed Book. Ed. by L. C. Wroth. New York 1938.

Konrad Haebler: Handbuch der Inkunabelkunde. Lpz. 1925.

D. C. McMurtrie: The Book. The Story of Printing and Bookmaking. 3. revised ed. London 1943.

H. Meisner und J. Luther: Die Erfindung der Buchdruckerkunst. Bielefeld u. Lpz. 1900.

Stanley Morison: Four Centuries of Fine Printing. 2. revised ed. London 1949.

Lauritz Nielsen: Boghistoriske Studier til dansk Bibliografi 1550-1600. Kbh. 1923.

Lauritz Nielsen: Dansk typografisk Atlas 1482-1600. Kbh. 1934.

C. Volmer Nordlunde: Bogskrifter og Bogtrykkere. Kbh. 1945.

Nils Nordqvist: Berömda boktryckare. Sthlm. 1954.

J. C. Oswald: A History of Printing. Its Development through 500 Years. London 1928.

Ejnar Philip og C. Volmer Nordlunde: Bogtrykkets fortid og nutid. (Kalligrafi og bogskrift. Fra Kelmscott Press til Penguin Books). Kbh. 1952.

H. R. Plomer: A short History of English Printing 1476-1900. London 1927.

Alfred W. Pollard: Fine Books. London 1912.

Printing. A History of the Art. ed. by R. A. Peddie. London 1927.

W. Ransom: Private Presses and the Books they have given us. London 1929.

Paul Renner: Die Kunst der Typographie. 2. Aufl. Berlin 1948.

Volmer Rosenkilde: Europaeiske bibeltryk, Omkring den Rosendahlske bibelsamling. Esbjerg 1952.

Aloys Ruppel: Johannes Gutenberg. Sein Leben und sein Werk. 2. Aufl. Berlin 1947.

F. A. Schmidt-Künsemüller: Die Erfinderung des Buchdrucks als techniches Phänomen. Mainz 1951.

Oliver Simon and Julius Rodenberg: Printing of To-Day. An illustrated Survey of Postwar-Typography in Europe and the United States. London 1928.

S. H. Steinberg: Five Hundred Years of Printing. Penguin Books 1955.

Jan Tschichold: Geschichte der Schrift in Bildern. Hamburg 1941.

Daniel Berkeley Updike: Printing Types, their History, Forms and Use. Vol. 1-2. Cambr., Mass. 1922.

Harold Williams: History of Book Clubs and Printing Societies in Great Britain and Ireland. (First Edition Club) London 1929.

E. Vouillième: Die deutschen Drucker des 15. Jahrhunderts. 2. Aufl. Berlin 1922.

Book Illustration

Anthologie du livre illustré par les peintres et sculpteurs de l'école de Paris. Avant-propos de Claude Roger-Marx. Genève 1946.

D. Bland: The Illustration of Books. London 1951.

A. Blum: Les origines du livre à gravure en France. Paris 1928.

Lothar Brieger: Das goldene Zeitalter der französischen Illustration. München 1924.

R. Brun: Le livre illustré en France au XVIe siècle. Paris 1930.

Henri Cohen: Guide de l'amateur de livres à gravure du 18. siècle. 6. éd. Paris 1912. [Nytryk af 4. éd. Lpz. 1924].

Walter Crane: On the Decorative Illustration of Books. 3. ed. London 1921.

A, J. J. Delen: Histoire de la gravure dans les anciens Pays-Bas et dans les provinces belges des origines jusqu'à la fin du XVIIIe siècle. Tome 1-2. Paris 1924-34.

Raymond Hesse: Le livre d'art du XIXe siècle à nos jours. Paris [u. aar].

Arthur M. Hind: History of Engraving and Etching. 3. ed.

London 1923.

Arthur M. Hind: An Introduction to a History of Woodcut. Vol. 1-2. London 1935.

Philip James: English Book Illustration 1800-1900. Harmondsworth 1947.

Niels J. Johnsen: Døler og troll. Fra norsk illustrasjonskunsts historie. Oslo 1935.

Paul Kristeller: Kupferstich und Holzschnitt in vier Jarhunderten. 4. Aufl. Berlin 1922.

Th. Kutschmann: Geschichte der deutschen Illustration vom ersten Auftreten des Holzschnitts bis auf die Gegenwart. Bd. 1-2. Goslar u. Berlin 1896-99.

Karl Madsen: Franske Illustratorer fra det XVIII Aarhundrede. Kbh. 1929.

Theodor Musper: Der Holzschnitt in fünf Jahrhunderten. Stuttg. 1944.

R. Muther: Die deutsche Buchillustration der Gotik und Frührenaissance. Bd. 1-2. München 1884.

B. H. Newdigate: The Art of the Book. (Studio. Special Number). London 1938.

Alfred W. Pollard: Early Illustrated Books. A History of the Decoration and Illustration of Books in the 15th and 16th Centuries. London 1917.

Felix Poppenberg: Buchkunst. (Die Kunst Bd. 57-58). Berlin 1908.

H. P. Rohde: Dansk Bogillustration 1800-1890. Kbh. 1949.

Arthur Rümann: Das illustrierte Buch des 19. Jahrhunderts in England, Frankreich und Deutschland. Lpz. 1930.

Arthur Rümann: Das deutsche illustrierte Buch des achtzehnten Jahrhunderts. Stuttg. 1931.

Max Sander: Die illustrierten französischen Bücher des 18. Jahrhunderts. Stuttg. 1926.

Max Sander: Le livre à figures italien. Milan 1942.

Albert Schramm: Der Bilderschmuck der Frühdrucke. Bd. 1-23. Lpz. 1922-43.

W. L. Schreiber: Der Buchholzschnitt im 15. Jahrhundert. München 1929.

Walter Schwartz: Dansk Illustrationskunst fra Valdemar Andersen til Ib Andersen. Kbh. 1949.

Jørgen Sthyr: Dansk Grafik 1500-1800. Kbh. 1943. -- 1800-1910. Kbh. 1949.

Georg Svensson: Modern svensk bokkonst. Sthlm. 1953.

F. Weitenkampf: The Illustrated Book. Cambr., Mass. 1938.

Book-Binding

Paul Adam: Der Bucheinband. Lpz. 1890.
William Barkell: Från papyrusrulle till partiband. Sthlm.
1950.
H. Béraldi: La reliure du 19e siècle. Tome 1-4. Paris
1895-97.
G. A. E. Bogeng: Der Bucheinband. Halle a. S. 1950.
W. S. Brassington: A History of the Art of Bookbinding.
London 1894.
H. O. Bøggild-Andersen og Edward C. J. Wolf: Bogbindets
Historie. Kbh. 1945.
Douglas B. Cockerell: Bookbinding and the Care of Books.
New ed. London 1948.
Danish Eighteenth Century Bindings 1730-1780. 102 Plates.
With an Introduction by Sofus Larsen and Anker Kyster.
Kbh. 1930.
E. Déville: La reliure française. Tome 1-2. Paris 1930-31
Edith Diehl: Bookbinding, its Background and Technique.
Vol. 1-2. New York 1946.
Carl Elberling: Breve fra en Bogelsker. Kbh. 1909.
Ernst Fischer: Bokbandets historia. Sthlm. 1922.
W. Fletcher: Bookbinding in England and France. Vol. 1-2.
London 1905.
E. P. Goldschmidt: Gothic and Renaissance Bookbindings.
Vol. 1-2. London 1928.
Léon Gruel: Manuel historique et bibliographique de l'ama-
teur des reliures. Paris 1887.
G. D. Hobson: Maioli, Canevari and others. London 1926.
G. D. Hobson: Bindings in Cambridge Libraries. London
1929.
G. D. Hobson: English Binding before 1500. London 1929.
G. D. Hobson: Les reliures à la fanfare. London 1935.
Herbert P. Horne: The Binding of Books. An Essay in the
History of Gold-tooled Bindings. London 1894.
Kunstfaerdige gamle Bogbind indtil 1850. Det danske Kunst-
industrimuseums Udstilling 1906. Med en Indledning af
Emil Hannover. Kbh. 1907.
E. Kyriss: Verzierte gotische Einbände im alten deutschen
Sprachgebiet. Stuttg. 1951.
Anker Kyster: Om Indbinding af Bøger. Holstebro 1920-35.
Hans Loubier: Der Bucheinband von seinen Anfängen bis zum
Ende des 18. Jahrhunderts. 2. Aufl. Lpz. 1926.
Ch. Meunier: La reliure française ancienne et moderne.
Paris 1910.
Marius Michel: La reliure française. Paris 1880.
Louis Marie Michon: La reliure française. Paris 1951.
Carl P. Nielsen og. R. Berg: Danmarks Bogbindere gennem

400 Aar. Kbh. 1926.

Axel Nilsson: Bokbandsdekorens stilutveckling. Göteborg 1922.

Sarah T. Prideaux: An Historical Sketch of Bookbinding. London 1893.

Ch. Ramsden: French Bookbinders 1789-1848. London 1950.

Ch. Ramsden: London Bookbinders 1780-1940. London 1956. -- Bookbinders of the United Kingdom (outside London) 1780-1940. London 1954.

J. Rudbeck: Svenska bokband under nyare tiden. Bidrag till svensk bokbinderhistoria. Bd. 1-3. Sthlm. 1910-14.

Heinrich Schreiber: Einführung in die Einbandkunde. Lpz. 1932.

The Book Trade

Aus Wissenschaft un d Antiquariat. Festschrift zum 50-jährigen Bestehen der Buchhandlung Gustav Fock. Lpz. 1929.

Der Buchhandel der Welt. Aufbau, Verkehrswesen, Anschriften des Buchhandels in Europa und U.S.A. Hrsg. von A. Druckenmüller. Stuttg. 1935.

Ed. Frommann: Aufsätze zur Geschichte des Buchhandels. Hft. 1-2. Jena 1881.

Friedrich Kapp und Joh. Goldfriedrich: Geschichte des deutschen Buchhandels. Bd. 1-4. Lpz. 1886-1913.

Henrik Koppel: Spredte Traek af Boghandelens Historie. Kbh. 1932.

Walter Krieg: Materialien zu einer Entwicklungsgeschichte der Bücherpreise und des Autoren-Honorars von 15. bis zum 20. Jahrhundert. Wien 1953.

Gerhard Menz: Deutsche Buchhändler. 24 Lebensbilder führender Männer des Buchhandels. Lpz. u. München 1925.

Gerhard Menz: Der deutsche Buchhandel. 2. Aufl. Gotha 1942.

F. A. Mumby: The Romance of Bookselling. 2. ed. London 1930.

Jean-Alexis Néret: Histoire illustrée de la librairie et du livre français des origines à nos jours. Paris 1953.

Camillus Nyrop: Bidrag til den danske Boghandels Historie. Del 1-2. Kbh. 1870.

W. Olbrich: Einführung in die Verlagskunde. 3. Aufl. Lpz. 1956.

M. Paschke und Philipp Rath: Lehrbuch des deutschen Buchhandels. Bd. 1-2. 6. Aufl. Lpz. 1922.

Marjorie Plant: The English Book Trade. An Economic History. London 1939.

Volmer Rosenkilde: Af Antikvarens Historie. (Saertr. af:

Mennesker og Bøger). Kbh. 1945.
Henrik Schück: Den svenska förlagsbokhandelns historia. Bd. 1-2. Sthlm. 1923.
V. Sønstevold og Harald L. Tveteras: Den norske bokhandelns historie. Bd. 1 ff. Oslo 1936 ff.
Friedrich Uhlig: Geschichte des Buches und des Buchhandels. Stuttg. 1953.

Libraries and Librarianship,
Book-Collecting and Exlibris

Ester Aarup Hansen: Exlibriskunstens Udvikling i Danmark. Kbh. 1944.
Jørgen Banke: Folkebibliotekernes Historie i Danmark indtil Aar 1920 i Omrids. Kbh. 1929.
G. A. E. Bogeng: Die grossen Bibliophilen. Geschichte der Büchersammler und ihrer Sammlungen. Bd. 1-3. Lpz. 1922.
G. A. E. Bogeng: Einführungin die Bibliophilie. Lpz. 1931.
Arthur E. Bostwick: The American Public Library. 4. ed. New York 1929.
Henri Bouchot: Les ex-libris et les marques de possession du livre. Paris 1891.
Margaret Burton: Famous Libraries of the World. Their History, Collections and Administration. London 1937.
G. H. Bushwell: The World's Earliest Libraries. London 1931.
Christian Callmer: Antike Bibliotheken. (Opuscula archaeologica. 3). Lund 1944 (Skrifter utg. av Svenska institutet i Rom. 10).
Carl L. Cannon: American Book Collectors and Collecting from Colonial Times to the Present. New York 1941.
C. M. Carlander: Svenska bibliotek och ex-libris. 2. uppl., bd. 1-4. Sthlm. 1896-1903.
J. Cerný: Paper and Books in Ancient Egypt. London 1952.
J. W. Clark: The Care of Books. London 1901.
Ch. J. Elton and Mary A. Elton: The Great Book Collectors. London 1893.
Arundell Esdaile: National Libraries of the World. London 1934.
William Younger Fletcher: English Book Collectors. London 1902.
Theodor Gottlieb: Ueber mittelalterliche Bibliotheken. Lpz. 1890.
Joannis Guigard: Nouvel armorial du bibliophile. Tome 1-2. Nouv. éd. Paris 1899.
W. J. Hardy: Bookplates. London 1893.

Arthur G. Hassø: Danske Exlibris. Kbh. 1942.
Alfred Hessel: History of Libraries, trans. with supplementary material by Reuben Peiss. ed. 2. New York, 1955.
Hugo Høgdahl: Norske exlibris og andre bokeiermerker. Oslo 1946.
Clément Janin: Essai sur la bibliophilie contemporaine de 1900 à 1928. Tome 1-2. Paris 1931.
A. Jörgensen: Bokägermärken i Finland. Helsingfors 1916.
Preben Kirkegaard: Folkebibliotekerne i Danmark. Kbh. 1948.
Kl. Löffler: Deutsche Klosterbibliotheken. 2 stark verm. Aufl. Bonn und Lpz. 1922.
F. S. Merryweather: Bibliomania in the Middle Ages. Revised ed. London 1933.
F. Milkau: Die Bibliotheken. (Kultur der Gegenwart Teil 1, Abt. 1). 2. Aufl. Lpz. 1912.
Otto Mühlbrecht: Die Bücherliebhaberei in ihrer Entwicklung bis zum Ende des 19. Jahrhunderts. 2. Aufl. Bielefeld und Lpz. 1898.
Lauritz Nielsen: Danske Privatbiblioteker gennem Tiderne. I: Indtil Udgangen af det 17. Aarhundrede. Kbh. 1946.
Carl S. Petersen: Afhandlinger til dansk Bog- og Bibliotekshistorie. Kbh. 1949.
Popular Libraries of the World. Ed. by Arthur E. Bostwick. (American Library Association). New York 1933.
Saymour de Ricci: English Collectors of Books and Manuscripts (1530-1930). Cambr. 1930.
Ernest A. Savage: The Story of Libraries and Book-Collecting. New York [u. aar].
W. Schürmeyer: Bibliotheksräume aus fünf Jahrhunderten. [U. st. og aar].
G. Seyler: Illustriertes Handbuch der Exlibris-Kunde. Berlin 1895.
Arthur Sjögren: Svenska kungliga och furstliga bokägaremärken. Sthlm. 1915.
A. Stalhane: Finska ex-libris. Helsingfors 1940.
J. W. Thompson: The Medieval Library. Cambr. 1939.
Svenska bibliotek. Under red. av J. Viktor Johansson. I. Sthlm. 1946.
O. Walde: Storhetstidens litterära krigsbyten. En kulturhistorisk-bibliografisk studie. I-II. Upps. og Sthlm. 1916-20.
M. Weitemeyer: Babylonske og assyriske arkiver og biblioteker. Kbh. 1955. (Studier fra Sprog- og Oldtidsforskning. 227).
W. von Zur Westen: Exlibris (Bucheignerzeichen). 3. Aufl. Bielefeld 1925.